The Cricket Captains
of England

ALAN GIBSON

The Cricket Captains of England

A SURVEY

CASSELL

LONDON

CASSELL LTD.
35 Red Lion Square, London WC1R 4SG
and at Sydney, Auckland, Toronto, Johannesburg,
an affiliate of
Macmillan Publishing Co., Inc.,
New York

First published 1979

ISBN 0 304 29779 8

Printed and bound in Great Britain at
The Camelot Press Ltd, Southampton

To
E.W.S.
with, as they say,
my humble affection

CONTENTS

ILLUSTRATIONS

following page 152

PREFACE

I am grateful to many friends for their help with this book, and to the House of Cassell, who may, I hope, still be counted as friends, since they have been very patient with me as I battled through it. I have not put in footnotes, because they would have been so numerous, but I have done my best to refer to my authorities, especially on any point of dispute, in the text.

I have never been much of a man for sums, and I am sure I will have made many statistical errors. I shall be deeply grateful to any reader who does not point them out to me.

Alan Gibson
High Littleton
Avon
1979

1

GREAT MEN
BEFORE AGAMEMNON

Vixere fortes ante Agamemnona
Multi; sed omnes illacrimabiles
Urgentur ignotique longa
    Nocte, carent quia vate sacro.
                        Horace

which may be roughly translated
and abbreviated to 'There were
great men before Agamemnon, but
the press hadn't got round to it'

The first English sporting team to tour abroad (or so I imagine) left our shores in 1586, under the captaincy of John Davis. Its destination was the Arctic Circle, where it took part in a series of athletic contests against the Eskimo. Like most touring teams, it won some and it lost some, though no detailed results survive. There were newspapers of a kind then, but they did not run to sports correspondents, and in any case there might have been a shortage of volunteers: intrepidly though our pressmen may now venture to Australia or America, Greenland in the sixteenth century might have daunted the bravest. The expenses would no doubt have been good, but you could not be sure of surviving to claim them, and an occasional whale steak did not represent much in the way of free-loading.

This is not just a little joke. Davis, one of the most courageous and selfless of the great Elizabethan sailors, had visited the Arctic before, and had tried to establish friendly relations with the Eskimo, without much success. He had taken out some musicians, who played old English folk tunes, while the seamen danced to them. The Eskimo were only mildly interested, and did not seek to compete with these early Cloggies.

But Davis had noticed they were an active people, who enjoyed wrestling, jumping, and other sports; so on his second trip he took some athletes with him. This did establish some kind of bond with the natives. 'Our men did overleape them, but we found them strong and nimble, and to have skil in wrestling, for

1

they cast some of our men that were good wrestlers.' As many of Davis's men came from Devon and Cornwall, famous wrestling counties, we may take it that the Eskimo standard was high. They were not, however, so good at football, of which they already had a version. 'Divers times did they weave us on shore to play with them at the foot-ball, and some of our company went on shore to play with them, and our men did cast them downe as soon as they did come to strike the ball'. Clearly the Eskimo had not learnt to tackle.

This tour is worth remembering, as an illustration (there are many to the contrary) of the hopeful belief that if different peoples can be brought to play games together, they will understand each other better, and grow fonder of each other. But there is no record of anything like cricket being played. It is not quite impossible, because cricket and similar bat-and-ball games were known in England at the time, but the records are scanty, and mostly refer to the south-east of the country. So, reluctantly, I cannot grant John Davis the honour of being our first touring captain.

That distinction would have gone to the third Duke of Dorset, J. F. Sackville, at the end of the eighteenth century, but for an unhappy misadventure. He was one of the many nobility and gentry who were enthusiasts for the game, and used to gather at Hambledon: a great backer of sides, and a considerable player himself. At one time he was Ambassador in Paris, and in 1789 he asked the Foreign Secretary, the Duke of Leeds (another cricketer), for a token of goodwill towards the French. Between them they planned a tour of English cricketers to Paris. It seems odd, because there was nobody obvious for them to play, but that is what they did. Unfortunately the French Revolution broke out, and the first the Duke of Dorset saw of his team was at Dover, they wondering whether to embark and he flying homewards. As Major Rowland Bowen has pointed out, this was the first cricket tour to be cancelled because of political events, though not the last.

By this time, plenty of matches were being played at home by sides called 'England versus Kent', 'England versus Hambledon', and so on; but if we started taking these into account we should soon be in trouble, as in many cases we do not know the detailed scores or the teams. We may, however, moving on to the nineteenth century, pause on the name of William Clarke. Clarke was born in 1798. He was a Nottingham bricklayer. He played for his county at the age of 18, but he was nearly 50 when he was first employed as a practice bowler at Lord's, where he soon made a reputation as one of the best in the country. In 1847, he and William Lillywhite took all 20 wickets for the Players against the Gentlemen. He spun the ball from leg, bowling at about the height of the hip, and there are many tales of his cunning. He was the founder of 'The All-England XI', which played its first match in 1846, against Twenty of Sheffield. The idea was that the best cricketers in the country should tour together, playing against local

2

sides. It was a business enterprise, though occasionally a leading amateur, such as Mynn or Felix, would play.

In order to make an even game of it, All-England customarily played against odds, usually 22. If the local sides still did not feel strong enough, they would engage a spare professional or two to play for them. One or two professionals, perhaps those who did not fit easily into the disciplines of a touring side, specialized in taking engagements for the opposition. Of one of these, William Caffyn tells a story in his capital book, *71 Not Out*. (Caffyn was a member of Clarke's team, and later had much to do with the advance of the game in Australia, where he coached.) The player concerned, he recalls, was about to be arrested for debt. The sum was only £12, and so he arranged with his creditor to be seized just before the start of play, on the ground of the club for whom he was playing. As both debtor and creditor had calculated, the club was so alarmed at the prospect of playing without their star guest that a whip-round raised the money.

The All-England XI had many adventures and many successes. F. S. Ashley-Cooper worked out that in the seven years 1847–53 Clarke himself took 2,385 wickets for them, an average of 340 per season. A booklet was published, for the benefit of local cricketers, entitled 'How to Play Clarke'. He did not like taking himself off, and of course he had plenty of batsmen to bowl at, but it is still a lot of wickets. Batting 22 may not have made much difference to the scores of the local side, but it did make a difference to the England batsmen. Imagine the difficulty of scoring runs, against any sort of bowling, with 22 men in the field, especially when everything has to be run out, and with the crowd on the side of the fieldsmen, eager to return the ball (quite the opposite when their own side was batting). The grounds were often small, the pitches almost inevitably rough. In 1855, for instance, Caffyn averaged 22 in 11-a-side matches, which would usually be played on better grounds, but only 16 for the whole season. In the same season John Wisden took 223 wickets in all matches at an average of five, and averaged 23 with the bat, and it was the second figure that was considered more remarkable.

It was Wisden, with Jemmy Dean (two Sussex men), who founded the United England XI in 1852. Old Clarke was a bit of an autocrat, and was reputed to be making money out of all proportion to the £4 a match (which usually lasted three days) which he paid his players. In any case, now that the career of a travelling cricket professional had been shown to be feasible (it could not have been done without the railway), more good players were coming forward than one XI could accommodate. The matches between the All-England and United XIs became the most important matches of the season, more so even than North versus South, much more so than Gentlemen versus Players – for this development of professional strength was too much for the amateurs, who between 1850 and

3

1865 lost every match but one. The England–United match first took place in 1857. Clarke, so long as he was in charge, would have nothing to do with it, and of course from his own point of view he was right, because the unique status of his side had gone. It is reported that 10,000 people at a time would attend these matches, which were sometimes played for the Cricketers' Friendly Fund ('after deducting all expenses', Caffyn says, a somewhat uncertain qualification). These two great XIs, which had a number of less successful imitators, undoubtedly did the game of cricket service, spreading it all over the British Isles. The wide interest they created proved to be, as county clubs emerged, their own undoing. But they lasted a long time, and no discussion of English cricket captains should omit the name of crusty old Clarke.

Nor should it omit that of George Parr. The formula which had worked so well for the professionals at home might surely be tried out abroad, and so it was that a representative team left Liverpool for North America in 1859. Six players were from the All-England XI, and six from the United. Fred Lillywhite accompanied them as scorer, reporter, and mentor, not to say Nestor. George Parr of Nottinghamshire was the captain. There were two other Nottinghamshire players, three from Cambridgeshire, two from Sussex, and four from Surrey. Wherever it went, the party was distinguished by Fred Lillywhite's portable scoring-booth and printing-press. The team were photographed before they started, against a suitable background of rigging (not actually on the ship they sailed on), in spotted shirts and striking attitudes. They had a rough passage, and Parr, a bad traveller, had consumed large quantities of gin-and-water before they arrived at Quebec.

Cricket was very popular then in the United States and Canada. At New York, 'ten thousand people' (though one must always mistrust such conveniently rounded figures) watched the match, all the ground could hold. The band played 'Rule, Britannia!' as the English began their innings. This was only 45 years after the Second American War, and only three years before the *Alabama* sailed from Liverpool, nearly producing a third. At Philadelphia the crowds were even larger.

All the matches were played against odds, and if the match ended early, as often it did, the Englishmen would divide forces and play an 11-a-side match, sharing the locals. In one of these additional matches, Parr was badly hit on the elbow by Jackson, the dreaded English fast bowler, and was unable to bat again during the tour. He did, however, make a public appearance in the last match, against a Combined XXII of Canada and the United States, when he volunteered to umpire. It was now the second half of October, and bitterly cold, and it has to be said that soon the umpire/captain abandoned his duties, retiring to the comforts of *hot* gin-and-water in the pavilion. His colleagues fielded in overcoats and gloves. On the second day there was no play because of snow, but the teams played a match at baseball instead.

In spite of the formidable travelling, and the fearful difficulties in transporting Lillywhite's scoring-booth, Parr's team won all its matches. They made themselves very popular, saw the Niagara Falls, and took home a profit of £90 a head. They had an even rougher passage back, and one of them, Jemmy Grundy, had a misunderstanding with the Customs over a box of cigars.

Parr had succeeded Clarke as the captain of the All-England XI, and was reckoned the champion of batsmen between Fuller Pilch and Richard Daft. He came to be called 'The Lion of the North', and he was a fine, courageous player, especially strong on the leg side. 'George Parr's tree' at Trent Bridge used to mark the spot where his favourite leg-hits went, and when he died, in 1891, a branch from it was placed among the wreaths upon his grave at Radcliffe-on-Trent, his lifelong home. He was a nervous and choleric man, but popular with his teams. He had bright blue eyes, ginger hair, mutton-chop whiskers with moustache (or without either, according to his mood), and was not much good at administration and not very patient with those who had to do it. I would guess that he was the kind of man who, in any period, would turn out to be a captain of England at something or other.

Two years later, in 1861, the first English team went to Australia. It would probably have gone to North America, had it not been for the outbreak of the American Civil War, which among rather more important consequences set back American cricket severely. This was not, as English standards then went, a very good side. The 'northern players' were unhappy about the terms offered by the sponsors, the Melbourne caterers Spiers & Pond. These were £150 a head, plus – that word which could mean so much then, as now – 'expenses'. 'The northern players' meant, in effect, Parr and his Nottinghamshire men. They refused to go. The team was raised principally through the efforts of Surrey, whose secretary came to an amiable arrangement with the representative of Spiers & Pond. There were seven Surrey players in the 12. Two Yorkshiremen, Iddison and Ned Stephenson, were enlisted – they would hardly at that stage of their careers have been first choices – and added much to the joviality of the tour, as well as its success. One cannot say quite so much, especially respecting the first part, of all the Yorkshiremen who have toured Australia since. Iddison wrote back home: 'We are made a great fuss of; the Queen herself could not have been treated better.' Ned made the witty remark, as they travelled through the Red Sea, that it looked no redder than any of the others he had seen, and stuffed a towel into the trombone of the cook at the ship's concert. Roaring Yorkshire stuff.

But it was Surrey's tour, essentially, and a Surrey man, H. H. Stephenson, was captain. They won six and lost two matches out of 12, all against odds. Stephenson, the captain, had much success as an after-dinner speaker, an accomplishment which many other captains had to learn, often painfully. Large crowds attended them. Stephenson was a notable cricketer, chiefly for his bowling, and his fast break-back (the arm had of course been getting above the shoulder by now, though an over-arm delivery was not legalized until 1864). He was also a powerful hitter and probably the second-best English wicket-keeper, Lockyer being, it was recognized, the best. He became coach at Uppingham, where he produced many admirable cricketers, and seems, towards the end of his life, to have been the most influential, not to say bossy, man in the school. No doubt a man who had led the first England side in Australia was entitled to be a little authoritative.

In 1863, the American Civil War was still on, never more so, and the second English side to Australia set out, a better and more representative side than the first, Parr captain. Again, all matches were against odds, and England were unbeaten, though they only scrambled home by one wicket, almost at the end of their tour, against Twenty-Two of New South Wales. An amateur went on this tour, the youthful E. M. Grace of Gloucestershire.

Now in 1854 old Clarke had brought the All-England down to Bristol to play against the West Gloucestershire club, on the Downs at Durdham. This was the first important match that W. G. Grace, aged six, remembered watching. In 1855, Clarke brought the side again, though he did not play himself, and was impressed by the play of W.G.'s eldest brother, E.M. E. M. Grace was then 13 years old. When he was asked to go to Australia, as the result of some extraordinary batting late in the season, he was 21. After watching the boy E.M., Clarke gave him a bat, and gave his mother a copy of a book which bore his name, inscribing it

Presented to MRS. GRACE
By William Clarke,
Secretary All-England XI.

The book ultimately came into the possession of W.G. Thus does one England captain edify and encourage another.

There was a lull in tours from England after this. Australia was such a long way away, and America, even when the war there was over, was bothered and restless and thinking of other things. But a lot a cricket was played, increasingly, in various parts of the world. Parr's second side had been the first from England to visit New Zealand. In the same year, cricket clubs were founded in the Transvaal and in Kingston, Jamaica, and in 1864 there took place the first known match between Madras and Calcutta. They were playing cricket in Valparaiso, and in 1866 came the first Argentinian hat-trick. In 1868 a team of

Australian aborigines visited Britain, and played a lot of cricket among their other entertainments, such as throwing boomerangs, but this, while a pleasing event both at the time and in retrospect, was one of history's freaks, and led to nothing.

In the same year a second English side went to North America. They drew against XXII of Canada, and beat XXII of the United States. Their captain was Edgar Willsher, who had caused such a stir at the Oval in 1862, when playing for 'England' against Surrey. He did not trouble to conceal the height at which his arm went over, well above shoulder-height, and was no-balled five times running by his old pal, John Lillywhite, whereupon he flung down the ball upon the pitch and left the field. The game was resumed the following day, after dropping the umpire, which as any cricketer to this day will tell you, is a plan with a lot to be said for it. Whether Willsher, in this unimportant tour, had any trouble with American umpires, I do not know.

In 1872 there came the third English tour to North America. The captain was R. A. Fitzgerald, although the dominating figure was that of W. G. Grace, now 24, and established as England's leading batsman: indeed, 'leading' does not quite fit the case. It was widely thought in England that there had never been a cricketer like him; it is still. But we shall have to deal with him again. Fitzgerald was secretary of the M.C.C., and all the team were members of M.C.C., and therefore amateur, so this tour was a departure from precedent, when the professionals had made all the running. Fitzgerald wrote an amusing book about it, *Wickets in the West*, but I must not dwell upon it, for even with Grace, the absence of professionals made it hopelessly far from an England XI. Not that it did badly, in terms of either results or attendance.

The following winter, 1873–4, Grace took a side to Australia, which played 15 matches, all against odds, and lost three. They won the most important one, against a combined Fifteen of New South Wales and Victoria. This was a strong team, which included four amateurs besides the captain. It was clear that Australian cricket had made great strides, especially in bowling.

And so we come to the tour of 1876–7. Two tours to Australia were planned that summer. James Lillywhite, Junior – yet another member of that famous cricketing family – was intending to take out a band of professionals, and G. F. Grace one which was to include some amateurs. Grace's fell through, after many of the preliminary arrangements had been made. Now this was to prove a matter of some importance. To English cricketers, this was just another tour, but Lillywhite's men were to play two matches against a Combined Australian *Eleven*, the first time such a thing had happened. As the years went by, and cricketers began to develop their passion for statistics, it became desirable to decide which matches should count in the records as 'Test matches', and 1877 was the obvious place to start. But if there had been *two* touring sides, the status

7

of the 11-a-side matches would have been demonstrably reduced, and perhaps a different starting-point would have been found.

However, Fred Grace did not go, and Lillywhite did, and so the match at Melbourne in 1877 became recognized as 'the first Test', and a hundred years later the centenary Test was played on the same ground, with exactly the same result, victory to Australia by 45 runs. From this point I have followed the generally recognized practice as to what was, and was not, a Test match. It leads to some absurdities. For instance, the standard of cricket on some of the early tours, particularly to South Africa, was a long way from a true international standard. I can, again, see no real reason why the 1929–30 England tour to New Zealand (captain, A. H. H. Gilligan) should be counted, and not that of 1935–6 (captain, E. R. T. Holmes). In February 1930, England began two Test matches on the same day, one at Auckland and one at Georgetown. But if you want to have statistics, you must agree on which matches to base them, or everyone would have his own, and it is more convenient to follow the accepted list. It does mean, however, that 'Test career records', at least up to the Second World War, are not quite always what they seem.

So they were making history, though they did not know it, the party of 12 professionals who set out in 1876. Let us consider these hardy pioneers a little.

Lillywhite, who was promoter and manager as well as captain, was a Sussex man, from West Hampnett, and 35 years old at the time of the first Test. He was a medium-paced left-arm bowler, in the steady, persistent style much admired at the time, and a good enough left-handed batsman to score the occasional century. He had visited Australia with the previous side. In the Tests (England won the second by four wickets, thus sharing the honours) he scored only 12 runs, but took eight wickets, and only Alfred Shaw took as many. They were the only two Tests that Lillywhite played in. Alfred Shaw was vice-captain, and assistant manager. There were two other Sussex men besides the captain, Charlwood and Southerton (though Southerton at the time was playing for Surrey). Jupp and Pooley were Surrey-born, Selby and Shaw from Nottinghamshire. There were five Yorkshiremen: Greenwood, Armitage, Hill, and – two of the great all-rounders – Emmett and Ulyett, Emmett growing old but Ulyett with many Tests in front of him. So the south, the Midlands and the north were all represented. Lillywhite paid them £150 each for the trip, except for Shaw, who was paid £300 because of his extra responsibilities. Lillywhite also paid them travelling expenses, first class. This was an important point. W. G. Grace's side had caused some unfavourable comment, especially in Australia, because the professionals had travelled second class, and the amateurs first. This even extended to the hotels where they stayed. It was for this reason that Shaw had declined the trip. Now W.G., perhaps unfairly, was said to have cost the Australians a lot of money by his requirements for 'expenses': so an all-professional team, with the terms set out, suited both the hosts and the guests well. They knew where they were.

It was beginning to be possible, and the Australians were soon to recognize the possibilities, for a man to be a professional cricketer all the year round: £150 for the winter, with free living, and colonial hospitality, was not so bad, even though the travelling was severe. It was better than a man might do at home as a bricklayer, or a stonemason, or even a publican (half Lillywhite's team were publicans at some stage of their lives). Such men were letting the future take care of itself, but nearly all working men had to do that anyway, in those unpensioned days.

Sea travel was becoming safe (as important a fact in the growth of tours as the railway had been to the All-England XI). You could expect to get to Australia on the new P. & O. steamships which came into service in the 1870s, but it would take you a long time: 48 days was an average. If you went, first class, by P. & O., you would be comfortable, by the standards of the time. The P. & O. put their first-class cabins on the top deck, surrounding a central dining-room, where there were long tables, with benches which could face either way, because you could switch their backs, and look at the table or the sea as you chose. Refrigeration was beginning, but livestock were still carried: cows, to provide fresh milk for the children, and sheep for meat, and hens for eggs.

I am indebted to Basil Greenhill, Director of the Greenwich Maritime Museum, for these details of how Lillywhite's men, and all the other touring sides of that period, travelled. 'The P. & O. really did their first-class passengers pretty well', he concludes. But 48 days was a long time, however many runs round the deck you took, and at the coaling stops – Malta, Suez, King George's Sound – the cricketers conceivably went ashore in pursuit of more urgent interests than keeping fit. They must have felt weary when at last they got there.

It was not, therefore, surprising that they soon lost a match (against odds). After this they were given a ticking off in *The Australasian*. The English, it said,

> . . . are by a long way the weakest side that have ever played in the colonies, notwithstanding the presence of Shaw, who is termed the premier bowler of England. If Ulyett, Emmett, and Hill are specimens of the best fast bowling in England, all we can say is, either they have not shown their proper form, or British bowling has sadly deteriorated.

It is not uncommon, to this day, for touring sides to be hailed as heroes on arrival, and dismissed as nobodies when things go wrong.

However, the attendances were good, and the early matches suggested that Lillywhite would make a profit, as he ultimately did – on this tour, though not on later ones. But they still had much travelling ahead, even when they had settled to form. Apart from their journeys within Australia, they had undertaken to go to

9

New Zealand (in the middle of the tour, with the big matches still to come). Touring in New Zealand then was even tougher than touring in Australia. It was in New Zealand that the English lost their wicket-keeper, Ed Pooley, in unfortunate circumstances. Pooley was a capable cricketer, and a popular one, but not one of Queen Victoria's more reliable citizens. He was to die in the workhouse, though he battled on for another 30 years. Alfred Shaw describes how

> We were playing against Eighteen of Canterbury, and in a discussion of the prospects of the match that occurred in an hotel bar at night, Pooley offered to take £1 to a shilling that he named the individual score of every member of the local team. It is a trick familiar to cricketers, and in the old days of matches against local eighteens and twenty-twos it was not infrequently worked off against the unwary. The bet being accepted, Pooley named a duck as the score of each batsman on the local side. A fair proportion of ducks was recorded, and Pooley claimed £1 for each of them, while prepared to pay one shilling for the other scores. The man with whom the bet had been made said it was a catch bet, and he declined to pay. The man's name was Donkin. His refusal to pay led to a scene of disorder. We next had to go to Otago, and at the close of the match there, Pooley was arrested on a charge of 'having at Christchurch maliciously injured property above the value of £5'; and another charge, of assaulting Donkin. For the assault he had £5 and costs to pay. In the other charge he had as partner in trouble Alf Bramall, a supernumerary attached to our team. The two were committed for trial, bail being allowed of £100. We never saw Pooley again during that tour.

Pooley's bail did not allow him to leave the country, and though he was acquitted of the major charge, and even had a public subscription raised for him by the New Zealanders – many of whom felt he had been inhospitably treated – the rest of the English team had to leave him behind, because they had to be back in Australia. Pooley ultimately trailed home on his own, thus missing playing in the first Test match. As it happened, he never had a chance to play in another.

It was suggested during this tour, both in Australia and New Zealand, that the English were too fond of diddling an innocent colonial, and of looking upon the girls when they were bonny, and the wine when it was red – even more when it was sparkling. This complaint also, whether true or not, remains a recognized accompaniment of any touring team which is not doing too well. The English would no doubt have pleaded justification for at least the last of these offences, because the travelling problems did give a man a thirst. After they had spent 80 hours on the road in New Zealand, wading and swimming through swollen streams on the way, they arrived in Christchurch just in time for the start of play. George Ulyett, no weakling he, but as strapping a man as ever came out of Yorkshire, said that 'We were so stiff, cold and sore with being wet and cramped up in the coach that we could scarcely bowl or run.' They only just managed to get the Eighteen of Canterbury out on the first day, and the local opinion was that the English might as well have stopped at home, instead of coming all that way to teach Canterbury folks how to play cricket. Ulyett goes on (A. W. Pullin took down his recollections):

> In the evening I told Lillywhite that we had been up to our necks in water, had no bed and nothing to eat, it was worth stretching a point, so we got him to allow us a case of champagne and we had a merry evening. The next day we went on to the field new men.

The early English touring sides were very fond of champagne, surprisingly – or so it seems to us, today, accustomed to watching the pints of beer go down. There are many instances of early English cricketers, in forlorn moments far from home, clamouring for champagne. I sometimes wonder if this is the origin of the term 'Pommy' (all the *Shorter Oxford* says is 'origin obscure'). Pommery was a well-known brand before the end of the century. After all, we were called 'Limeys' by the Americans because our seamen drank lime-juice, as a precaution against the scurvy.

Well, while I am indulging in such speculations, the 1876–7 tourists are on their way back to Australia, and another rough trip they had, arriving several days late with no proper time to rest. 'Not one of us was fit to play cricket', writes Shaw: 'I was simply spun out of myself.' There was probably some substance in this excuse. Armitage, who was the fattest member of the side, and a particularly bad traveller, bowled a ball to Bannerman which went for an overhead wide; and then rolled the next one along the ground. But only two wides were bowled in the innings, and Armitage was not primarily a bowler. It was more important that he dropped Bannerman, a simple catch at mid-off, before the Australian No. 1 had reached double figures. Bannerman went on to 165 (retired hurt) and effectively settled the match. This was a most extraordinary performance as scores went in those days. No other Australian, in either innings, scored more than 20, and the highest English score was 63, by Jupp.

If Lillywhite's men were not the best 11 cricketers in England, they were not so far from it, a tried professional XI, and whatever their handicaps, they had had to give the colonials best. *The Melbourne Age* had no doubt of the significance of the victory.

> Such an event would not have been dreamed of as coming within the limits of possibility ten or fifteen years ago, and it is a crushing reply to those unpatriotic theorists who would have us believe that the Australian race is deteriorating from the Imperial type, or that lengthened existence under Australian suns would kill out the Briton in the blood.

Readers of *The Times* in London had to wait two months for their account, which ultimately came in their 'Melbourne Letter', immediately after a description of a first-class rumpus in the Victorian Parliament, and just before the latest population statistics. It is a shade patronizing.

> You know the result of our great cricket match. To use Mr. Trollope's word, Australians will 'blow' about it for some time to come. It was played on the ground of the Melbourne Club, between Lillywhite's eleven and a combined eleven of New South Wales and Victoria. We are told that it is the first match in which an English professional eleven has been beaten out of England. The game was watched with intense excitement by enthusiastic crowds, and those who could not get to the ground clustered round the newspaper offices to see the last despatches from the seat of war placarded on the door posts. It began and ended in good temper, and Lillywhite's pecuniary success must have consoled him for his defeat.

The reference to Trollope concerns some unflattering remarks he had made in a book about his Australian travels. After the victory, some triumphant verses appeared in *The Australasian*, called 'The Brazen Trumpet', and beginning

> Anthony Trollope
> Says we can wallop
> The whole of creation at 'blowing',
> It's well in a way,
> But then he don't say
> We blow about nothing worth showing!

Shaw, in his reminiscences, gives the full score of the match, but is careful to refer to the English XI as 'Lillywhite's Eleven'. The excitement in England was not great, especially as the second Test, a fortnight later on the same ground, was won.

That brings me to a last curious point about this famous occasion. When G. F. Grace was still planning his tour, he had booked the Melbourne ground, the big ground, the home of the Melbourne Cricket Club. Lillywhite's agent had to be content with booking the East Melbourne ground, and the East Melbourne club duly went to much trouble and expense in making preparations. However, when Grace withdrew, Lillywhite naturally wanted to switch grounds, and this did not please the East Melbourne club at all. There were threats of legal proceedings. In the end an amicable settlement was reached. Lillywhite paid East Melbourne £230, and gave free admission to their members, of whom there were 500. He was not a mean man, which was one reason why he never made much money out of his various cricketing ventures. So Test cricket might have begun upon a relatively obscure ground, not at its most famous home, barring possibly one. There were several arguments during the tour, about such matters as rolling the pitch, and the hours of play. The Englishmen, their thoughts directed to the financial benefits, usually gave way. Nevertheless, there were times when feeling ran high. During the match against Fifteen of New South Wales, a lady wrote to Lillywhite imploring him to win, 'as it would not be safe for any Englishman or woman to walk the streets of Sydney if New South Wales were victorious'.

James Lillywhite, for all his adventures and misadventures, was England's first Test captain, as these things came to be reckoned, and he ended with a 50/50 record, slightly above average. What is more, he lived long enough to realize something of what he had started. He outlived all the other members of his team, and died in 1929, aged 87, when A. P. F. Chapman had just been to Australia (Lillywhite was nearly 60 when Chapman was born), and beaten them, 4–1, before record crowds.

There had been discussion from time to time about the possibility of an Australian tour of England. At the farewell dinner in 1874, W.G. had told the Australians, 'If you ever come to England, and your bowlers are as good there as they are here, you will make a name for yourselves.' Lillywhite and Shaw offered to undertake the financing and organization of a tour. After the Melbourne victory, the leading Australians decided to go ahead on their own account, though Lillywhite acted as their match-making agent. He arranged 40 matches for the 1878 season, 21 of them against odds. There was no match against 'England', but they were due to meet M.C.C. at Lord's on May 27.

There was no special excitement beforehand. While Lillywhite's team had confirmed reports of rapid development in the colonies, they had not, one conjectures, minimized their own difficulties. M.C.C. put out a side thought to be stronger than Lillywhite's. Besides, England was England, and Lord's was Lord's, and W.G. was W.G. It was the Australian win by nine wickets, in a single day, which marked the beginning for Englishmen, indeed for many Australians too. M.C.C. scored 33 and 19, Australia 41 and 12 for 1. The crowd flocked to the ground as word got round of the extraordinary cricket. 'The wicket', wrote W.G. (who scored 4 and 0), 'was as bad as it could be, and small scoring was expected; but no one dreamt for a moment that in the Australian eleven there were two bowlers possessing the powers which Messrs. Spofforth and Boyle displayed.' Although this match does not rank as a Test, it had more to do with the development of international cricket than any other that has been played.

The 1878 Australian side lost only four matches on level terms – against Nottinghamshire (their first one), Yorkshire, Cambridge University and the Gentlemen of England. Well before the summer's end, English cricketers were contemplating another trip abroad. Lillywhite and Shaw were ready to try again, but did not press their claims when it became known that the Melbourne Cricket Club had invited Lord Harris to take out a team, and that Lord Harris was willing to go.

Lord Harris was to become a dominant figure in English cricket, and his name will recur in this tale, but his personal impact in Tests, as player and captain, was slight. He played once in Australia in 1879, once in England in 1880, and twice in England in 1884. He was naturally captain in all of them. I do not say 'naturally' with any sarcasm. The position of a peer of the realm, a fourth baron, was then such that it was more comfortable for everyone if he was captain; and Harris was a good cricketer, a very knowledgeable one. He had toured America with R. A. Fitzgerald, though he had not then succeeded to the peerage.

I find it difficult to warm to Lord Harris. In a memorial tribute in *Wisden*, the secretary of M.C.C. wrote 'Unbeknown to some, he was the kindest and most affectionate of men', which sounds rather too much like the character in *Oklahoma* who loved everybody and everything – 'only he never let on, so nobody ever knowed it'. I once, indeed, in print, called him an antediluvian old tyrant, but that was an immature view. He was more complex than that, and might make a rewarding study for a psychiatrist with a taste for cricket, or the other way round. Here I confine myself to a note on his England captaincy. Of his four matches, he won two, drew one, and lost one. His batting average was 29 for six innings, once not out. He bowled a few overs but did not take a wicket.

He was fearless against fast bowling, strong in the drive and the cut. Whether he would have played for England had he been born, say, George Harris of West Hampnett, we cannot be sure, but plenty of worse cricketers have done. In any case these are profitless thoughts, and possibly blasphemous, for he did not doubt that it was by the divine will that he was born to the ermine, and to Kent (though despite his passion for that county, he was not born there: his birthplace was St Anne's, Trinidad). His devotion to the game was lifelong, both as player and administrator. In 1862, at the age of 11, he was practising at Lord's, and in 1930, in a 2nd XI match, he was playing at Eton on the Fourth of June. A year before that, he had played at Lord's for the last time, for M.C.C. *v.* Indian Gymkhana. A young Bill Bowes was playing for M.C.C., and has left us an interesting account of the occasion in his book, *Express Deliveries*.

Although Lord Harris's England captaincy was brief, it was important. Had he acted differently, he could have wrecked Anglo-Australian cricket, or at least delayed it and changed its nature. The team he took to Australia was not a strong one. It had been intended that it should consist entirely of amateurs, but when it became plain that not enough of the best ones could go, Emmett and Ulyett were enlisted. Even so, the bowling was weak and the tail was long. Australia won the only Test by ten wickets, Harris making more runs than any other Englishman (Spofforth took 13 wickets in this match). There were four other matches on level

14

terms, two against Victoria and two against New South Wales. The tourists won one, lost one, against both opponents. It was in the second match against New South Wales that there occurred one of cricket's early riots.

The details are confused, but the outline of events is clear. Murdoch, who had scored 82 not out for New South Wales in the first innings, was given run out for 10 in the second. The umpire was Coulthard. He is called in some accounts 'the English umpire', but this is misleading. He was a Victorian, whom the English team had engaged to accompany them. Instead of the next batsman coming in, D. W. Gregory, the Australian captain, appeared at the gate. Harris walked over to speak to him, and Gregory lodged an objection against Coulthard's umpiring. The crowd was in a high state of wrath and invaded the pitch. Harris returned to the middle of the field and, in defending Coulthard, was struck by a stick. A. N. Hornby, a muscular man though not a very big one, seized the offender and pulled him off to the pavilion. Hornby in turn was assaulted, and his shirt almost torn from his back. Ulyett and Emmett each seized a stump and escorted off their captain, with some assistance from the members. The field was cleared, but when the Englishmen came back, with Coulthard, the crowd came on again. Once more it was cleared, once more Harris led out his men, and though the Australians did not follow, he stayed there until the close of play. He did not want New South Wales to claim the match.

Tempers had cooled a little by the morning, apologies were made, and the match went on. Harris sent a complete account of the affair to the English press. When this became known in Australia, it stirred the embers. What is more, the incident attracted much attention in England. Disputes about umpiring were far from new, but the 1878 tourists had not earned a very good reputation in this respect. It can be seen therefore that the Australian side which set out for England in 1880 could not be certain of its welcome.

To add to their problems, rather perplexingly, they had not planned the tour properly. It was not until late in the spring that anyone in England was sure they were coming at all, and by that time the summer's programme (to be sure, nothing like so crowded as it is today) had been settled. They had no Lillywhite as match-maker. After the trouble at Sydney, English counties were not predisposed to put themselves out to give the tourists a game. The Australians found themselves playing a series of minor matches against odds. Yorkshire gave them a couple of unofficial matches. W.G. tried to raise a side against them which would have some sort of representative nature, but did not succeed. They tactfully offered to play an English XI for the benefit of the Cricketers' Fund, but the offer was declined. However, they increased in popularity – Murdoch, their captain, struck a more sympathetic note with the English public than his predecessor Gregory had done – and at the end of the season, a Test match was arranged at the Oval. C. W. Alcock, the Surrey secretary, was responsible for the arrangements, and persuaded Harris to impart the stamp of authority by collecting and captaining the English team. This was undoubtedly a generous and far-reaching action on Harris's part. Not all his colleagues, it seems, were so forgiving. Hornby, Emmett and Ulyett declined invitations to play. But it was a strong side, with all three Grace brothers playing. Australia, short of practice against the best opposition, and, even more important, without Spofforth, who was injured, were beaten by five wickets (England 420 and 57 for 5, Australia 149 and 327), but it was an excellent match, and Test cricket was now fairly launched in both countries.

In fact for the next decade there was a good deal too much of it, with teams setting off every year in one direction or the other. These teams were often unrepresentative. Many leading English amateurs were unable to tour, and even some professionals did not wish to. Several Australian sides were below strength because of disputes over terms and organization. No general pattern of management emerged on either side. Some English tours were straightforward professional ventures, some mixed affairs, with amateur leadership and professional stiffening, and terms arranged on a catch-as-catch-can basis (on which it was not impossible for an amateur to do quite nicely). The professional tours continued for some years under the aegis of Lillywhite and his partners, Shaw and a little later Shrewsbury. To these latter two I now turn.

Alfred Shaw was captain of England four times, all on the tour of 1881–2, when two matches were drawn and two lost. Arthur Shrewsbury was captain on all five occasions in the 1884–5 series, and twice more in 1886–7. Of Shrewsbury's matches, five were won and two lost. Both were Nottinghamshire men, Shaw from Burton Joyce, Shrewsbury from New Lenton. Shaw was born in 1842, Shrewsbury 14 years later. Shaw was the best defensive bowler of his time, and Shrewsbury the best defensive batsman. W.G. has said that he did not find it difficult to play Shaw on a good wicket, but he had to be very patient. On one occasion he was asked whom he thought to be the best English batsman of his time – this was at the end of his career – after himself, and his answer was 'Give me Arthur!' The Lillywhite–Shaw–Shrewsbury tours seem on the whole to have been efficiently and happily run. There were unpleasant incidents, but nothing so bad as the Sydney riot.

It was after that first, 1876–7 tour, that Lillywhite asked Shaw to partner him in organizing future visits to Australia. Shaw suggested that 'as the financial risk was great, it would be better to have an extra pair of shoulders to assist in bearing it', and so Shrewsbury was brought in. Because of the intervening tour of Harris, it was 1881 before the triumvirate put their fortunes to the test.

That year they travelled via America, losing money on the matches they played there. They had intended to take in New Zealand as well, but could not reach a satisfactory arrangement with the New Zealand authorities. They began well enough in Australia. They beat New South Wales. In this match Shaw bowled 29 (four-ball) overs in an innings, 25 of them maidens, for 5 runs and 3 wickets. They beat Victoria. Twenty thousand people watched play on the second day, a record for Australia. The Englishmen were 105 behind on the first innings, and had to follow on, but Shrewsbury then scored 80 not out. However, Victoria needed only 94 in the last innings.

Now on the 20th of December, the last day of the match, there was a boat to be caught for Adelaide, at one o'clock in the afternoon. The Victorians were anxious to play the match out, understandably. Shaw and Lillywhite consulted, and said that they would be happy to agree, if the sailing of the boat was delayed until seven in the evening. To their surprise the steamship company agreed. To the equal surprise of the Victorians, they were bowled out for 75. Lillywhite had given up big matches, and was travelling as joint-manager and umpire. H. F. Boyle, who was more famous as a bowler than a batsman (his Test match batting average was under 13), scored 43 in this innings, after the first six wickets had fallen for 7. Quite early in his innings, Shaw appealed against him for a catch at the wicket. Lillywhite gave him not out. 'Good gracious, Jim!' said Shaw, 'You've lost us the match.' At least that is what Shaw says he said, but I dare say it was a little more acerbic. Perhaps it was as well for the happiness of the business arrangement that it turned out not to matter.

There was still more bother to this match. Heavy betting was going on, and two of the English players were accused of trying to give the match away. Shaw writes

> I gave no credence to it at the time I heard of it, but certain cases of misfielding compelled me to come to the conclusion that the rumours were not without foundation. Whatever the scheme actually was, it failed. A remarkably curious circumstance was that after one ridiculously easy catch had been dropped, a batsman was out by the ball going up inside the fieldsman's arm and sticking there – not, I have reason to think, with the catcher's intentional aid.

He later says,

> The players implicated in the unsavoury business are . . . both dead, and it is but justice to their memory to say that both indignantly denied the allegation made, and that though my co-managers and myself made every effort to probe the facts and find out who it was that had offered the alleged bribes, we were unable to obtain any evidence to which credence could be given, and the whole matter was therefore allowed to drop.

All the same, there was a fight, three English players involved, on the boat to Adelaide. The third of them, the man who had made the accusation, was

W. E. Midwinter, who is the only man who has played for England against Australia, and Australia against England. I must not be tempted into an aside, which would develop into a chapter, about Midwinter; but I can refer you to an article by Grahame Parker, the then Gloucestershire secretary, in *Wisden* for 1971. *Wisden* is usually a source for researchers rather than the place where they display the results, but years of careful work had been done by Parker, a true scholar, before that article was written. He does not, however, throw any light on the question of bribery on the 1881–2 tour.

After those invigorating wins against the two principal states, the rest of that tour was a disappointment. England had, probably, slightly the better of the drawn first Test, and the drawn last, but were well beaten in between, twice. The Australian side of 1882 was in the making.

It may be as well to take a jump in the narrative, omitting the stirring events of the English summer of 1882, and the following winter, and go with Lillywhite and Company to Australia again for their last tours. The 1884 side was, Shaw considered, the best ever to leave England, and he wrote this in 1901. The rubber was won, 3–2, Shrewsbury captain. Lillywhite and Shaw made the trip, but confined themselves to management and umpiring, where the important matches were concerned. The remaining 11 played in all five Tests.

On the way out, going by Suez, they visited the Pyramids, and the place where Moses was found in the bulrushes, in an expedition organized by the resourceful Mr Thomas Cook, who was travelling on the same ship, seeking to expand the Egyptian connections of his promising travel agency. This was the first side to play a Test match at Adelaide. The English and Australian sides were in dispute about the division of the takings. The South Australian Cricket Association mediated, and a settlement was reached, though the Englishmen felt hard done by. Then Murdoch, established now as Australia's captain, refused to allow Lillywhite to umpire. (At this point in the story, it does just occur to me that Lillywhite, struggling for money, may have been susceptible to the little tap on the hip pocket. Why was Shaw so cross about that lbw decision on the previous tour?)

Two local umpires officiated in the first Adelaide Test, without giving much satisfaction to either side. Umpiring was becoming a problem, in both countries. An umpire's fees and travelling expenses meant that much less in the kitty, but it was not the kind of job which could be doubled with that of a visiting manager. The Australians accepted Lillywhite as umpire for the next Test of this 1884–5 tour, but after that the practice ceased.

The task of umpires was becoming more difficult. After that Adelaide Test, the local newspaper, *The Advertiser*, mentioned that 'the English have the irritating habit of appealing in chorus at every possible opportunity, presumably with the motive of discommoding the batsmen. The sooner this undesirable habit is corrected the better. Scott fell a victim to one of many appeals and retired with the accusation of putting his leg in front.' In the match, three batsmen were given out leg-before, a number which would not seem excessive today. But the undesirable habit, alas! has never been corrected, on either side. Within the last few years I have known both English and Australian captains who follow the plan, 'If it's close, *everybody* goes up for it.' It does not excuse them that the precedents go back a long way.

The dauntless trio set off again, in 1886. Lillywhite and Shaw had now almost completely ceased playing, and when one of the active 11 was injured, they had to call upon R. Wood, 'a player engaged at Melbourne, who hailed from Lancashire', in Shaw's description. Thus Wood achieved his place in *Wisden* among the Test cricketers, though he never rose so high as the 'Births and Deaths'. He played in the second Test, batted No. 10, scored 6 and 0 (hit wicket bowled Midwinter in the second innings) and did not bowl.

South Australia was left out of the itinerary this time, and also New Zealand, after some sharp correspondence between Lillywhite and the secretary of the Auckland Cricket Association ('I should have thought that they would have welcomed the English team to New Zealand, if only to improve their cricket'). Both Tests in Australia were played at Sydney. England won them, the first narrowly. A third match was planned at Melbourne, on the East Melbourne ground, the Melbourne Club holding aloof; and the Sydney players were unable to take part (this tells you a good deal about the bitterness in Australian cricket at that time). So the putative Test was replaced by a match between Smokers and Non-Smokers (not very strictly identified), which became famous because it produced the record innings total for a first-class match. The Non-Smokers scored 803 for 9, 236 of them by Shrewsbury, the English captain.

There were complaints on this tour about the slow batting of the Englishmen. It was not a specially strong side: six of them came from Nottinghamshire, which was disproportionate even at a time when that county was producing a flow of fine cricketers. The slow batting had some excuse in the bad pitches. Australian pitches were by then very good, on the main grounds, but this English side were 'the great destroyers of Colonial drought – the providentially sent water diviners, who produced deluges at call'. The phrase is Shaw's – though possibly his editor, A. W. Pullin, had something to do with it.

The Englishman whose injury had given Wood his brief moment of glory was Barnes, a tough Nottinghamshire professional who played in 21 Tests, scored 725 runs at an average of 23, and took 51 wickets at an average of 15. In the first Test of this tour he took eight wickets, getting McDonnell, the Australian captain, out twice, the second time leg-before. There was a row between them afterwards. It ended when McDonnell ducked a swing from Barnes, who hit the wall and put his hand out of action for some time to come. The comment by Shaw is,

> Personally, I think both were to blame, in that they both lost their tempers, and therefore their sense of self-respect . . . I think both were genuinely sorry for the fracas afterwards. Both were fine cricketers. Alas, that death should have claimed them so soon!

So that had not been, one way and another, a very successful tour; but off they set again, the following winter, 1887–8, for the last time. It was not only the last effort of the triumvirate, it was the last of the old professional tours to Australia. Sixty-seven years were to pass before another English captain in Australia was an acknowledged professional. The events of this Australian season demonstrated that the organization of international cricket had fallen far behind its popularity, and that there was a need, if it was not to collapse in a haphazard muddle, for responsible and representative leadership. The separation between the amateur and professional approaches in England had, not indeed its parallel, but its counterpart, in the separation between the Melbourne and Sydney interests (with Adelaide beginning to put a word in) in Australia. The absurdity which had nearly happened in 1876, did happen in 1887: two English sides touring Australia simultaneously. Shaw and company had agreed to an offer made under the auspices of Sydney. The Melbourne Club asked the Hon. M. B. Hawke to bring out a side. Both these sides won victories over 'Combined Australia', but these matches are not reckoned as Tests, nor is there any good reason why they should be. The English teams provided a joint XI to play a joint Australian XI at Sydney in a match which *is* recognized as a Test. It was all a little farcical, but there is no doubt that much talent was assembled for the occasion. The match counts as a win to England, a low-scoring game in wet weather. The English captain for the match was W. W. Read. He was captain of neither of the two touring teams.

It gets very confusing. Hawke's team had been led by the Honourable in person, but he was summoned home because his father had died, and G. F. Vernon took over the leadership of his party. The Shaw–Shrewsbury–Lillywhite party did not include Shaw, who stayed at home; and, possibly in an attempt to give Sydney some social status comparable with that of Melbourne, they had invited an amateur to be captain, one C. A. Smith of Sussex. But neither Smith nor Vernon played in the Test, that is to say the match where the English teams combined. Walter Read, a Surrey amateur and one of the leading batsmen of his day, therefore led England against Australia. Hawke and Smith led Test teams on other occasions as we shall see, though not Vernon.

The Melbourne Cricket Club lost £4,000 on the tour, according to Shaw. 'This they could afford', he adds with some bitterness. The triumvirate lost £2,400. All the burden fell on Shaw and Shrewsbury, for Lillywhite defaulted.

Here is another oddity. The reason Shaw had stayed at home had been to organize a football trip to Australia, which was to follow immediately upon the cricket one. It is hard to tell whether this was something to which he and Shrewsbury were already committed, or whether it was a last desperate throw to recoup their fortunes. The football side duly went to Australia and New Zealand. They did pretty well under Rugby Union rules, winning 27 matches, drawing six, and losing two. But any financial success depended on the matches played under 'Victorian Rules', or Australian Rules as the game is now called. 'We thought the team we took out would readily pick up the game', says Shaw a touch pathetically; but of course they did not, and were outclassed, and there was a further debit. Most of the English football team came from the north of England, where the leading teams were within a few years of breaking away from the Rugby Football Union because of disagreement over 'broken-time payments'. It seems astonishing that the R.F.U. should have sanctioned the tour at all. 'If a football professional is a man who undertakes a tour for the money he can make out of it', wrote Shaw, 'then there was no professional in our team of 1888.' But that was not, quite, how the R.F.U. defined 'a football professional' then, nor even now.

One of the football team was A. E. Stoddart, who had gone out to Australia under Hawke, and stayed on. He was the only Englishman who managed to play Victorian Rules almost as well as he did Rugby. This laid the foundation of an all-round sporting reputation in Australia which perhaps no England captain (which Stoddart was to become) has ever surpassed. When R. L. Seddon, the football captain, was drowned in a sculling misadventure, Stoddart took over from him, and also became assistant manager, under Shrewsbury.

Shaw went out to Australia yet again, in 1891, as manager to Lord Sheffield's team. He was probably happier in the less responsible position. He took employment at home under Sheffield, a Sussex magnate, and after an interval of seven years returned to first-class cricket to play a season for Sussex, not unsuccessfully. Shrewsbury played his last, and twenty-third Test, in 1893 (1,277 runs, average 35·47). He continued playing county cricket for a while. He died in 1903, when he was only 47, by his own hand. He had always been inclined to melancholy, and his financial difficulties oppressed him, though he was prompted to take the last step by a belief that he was suffering from an incurable illness.

We must not contemn, nor patronize the efforts of these three early professional captains of England, any more than we should those of men like Clarke and Parr, who carried the game though Britain and then across the world. They were not educated men, in the sense Lord Harris would have used the word.

It was remarkable that they should have done all they did, even if in the end the sums did not work out right. It was good fortune that the professional development of English cricket was in such hands at such a time. 'Shaw's name', wrote Altham, 'stood for hard work, clean living, and straight dealing', and the same high authority said of Shrewsbury that 'he enjoyed the respect and admiration of everyone associated with him'.

Shaw died four years after Shrewsbury, in 1907. 'Bury me 22 yards from Arthur', he had said, 'so I can send him down a ball now and then'. Later a zealot measured the distance between the graves and found it was 27 yards. He complained to the county committee, but was reassured: 'Alfred always took a five-yards run'.

Here we leave the triumvirate, and retrace our steps to catch up with one or two others. The 'real' Tests, for Englishmen, were those played in England. Here are the captains for home matches in the period 1882–8:

1882: A. N. Hornby (1)
1884: A. N. Hornby (1); Lord Harris (2)
1886: A. G. Steel (3)
1888: A. G. Steel (1); W. G. Grace (2)

There was also a tour of Australia, an important one which we have not yet noticed, in 1882–3, when the captain was the Hon. Ivo Bligh.

It is a little puzzling why Hornby was captain in 1882, because although Lord Harris did not choose or was not chosen to play, there was still an Honourable (A. Lyttelton) in the side, to say nothing of a 34-year-old bearded character who had long been established both as the best batsman in the land and the captain of his county. But Hornby was worthy of his rank as a captain of England, even though his figures do not immediately suggest it. He played for his country three times, and his scores were 2, 4, 2, 9, 0 and 4.

Australia won at the Oval in 1882 by 7 runs. Hornby has been criticized for putting in C. T. Studd as late as No. 10 in the second innings. Two wickets fell at the other end, and Studd never had a ball. But the England batting was, at least on paper, so strong that Hornby himself had gone in at No. 10 in the first innings. His Lancashire opening partner, Barlow, was playing, and had opened the first innings with Grace. In the second innings Hornby decided to go in himself with Grace, to give a lead, with Barlow at No. 3. These seem sensible tactics on the face of it. No doubt Studd was dropped down the order because he had scored 0 in the first innings, and also because he was so nervous that – or so it was said – he was walking round the pavilion wrapped in a blanket. On the other hand, Studd had scored two centuries against the Australians that season. He was a sensitive and attractive character, but edgy. When Peate, the No. 11, got out to a wild swipe, he excused himself by saying 'I couldn't trust Maister Studd', and this has always been thought of as a comical remark by a non-batting Yorkshire slow left-arm bowler, but it may have had a touch of truth in it.

Anyway, as Spofforth bowled that day, it is hard to imagine any change in the batting order changing the result. Australia scored 63 and 122, England 101 and 77.

Some of the stories of the tension at the end may have been exaggerated in retrospect – how the scorer wrote down the name 'Peate' like 'Geese'; how a man dropped dead, and another chewed lumps from the handle of his umbrella; how one English batsman came in ashen even to the lips; how, when the last wicket fell, for a few seconds the crowd was like one man stunned; how George Giffen (who had scored 2 and 0) was embraced by the mother of the Australian manager – but over all the years there has seldom been a more gripping finish to a Test, and this match, along with the victory over M.C.C. at Lord's four years earlier, gave Australian cricket a standing in this country which it has never lost.

In the first Test of 1884, at Old Trafford, Hornby was captain again. The match was drawn, Australia having the better of it. Hornby went in first with Grace and was stumped twice, which gives some idea of what he thought was the proper way to open an innings. He always liked to be on the attack. He was very sharp between the wickets. He would run Barlow out, it was said, and then give him a sovereign; but in spite of the risks he took, this did not happen very often. Indeed, they were famous for the way they ran together, and Francis Thompson's much-quoted line about the 'run-stealers' was keenly observed as well as nostalgically remembered.

Thompson's poem, of which only the latter part is now widely recalled, had a curious and sad origin. Thompson was born in Lancashire, at Preston, in 1859 (Hornby at Blackburn in 1847; Barlow at Bolton in 1850 – not 20 miles separated the three of them). As a boy and young man Thompson watched Lancashire play cricket, watched them devotedly. The match between Lancashire and Gloucestershire, at Manchester in 1878, was one he always remembered. For many years he could recite the names of all the players. Thompson did not have a very successful personal life, as these things are outwardly judged: failed for the priesthood, failed at medicine, row with family, walked to London, took to opium, underneath the arches, down and out. In his later life he had made a reputation as a writer, found some good friends, and was not seriously short of money. 'But' – in Holbrook Jackson's words – 'opium and privation are exacting mistresses.' He died of tuberculosis at the age of 48 (Hornby lived to 78, Barlow to 69). A few years before his death he was asked if he would like to watch Lancashire play at Lord's. He said he would, but then could not face it – too many memories, or just preoccupied with getting his next fix? He wrote the poem instead. He may have written it in order to get an advance from his publisher, or as a kind of apology to his friends for not turning up. This is why, although the poem was published under the title 'At Lord's', there is nothing about Lord's in it. 'It is Glo'ster coming North, the irresistible . . .'

This day of seventy-eight they are come up North against thee,
This day of seventy-eight, long ago!
The champion of the centuries, he cometh up against thee,
With his brethren, every one a famous foe!
The long-whiskered Doctor, that laugheth rules to scorn,
While the bowler, pitched against him, bans the day that he was born;
And G.F. with his science makes the fairest length forlorn;
They are come from the West to work thee woe!

It is little I repair to the matches of the Southron folk,
Though my own red roses there may blow;
It is little I repair to the matches of the Southron folk,
Though the red roses crest the caps, I know.
For the field is full of shades as I near the shadowy coast,
And a ghostly batsman plays to the bowling of a ghost,
And I look through my tears on a soundless-clapping host,
As the run-stealers flicker to and fro,
   To and fro,
O my Hornby and my Barlow long ago!

I wonder if Hornby or Barlow ever read the poem.

Francis Thompson had a curiously compelling relationship with cricket. He lived for a while at Storrington, in Sussex, the village about which Hugh de Selincourt was to write, disguised as Tillingfold, in *The Cricket Match*. He died at St John's Wood. However, for all his wayward and attractive genius, he never captained England, and it is time I got back to Hornby. From first appearance to last, he played 30 years for Lancashire, most of them as captain. After that he interested himself in the administration of the county club, until his death. His son, A. H. Hornby, though not so good a cricketer as his father, was also a captain of Lancashire and, in a sense, of England, since he led the first M.C.C. side to Holland, in 1902.

Hornby was a light, nimble, though strong man, nicknamed 'Monkey' from his schooldays. When he was first chosen to play for Harrow, at the age of 17, he weighed less than six stone. In his prime, at five feet nine, he weighed 11 stone. All through the 1870s, apart from one season when he was injured, his was one of the leading national averages, and he kept popping up in the list until the 1890s. His best season was 1881, when he was top with 1,531 runs at 41·14, four runs an innings more than Grace. That year Lancashire won the championship, and they also shared it three times under Hornby's captaincy. He was as well known for his Rugby football as his cricket. He played nine times for England at Rugby in the years 1877–82, at three-quarter or full-back. As he did not begin his international career until he was 30, this was a considerable achievement. He was made captain for his last match, against Scotland at Manchester, and so became the first man to have led England at both cricket and football. This last match, however, was not among his happier experiences. The report printed in Marshall (*Football: The Rugby Union Game*) says severely:

> Hornby was unequal to the task of keeping the Scotsmen out. His tackling was good, but in fielding the ball and in punting he was far removed from his best form.

He could have had another match against Scotland after that, all the same, but declined the invitation. It would, he said, interfere with his shooting, which was going particular well at the time.

He was a Justice of the Peace, I dare say sometimes a little testy and impetuous in his decisions, a man much admired, much loved, and much joked about in Lancashire (where it is a sure sign of confidence if they make jokes about you). One must be careful of generalizing about local qualities, but I cannot help thinking of him as a characteristic Lancastrian.

After Hornby had first led England, in 1882, there came Bligh's tour, and here, as any cricket chronicler must, I have to face the legend of the Ashes, which, as conceived today, has done even more harm to cricket than the myth of William Webb Ellis has done to Rugby football. The Ashes, however, have more documentation than the Ellis tale. With apologies, therefore, to those of you who are sick of seeing it in print, I reproduce the *Sporting Times* announcement:

In Affectionate Remembrance

of

ENGLISH CRICKET

which died at the Oval

on

29th August, 1882.

Deeply lamented by a large circle

Of Sorrowing Friends and Acquaintances

R. I. P.

N.B. The body will be cremated, and the Ashes taken to Australia.

It was no more than a tolerable joke, and nobody could have foreseen that in 1977 another would appear, this time in *The Times*, commemorating the death of international cricket, 'which died at Hove'. I believe some Australian journalists were responsible for putting it in (the 1977 one, I mean), but that takes me long ahead of my story.

The original idea of Bligh's tour, leaving for Australia in the autumn of 1882, had been that the team should be made up of Cambridge men. Cambridge had a marvellous record against Australians in those days, and one Australian is supposed to have said 'Show us a light blue cap and we'll run!' This was too ambitious a project, but there were still eight amateurs to four professionals in Bligh's twelve, and one of the professionals, their only fast bowler, Morley of Nottinghamshire, was injured in a ship collision at Colombo on the way out. Morley's injury kept him out of the first Test, handicapped him in the others, and is said to have been the cause of his early death, but as he bowled 150 overs in the rest of the series the wounds cannot have been too gaping.

At a dinner in London before the party left, Bligh declared that he hoped to recover 'those Ashes', which was no more than another tolerable joke. He had undertaken to play three matches against the same team as Murdoch had recently brought to England. When Bligh had won the third match, giving him a lead of 2–1, some Melbourne ladies burnt a bail, or bails, and placed their ashes in the little urn which now rests at Lord's. It was presented to Bligh, since the defeat at the Oval had been revenged, and the Ashes were judged to be recovered. It was obviously no more than a lark, and Bligh was a handsome young man, and the belles of Melbourne were full of fun (he married one of them). Until Bligh's death, the urn stood on his study mantelpiece.

All very jolly, but a fourth match was played by the tourists, this time against the full strength of Australia, not just Murdoch's men, and Australia won the match, so the rubber is recorded in the books as drawn, 2–2. There was controversy about this at the time and has been ever since. It is an early example of the statistical scarlet fever which is liable to overtake cricketers. An admirable writer called R. L. Hodgson (he wrote under the pseudonym of 'Country Vicar'), who knew Bligh well, maintained that the fourth match was an afterthought, and ought not to be counted in the official series; according to him, this was also Bligh's view. But this cannot be quite right, for Bowen has demonstrated that a fourth match was scheduled, and possibly a fifth. One might indeed make a case for saying that the fourth match was the only one which should count. I recommend those of you who wish to delve further into this interesting, though intrinsically unimportant, subject, to an article in the spring annual of *The Cricketer* for 1972, by Ralph Barker, which sums up the evidence impartially, without reaching any conclusive judgment.

Gradually, the term 'Ashes' crept into general use, or misuse. It spread in Australia before it did in England. George Giffen, in his memoirs, used the term as if it was familiar, but it was P. F. Warner's book, *How We Recovered the Ashes*, after the 1903–4 tour, which popularized it over here.

As for Ivo Bligh: his Test cricket was restricted to that one tour. He was not a success as a player, making only 62 runs at an average of 10·33, but he was a useful enough cricketer, who made many runs for Eton, Cambridge, and Kent. He was an old-style amateur batsman, a dasher, six feet four inches tall, his favourite stroke the cut. He was 28 when he led England and 70 when he died, the eighth Earl of Darnley.

A. G. Steel captained England four times, in the three Tests of 1886 and the first of 1888. In 1886 the Australians were beaten by four wickets, by an innings and 106, and an innings and 217: a fair whacking. England lost the first of 1888. It is hard to say how good a captain Steel was. English cricket was strong at the time, and Australian riven by discord. It would have taken a bad English captain to lose that year. As a player, Steel was one of the masters, a batsman and a leg-spinner. His name used to be mentioned when people played the old game of picking all-time XIs (I remember he was in mine when I was a boy, but this was possibly because his Christian names were Allan Gibson). Altham wrote in 1926, 'Even today he must be written down as the best leg-break bowler in history'. In all Steel played in 13 Tests, scoring 600 runs at an average of 35·29, which was very high for that period, and more than acceptable even today. His bowling figures were not quite so good: 29 wickets at an average of 20·86. He was a Lancastrian, educated at Marlborough and Cambridge. He was held to be the best schoolboy cricketer known until that time, and made a bigger impact upon the university than any other freshman. (He was 20 when he went up to Cambridge, but that was not then uncommon.) He was President of M.C.C. in 1902, and died in 1914, only 55 years old. He used to wear a pill-box cap, a lavish moustache, a shirt buttoned to the neck, and a swaggering sash – at least that was how he liked to be photographed, the pattern of a Victorian gentleman-cricketer. Because of what W.G. called 'professional and other duties', he could not play regularly once his Cambridge days were over, but he had the gift of arriving in the middle of the season and jumping straight into form, a gift shared by F. S. Jackson, and to some extent by MacLaren.

Steel was on the wrong end of one of cricket's most repeated stories. He was bowling when C. I. Thornton hit the ball into Trafalgar Square at Scarborough, a very large carry, over the stand, towards the northern end. C. I. Thornton, the king of the Scarborough Festival for many years, mentioned this feat some years later to a lady. 'Trafalgar Square!' she said in astonishment. 'From Lord's or the Oval?' Whatever may be the historicity of the sequel, there is no doubt about the hit. An old man at Scarborough once purported to show me the exact spot in the Square where the ball landed.

Steel had played in the first English Test in 1880, somewhat grudgingly, because he was shooting in Scotland (like Hornby, he was a great one for the guns). He was not a tall man – a head shorter than Bligh – but had a comparable reputation as a cutter of the ball. His bowling action was often commented upon approvingly for its simplicity and rhythm. He could bowl both the off-break and the leg-break (the googly of course had not yet been invented). He would occasionally, R. H. Lyttelton tells us, 'alter the movements of his body, roll himself up into a ball and shoot out quite a fast one'. He never, adds the same authority, 'bowled for maidens', which Shaw and his school of course did. One can see why he was considered such an exciting cricketer.

Perhaps this is the point to say a word about Walter Read, captain against Australia in the one Test of the two-tour winter, 1887–8. He was also captain against South Africa at Cape Town in 1892, a match ranked as a Test, though nobody in England considered it as such at the time. Both matches were won, so Read had 100% success as England's captain, which can be said of nobody else who led them more than once: a curious record of no significance whatsoever.

But if Walter Read was only a fortuitous England captain, he was more of a character, and more of a player, than many who achieved the position more formally. He was an amateur, and batted like one – high backlift, always ready to use his feet to go down the pitch. He played in 18 Tests, 17 of them against Australia. He was, it might be said, in another respect one of the first of the 'modern amateurs', the men who did not have much in the way of private means, but retained their gentlemanly status, managing somehow to make a sufficient income out of the game. In his later years, while he was assistant secretary to Surrey (a post in which his duties did not prevent him from playing a full season for them) he was granted a benefit, the old fixture of Surrey v. England being revived for the purpose.

He was born in Surrey, at Reigate, and died there, at Addiscombe, aged 50, in 1906. He was not a product of one of the notable public schools or universities, though he came from a good family. He had a trial for Surrey at the age of 17, and was in the county side a year later. By 1875 he was head of their batting averages. By 1877 he was playing for the Gentlemen. He could bowl lobs usefully, and was a handy wicket-keeper when needed, once keeping wicket for Surrey at Huddersfield, and not conceding a bye, while Yorkshire scored 388. Batsmen in those days, to be sure, disliked letting balls pass their bat, even if they were only playing defensively. There was very little shouldering arms outside the off stump (in this respect, you might say that Bradman was the last of the Victorians, the true heir of Grace).

But after his batting, his chief fame was for close fielding. In the second Test of Bligh's tour, Bates – who bowled medium to slow off-breaks – had taken the wickets of McDonnell and Giffen with successive balls. The next man in was the huge Bonnor, the most famous hitter of his time. A. G. Steel describes what happened next in the *Badminton Book of Cricket*:

Somebody suggested that, in the faint hope of securing a 'hat' for Bates, we should bring a silly mid-on. Bates faithfully promised to bowl a fast shortish ball between the leg and the wicket, and said he was quite certain that Bonnor would play slowly forward to it. Acting on the faith of this, W.W. Read boldly volunteered to stand silly mid-on. In came the giant – loud were the shouts of welcome from the larrikins' throats . . . as Bates began to walk to the wicket to bowl, nearer and nearer crept our brave mid-on; a slow forward stroke to a fast shortish leg stump ball landed the ball in his hands not more than six feet from the bat. The crowd could not believe it and Bonnor was simply thunderstruck at mid-on's impertinence; but Bates had done the hat-trick for all that, and what is more, he got a very smart silver hat for his pains.

Read's batting average in Tests was nearly 28. His most famous innings was at the Oval in 1884, when Lord Harris was captain. Australia won the toss and scored 551, a record, Murdoch 211 of them, another record. This was the occasion when every man on the English side bowled, the most successful being the wicket-keeper, Alfred Lyttelton. England had lost eight wickets for 181 when Walter Read went in. It was said that he was in a towering rage at being put in so low in the order. Certainly towering rages were one of the things he was good at. It was about three o'clock on the last afternoon when he went in, and there was just a chance that Australia might break through and square the rubber. He scored 100 in two hours, and when he was out the match was safe. The ninth wicket partnership put on 151. His partner was Scotton, a dour professional left-hander from Nottinghamshire, who scored 90 in five hours and three-quarters. He had opened the innings and was last out.

Two years later, also at the Oval, Scotton scored 34 in three and three-quarter hours. As in the same innings, Grace scored 170 and Read 94, the spectators did not have much to complain about, but this prompted *Punch* to publish a Tennysonian parody which will be none the worse for being quoted again.

> Block, block, block,
>> At the foot of thy wicket, O Scotton!
> And I would that my tongue could utter
>> My boredom. You *won't* put the pot on!
> Oh, nice for the bowler, my boy,
>> That each ball like a barndoor you play!
> Oh, nice for yourself, I suppose,
>> That you stick at the wickets all day!

And the clock's slow hands go on,
  And you still keep up your sticks;
But oh! for the lift of a smiting hand,
  And the sound of a swipe for six!
Block, block, block,
  At the foot of thy wicket, ah do!
But one hour of Grace or Walter Read
  Were worth a week of you!

Read's tour of South Africa, incidentally, included a match against Eighteen Malays, so far the only occasion an English team has met a non-white team there. It was quite a strong team, though seven of the Test side only played for England on the one occasion. The best batsman, Murdoch, and the best bowler, Ferris, were Australians who had settled in England. That was the second tour to South Africa. The first, in 1888–9, had been led by C. A. Smith.

All matches on the 1888–9 tour were played against odds, except the two subsequently raised to Test status. Altham says the standard of the tourists was 'about that of a weak county', which seems a little hard for one which included Abel, Ulyett, Briggs and J. M. Read, who won 88 England caps between them. Of the remainder, however, only one otherwise played for England. They were much too good for the South Africans. Briggs, during the tour, took nearly 300 wickets at an average of about 5, and the captain himself took 130 at under 8.

C. Aubrey Smith ultimately became, I should say without question, the most widely-known man ever to have captained England at cricket. Millions knew of him who had scarcely so much as heard of the game. Let us look at his cricketing career first. He was born in London in 1863, a doctor's son, and played successfully for Charterhouse and Cambridge. He also played for Sussex from 1882 to 1896, irregularly, and was the county captain from 1887 to 1889. Although he had been captain of the Shaw–Shrewsbury team in 1887–8, he did not play in the representative match. He was a fast-medium bowler, what we would nowadays call an off-cutter; a tall man who batted much in the manner of Ivo Bligh, though not so well. He did come off with the bat from time to time – he scored 142 against Hampshire at Hove – but his bowling was his strength. Because of an oddity in his action, he became known as 'Round-the-Corner Smith'. It is not quite clear from the accounts what this oddity was. W. G. Grace, in a paragraph on the advantages which sometimes attend peculiar actions, said 'When Smith begins his run he is behind the umpire and out of sight of the batsman; and I can assure you it is rather startling when he suddenly appears at the bowling crease.' He contrasts him with Spofforth, who 'goes to the other extreme, starting some yards on the offside of the batsman, and giving the impression that he is aiming at a point nearer short-leg than the wicket'.

Yet Smith is also said, by *Wisden*, sometimes to have started his run from mid-off, in which case, even if he bowled round the wicket, it is hard to see why his appearance 'round the corner' could have been startling. No doubt he was a whimsical man, who changed his style to suit his mood.

Dennis Castle has told me of an old Sussex member, who had watched cricket at Hove for many years, who would say 'Good player, that fellow Smith. Pity he became a mummer.' Smith's acting career was no better than all right, until the invention of the moving picture. Then, seeing the opportunities of his profile and accent, relatively late in life, he became every American's idea of an English aristocrat. He moved to Hollywood. Beginning in butlerish parts, he rapidly became the Duke of Wellington. Most Englishmen, even, of about my age, when they think of the Duke of Wellington, recall an image of C. Aubrey Smith. He became, if not quite a star, a sub-star. The Gables and the Garbos might come above him on the hoardings, but just below them there would be a substantially-sized 'WITH C. AUBREY SMITH'. He was a good actor, better indeed than he was made to appear by being so relentlessly type-cast on the films, and became a kind of unofficial president of the English colony in Hollywood. He was captain of the Hollywood Cricket Club until a few years before his death. Evelyn Waugh must have had him in mind, to say the least, when he portrayed Sir Ambrose Abercrombie in *The Loved One*.

Aubrey Smith was knighted in 1944, for 'services to Anglo–American friendship'. He returned to England often, even in his later years, and was usually to be seen at a Lord's Test match. Sir Home Gordon recalls going with him to Hove, when for once the small boys with their autograph books totally neglected the cricketers. His last visit was in 1947, when he saw a partnership of 370 for England's third wicket between Edrich and Compton, and an England victory by 10 wickets. It was the sixty-sixth ranking match between the countries, and he had played in the first, 58 years earlier, when England won by eight wickets. He scored only 3 in his only Test appearance, but took 7 wickets for 61.

He could not play in the remaining Test of that tour, so England were led by M. P. Bowden, a quiz question if ever there was one. Bowden was primarily a wicket-keeper, though he did not keep wicket in his two Tests, since Wood was thought to be better. In his Test innings Bowden scored 0, run out, and 25. He had been at school at Dulwich, and played for Surrey before he was 18. He did not get many opportunities to keep wicket, because Wood was the regular Surrey wicket-keeper. In 1887, when Wood was injured, and Bowden kept wicket against Gloucestershire, *Wisden* states that he 'by no means shone'. Indeed he had to be replaced, first by Abel and then by Walter Read. However, the following year he kept wicket for the Gentlemen, and he won praise in that capacity on occasions in South Africa, so he must have improved. When not keeping wicket, he was a fast outfield. He had been chosen for the trip after a successful batting season in 1888, one of Surrey's championship years. When they scored 698, beating Sussex by an innings and 485, Walter Read made 171, and Bowden 189 not out. Surrey's was the highest score in county cricket up till that time, and their margin of victory is still the largest in a championship match.

At the end of that tour, Smith and Bowden stayed on in South Africa, setting up a stockbroking business. It did not prosper. Smith soon came home, though not before captaining Transvaal in the first Currie Cup match. Bowden on his debut in South African cricket scored 126 not out for Transvaal against Kimberley. He remains the youngest cricket captain England has ever had, about $23\frac{1}{2}$, and he died the youngest, in South Africa aged 26, a record of which few will seek to deprive him.

The third tour of South Africa – Walter Read's coming between – was led by Lord Hawke, in 1895-6. Here we approach another mighty name. England won all three Tests easily. The South Africans had in the meantime toured England, and though they played no matches recognized as Tests, had beaten M.C.C. at Lord's, so they were coming along. Hawke's team included Fry, Hayward, and Lohmann, three of the great ones; and also S. M. J. Woods, another Australian who had settled in England. South Africa had an Englishman, Frank Hearne, who had stayed on to coach there after the 1889 tour.

Hawke played in the first representative match, but had been unwell, and did not lead the side, at least not officially. Thus the name of Sir T. C. O'Brien, Bart., is numbered among the captains of England. Timothy O'Brien was an Irishman, born in Dublin in 1861. He learnt his cricket at Downside, a Catholic school in Somerset which has produced countless good cricketers. From there he went to St Charles College, Notting Hill. This gave him a qualification for Middlesex, for whom he first played in 1881. He went up to Oxford at the age of 23, chiefly with the intention of getting a Blue, which he did as a freshman. A Blue was at this time considered rather a higher honour than playing for a county. It was even better, of course, to play for the Gentlemen, and after 1882 it became increasingly accepted that the highest honour of all was to play for England, at home. We were still in the period when even a professional, so far as the honour and glory went, would rather have been chosen for the Players than for an overseas tour.

The attraction of tours was, for an amateur, the experience, the possibilities of fun, and – in some cases – the perquisites. For a professional, the attraction was the pay – the security of a winter's work in pleasant conditions, more lucrative, than he could expect down the mine, in the fields, or behind the bar. As I explained, I have followed the categorization of Tests commonly accepted today, but it needs to be constantly remembered that success in these early international matches was not a sure index to public esteem. A hundred in the university match, or in a high-class fixture, counted more to a man's reputation than a hundred at Cape Town, or even Sydney. Thus when Bowden died, what was remembered was his 189 against Sussex, not that he had been captain of 'England'. And who thought the less of Timothy O'Brien because his Test average, in eight innings, was 7·37? He scored many vigorous runs for Oxford and Middlesex. W.G. named him as one of the half-dozen best batsmen of his time, though W.G.'s pronouncements upon such subjects were inclined to be a little quirky and inconsistent (probably it depended on the views of his literary ghost). O'Brien was an ebullient character, of the kind Englishmen expect Irishmen to be, a high flyer in style and temper. Once he threatened to fight W.G. at the wicket.

O'Brien had a successful first season with Oxford, except in the University match itself, when he made a pair of noughts. He scored 92 against the Australians, on the only occasion Oxford have ever beaten them. He also scored 72 against the Australians for M.C.C., and was chosen for the Manchester Test in 1884, and chosen at Lord's four years later. These were his only Tests except for his three in South Africa. He had toured Australia with Hawke, but did not play in the Test.

He did better in his second University match, and altogether made over 7,000 runs for Middlesex, at an average of 30. He was another of those who did not play all the time, but was picked when available. It must have been irritating for the young professionals, even in those days – bowling to a man in the nets all afternoon, to get him into form, so that he could take your place in the side. But it was never doubted that O'Brien should play when he could. He was good enough, when nearly 53, to return to first-class cricket, and score 111 and 90 for Lionel Robinson's XI against Oxford – thus confirming many strongly expressed views about the slackness and incompetence of the younger generation, views current in 1914, before they all went off to die.

He might have had a third Blue, and a fourth, had he taken the precaution of passing the Oxford entrance examination. At about the same time, his friend Sam Woods was facing a similar problem at Cambridge. (I know this is an old story, but what is the purpose of books such as this if we are not allowed to recall old stories?) Alarm and despondency spread through Cambridge when it was known that Sam Woods, after a couple of years of residence, was up for his 'Little Go'. What, Cambridge men asked themselves, would the hopes be at Lord's, without the fast bowler? And in the Rugby match without the leader of the forwards? Sam was no scholar, and there were gloomy prognostications as he made his way towards the Examination Schools, in the unaccustomed dignity of subfusc. The examiners were lenient, and only asked Sam two questions. The first was his name. The second was 'What was the name of the first king of Israel?' Sam, who had been doing some desperate if belated study, triumphantly replied 'Saul', and was allowed to depart. Dazzled by success, he spoilt the effect by turning round at the door – he did not want all that work to be wasted – and adding 'Also called Paul'.

This in turn reminds me of another cricketer called Jordan, who intended to be either a lawyer or a doctor, I cannot remember which, and had much trouble passing his examinations. When at last he scrambled through, he sent a telegram to his family, saying

ANCIENT AND MODERN NUMBER TWO FIVE FOUR
VERSE FIVE FORTISSIMO

The relevant lines in the hymn, which begins 'Art thou weary, art thou languid?', are

> Sorrow vanquished, labour ended,
> Jordan passed.

I digress; and I digress a little more, as I always do when Sam Woods comes into the conversation, by recalling a famous breakfast-party at Cambridge. Sam Woods and his rooms-mate Gregor MacGregor (who kept wicket for Cambridge, Middlesex, and England) decided to invite the amateurs of C. I. Thornton's XI (O'Brien one of them) for breakfast on the third day of the match. They provided a great dish of hot lobsters, and quantities of beer. The guests were alarmed at such fare at such an hour, and cried out for bacon and eggs and coffee, which were brought. They lived well, those distant undergraduates. It is said that Sam and MacGregor ate all the lobster between them, and drank all the beer, and then they started cricket, and Sam took all ten wickets in an innings. The ten wickets are certainly historical, but the rest of the tale cannot be quite correct. Sam says in his reminiscences (a good book, I suppose ghosted but not noticeably so) that 'one or two of them tried it and ate well'. I would bet that Timothy O'Brien was one of those who tried it.

But O'Brien, whether because he did not know the name of the first king of Israel, or whether he did not care, went down at the end of his second year at Oxford. He inherited the baronetcy, from an uncle, just before he stumbled on the captaincy of England. Sir Home Gordon, another baronet, a man who approved of the aristocracy, has some amusing things to say about O'Brien in his book, *Background of Cricket*. (This is not an altogether reliable and admirable book, indeed I once heard E. W. Swanton describe it as 'Backside of Cricket', but it can be illuminating.) O'Brien, says Sir Home, 'is alleged to have been once seen in the Parks fielding in a mackintosh under an umbrella'. He also says: 'He was a fine captain, who possessed a unique habit. Directly he went in, he invariably, after his first over, ascertained for himself that the wickets were pitched in due alignment.' Here was the Irishman making sure the English were up to no tricks.

He died at the age of 87, and was the senior English Test player at the time of his death. Aubrey Smith, against whom he had played in both his University matches, succeeded to this distinction, but died 11 days later.

Lord Hawke, who was able to captain his sides personally in the second and third Tests of the 1895–6 tour, was born in 1860 and died in 1938. His first-class cricket career lasted from 1881 to 1911, though he did not play regularly in the last few years. He was a kind of north of England Harris, though a lesser man; the benevolent despot of Yorkshire cricket. I do not attempt here a full survey of his remarkable career, but one or two points must be made. He led Yorkshire to its first championship. He led the way in making large and necessary improvements in the lot of the professional cricketer. He became both Treasurer and President of M.C.C. He was chairman of selectors from 1899 to 1909, not a role in which he shone.

As a cricketer, he was not up to England standard. In strict terms of cricketing merit, he was not worth his place in the great Yorkshire sides which he captained at the beginning of the twentieth century. Nevertheless he was not a negligible player, and would have been an asset to most county sides. Peter Thomas, in his invaluable *Yorkshire Cricketers, 1839–1939*, gives a list of his best performances, and points out that he scored 50 at least once against every other county, and seven times against Lancashire. He did best against the best opposition, because there was more need. He would have scored many more runs had he batted higher in the order. Once he decided he would like a knock, and put himself down as No. 3 against Derbyshire at Chesterfield. He sat with his pads on while Brown and Tunnicliffe made 554 for the first wicket (then the record) and thereafter retreated to his usual modest place in the order.

He became a good fieldsman after a slow start, which rather put the Bramall Lane grinders against him. His Test career was limited to the three matches of 1895–6, and two more on a second tour of South Africa in 1898–9. His batting average was 7·85, which at least put him ahead of Timothy O'Brien. He did not bowl – and nor, now I come to think of it, did O'Brien, even when he was captain. This was rather odd, for he was always swinging his arm over in the hope of catching his captain's eye, and once got W.G. out at Cheltenham, when all the regular bowlers had failed, or retreated to the beer tent, or possibly the famous gentlemen's lavatory tent (which, I need scarcely remind you, was a trophy secured by the Glorious Gloucesters after the relief of Ladysmith, and is still religiously kept intact).

But if he had shortcomings as a player, Hawke deserves his place as an England captain, because few men have done more in spreading and en-couraging the game across the world. Apart from the trip to Australia, when he had to return, and the two to South Africa, he took sides twice to India and Ceylon, twice to Canada and the United States, once to the West Indies (where again there was a clash of arrangements, with two sides touring), a third time to South Africa (with no Tests played) and to New Zealand. His sides won many more matches than they lost, and if there was occasionally a certain stiffness in social relations, it was no more than was generally acceptable in a peer of the realm. He always insisted that his side should accompany him to church on Sundays. Timothy O'Brien no doubt managed to dodge this, as an earnest Roman Catholic.

Hawke was not born to the peerage – his father was a country parson, until the deaths of the two childless brothers changed the line – but took to it like a duck to water, if he would not resent the analogy. There was one odd thing about him. He was not a Yorkshireman. Even by his time, the county had established the rule, to which they have clung in good times and bad, that only Yorkshiremen-born play for Yorkshire. Hawke's family home was at Tadcaster, but he was not born there. He was born in Lincolnshire. Hawke's dispensation cannot have been unconnected with the fact that he was, by then, a prospective peer. He was within his legal rights – there was a 'family home' qualification in the championship regulations – but it was another obstacle he had to overcome with the grinders. There is a story of an argument at a Lancashire–Yorkshire match. Lancashire, with several importations in the side, were getting the better of things, and a Yorkshireman pointed out that at least *his* side were home-bred. The name of Hawke was produced as a counter, whereat the Yorkshireman said, 'If a cat has kittens in a fish-and-chip shop, does that make them kippers?' Good repartee, yet some Yorkshiremen had an uncomfortable feeling that a properly brought-up cat had no business having her kittens in a fish-and-chip shop.

In the 1920s Hawke published his *Recollections and Reminiscences*. It is a book full of interest although, indeed partly because, it has some comically aristocratic touches. Herbert Farjeon, who wrote amusingly about it, particularly relished the sentence, concerning Rhodes, 'The presentation of his portrait to me last year was the crowning tribute to his wonderful career'. I also enjoyed his comment on Barlow, Louis Hall, and the Hearne family. They were, he wrote, 'the earliest to be gentlemen-professionals. Higher praise cannot be given.' But it is also true, as Patrick Morrah has written, that 'in the entire history of cricket no man did more for the professional than he'.

Hawke's two tours take the story of South African Tests up to the end of the century. The two Tests of 1898–9 were won, but the first by only 32 runs, and it was a strong English side, with Tyldesley (who scored a century in the second Test), Albert Trott (who had played successfully for Australia before coming to England and qualifying for Middlesex), P. F. Warner, Frank Mitchell (a Yorkshireman who was later to captain South Africa himself) and Schofield

Haigh, one of the great Yorkshire bowlers. It was clear that something near the best would soon be needed to take on the South Africans.

Let us survey the field as we have seen it, since Test matches began. There have been Lillywhite, Shaw and Shrewsbury, the cautious old professionals; Harris, Bligh and Hawke, the aristocrats; Hornby and Steel, commoners but gentlemen, true amateurs who would weigh up the relative attractions of cricket and shooting; Read, an amateur who owed at least part of his living to the game; Smith, who despite his assorted, up-and-down life, won fame in the end as the aristocratic type *par excellence*; the shadowy Bowden, his business partner; and O'Brien, not a man for a category, but a baronet. Plenty of blue blood there.

And now let us return to the Australians. For the first Test of 1888, at Lord's A. G. Steel was captain again. Australia won a low-scoring match by 61 runs, and were a strong side, the best since the heroes of 1882. Steel played no further Test cricket that summer, or, as it turned out, ever. For the second match, at the Oval – the side chosen as usual by the ground authority – the Surrey committee turned, for a captain, to William Gilbert Grace.

2

THE DAYS OF GRACE

Give me a look, give me a face,
That makes simplicity a grace
Ben Jonson

It seems odd, on the face of it, that Grace had not captained England before. He had been first choice for every home Test, since they began. He had been 32 when the first was played in 1880, his dominance already beyond dispute, with tours of America and Australia behind him. He was enormously popular with the public, and well enough liked by the cricketers, though inclined to touches of what Stephen Potter called gamesmanship. But he was not, nor did he ever become, one of the inner circle of Marylebone. He was the son of a Gloucestershire country doctor, with no blue blood, no University, no public school. At the age of 14 he had scored 32 against Tarrant and Jackson, the fastest bowlers in England, for Twenty-Two of Bristol against All-England, on Durdham Down. They must have been trying, because the All-England XI were beaten. I lived for several years a couple of hundred yards from Durdham Down, and when I walked upon it, which was nearly every day if I was not away from home, I thought of that innings, and of the fearless, beardless boy. Yet it was not the same thing as Eton and Trinity, or Winchester and New College, and Gloucestershire did not have a Test match ground, and could not choose Test match captains. So, for England, Grace played on under the others, until there was really no one else left to pick, and became captain of England at the age of 40.

There are several good biographies of Grace, the best of them a delightful little book by Bernard Darwin. There is one matter, however, which the modern generation might not gather even from that book, because Darwin took it for granted: that is how very, very good a cricketer Grace was. Today, we have this obsession with Test matches, and Test match figures, and the prolixity of Test matches has caused a statistical inflation. How many Tests, a man will ask you, even on a Gloucestershire ground, did Grace play in? 'Only 22.' What is that, compared with Hammond's 85, or Evans's 91, or Cowdrey's 118, or Barrington's 250? (I may have got Barrington's total wrong. Perhaps it only *seemed* 250.) A man at Bristol once pointed out to me, knowledgeably, that David Allen, a worthy off-spinner if you remember, had now 'overtaken' Grace in Test appearances. What, such men would say, was Grace's Test batting average? (It was 32·29.) How many Test centuries did he score? (Two.) What was his bowling like? (Nine wickets at 26.) Compare with that, etcetera – and just look at the lumbering old blighter, look at his photographs, look at his stance, look at the way he sticks his toe in the air . . . and so the cry of 'Peanuts!' goes up, from those who are accustomed to work themselves into a state of sub-choral hysteria whenever Bonks or Bash makes an epoch-making 50 in the John Player League.

So I feel that I must remind you of the supremacy of W. G. Grace as a cricketer, and short of writing quite a different book, this may simply be done by looking at the English averages for the years of his prime. For whatever the changes in pitches, and publicity, whatever the increase in the game of 'science' (a word beloved by current cricketers, to whom it rarely occurs that the basis of science is experiment), you can only judge a cricketer in relation to what he did compared with the others of his time. No cricketer stands this comparison so well as Grace, except Bradman. And though I think Englishmen should long have recognized that Bradman was the best of all batsmen, his circumstances were easier, and he did not bowl. Grace remains the greatest of all cricketers.

In 1866, the season during which he reached his eighteenth birthday, Grace headed the first-class averages, with 42. I take the following figures from the appendix to Grace's book *Cricket,* published in 1891. I doubt if modern statisticians would agree with them, because there has been much dispute as to what constituted, or ought to have constituted, a first-class match. I can see Bill Frindall and Irving Rosenwater taking off their coats already. Furthermore, I cannot give you the decimal points. Methven Brownlee, who compiled Grace's statistical appendix as well as writing most of the book, gives them, but not in the modern style. His 'decimal portions' merely represent surplus runs or balls. Nevertheless I have no doubt of the weight these figures carry.

In 1867, Grace was only sixth in the batting averages. Not too much importance should be put upon these early averages, because few first-class matches, by the standards of the statisticians then or now, were played. In 1868, though, Grace was head of the averages again, with 588 runs in nine completed innings, average 65. The next man, R. A. H. Mitchell, a famous coach, averaged 41. In 1869, Grace was again first, averaging 58 in 23 completed innings, almost ten higher than Richard Daft of Nottinghamshire, who came second. In 1870 Daft pressed him more closely. Grace still led the list with an average of 54 in 33 completed innings, but Daft averaged 51, though only in 11. Now we come to the great decade.

1871	Completed Innings	Runs	Highest Score	Average
W. G. Grace	35	2,739	268	78
T. G. Matthews	7	277	201	39
Daft	15	565	92	37

Matthews was a Gloucestershire man, only a little older than W.G., who did not later play much. The only other batsman to score even a thousand runs that season was 'Young Stonewall' Jupp, who was to open with Selby for James Lillywhite. It is of Jupp that Altham tells a story, that he was playing in a match at Dorking, where he was born, and was bowled first ball. 'Ain't you going out, Harry?' they asked him. 'No,' he replied, 'not at Dorking.' I have heard just such a story of W.G. He attracted other men's tales.

1872	Completed Innings	Runs	Highest Score	Average
W. G. Grace	26	1,485	170*	57
Selby	9	377	128*	41
Daft	17	589	102	34

* Not Out

Jupp scored a thousand runs again this season, and so did Richard Humphrey, another Surrey professional, but their averages were a long way down the list.

1873	Completed Innings	Runs	Highest Score	Average
W. G. Grace	30	2,139	192*	71
F. Townsend	5	261	136	52
J. M. Cotterill	6	248	78	41

* Not Out

Jupp scored 996 runs, average 24, but only came thirteenth in the averages. E. M. Grace came tenth, average 29, and G. F. Grace ninth, average 30. Townsend was a member of a well-known Gloucestershire cricketing family.

Cotterill was a Sussex man, one of the leading amateurs over several seasons, whose career was curtailed by his medical practice in Edinburgh. He was an expert at throwing the cricket ball, a contest which then featured prominently in sports meetings. He had a close contest with W.G. at the Eastbourne Sports in 1870. W.G., three years the older man, won with a throw of 116 yards, but Cotterill surpassed this distance a year or two later.

1874	Completed Innings	Runs	Highest Score	Average
W. G. Grace	31	1,658	179	53
Jupp	35	1,275	154	36
C. S. Gordon	5	183	96	36

Gordon was yet another Gloucestershire man, later Brigadier-General Gordon-Stewart. Lord Harris was fourth this year (29, in eight innings), Hornby fifth, Fred Grace sixth, Cotterill seventh.

1875	Completed Innings	Runs	Highest Score	Average
Barlow	10	388	87	38
J. M. Cotterill	12	430	191	35
E. M. Grace	6	214	71	35

So now we have young Barlow making an appearance. He had been a porter at a Lancashire railway station. Hornby had observed him batting one day against the station-master, and asked if he might have an over or two himself. 'Ay, do', he was told, 'he's been in for a fortnight.' I wonder if Francis Thompson ever knew this story. Harris is in sixth place, Walter Read eighth, Hornby ninth. The prospective candidates for the England captaincy were beginning to emerge. Fred Grace was eleventh, and just missed his thousand.

And where was 'The Champion', as W.G. was now known? It has to be confessed that he came a miserable seventh, a place behind Harris, which may have irked him a little. He claimed never to be worried about figures, but frequently showed himself sharply aware of them. He still scored 1,498 runs, 500 more than anyone else, but it was a little disappointing by his own standards.

And then your eye drifts down the page to the bowling averages, and you see that in this season W. G. Grace is fourth, average 12, 192 wickets – 30 more than Alfred Shaw. There was no keeping him out of the picture.

1876	Completed Innings	Runs	Highest Score	Average
W. G. Grace	42	2,622	344	62
C. J. Ottaway	6	374	112	62
W. W. Read	14	588	106	42

Back to normal. Ephraim Lockwood of Yorkshire was the only other man to pass a thousand runs. W. R. Gilbert, a name which will recur, was fifth in the averages. W.G.'s 344 against Kent was the highest in first-class cricket to that time. He followed it with 177 against Nottinghamshire and 318, not out, against Yorkshire – 839 runs in eight days.

1877	Completed Innings	Runs	Highest Score	Average
W. G. Grace	37	1,474	261	39
W. W. Read	11	399	140	36
A. P. Lucas	24	832	115	34

The only other batsman to score a thousand runs was again Lockwood, whose average was 14 runs less. Grace came fourth in the bowling averages, taking 179 wickets at under 13. Nobody else took so many wickets.

1878	Completed Innings	Runs	Highest Score	Average
Selby	30	909	107	30
Ulyett	46	1,347	109	29
W. G. Grace	38	1,115	116	29

This again was a year of relative failure, since he neither headed the averages nor scored the most runs. He was only tenth in the bowling. He took 148 wickets, but Steel, Shaw and Morley took more. Ulyett was the hero of the season, though his bowling had not yet fully developed. It is interesting to see some of Lillywhite's men to the fore.

1879	Completed Innings	Runs	Highest Score	Average
W. G. Grace	25	880	123	35
A. N. Hornby	20	606	64*	30
Hon. A. Lyttelton	24	688	102	28

* Not Out

Once more, back to normal, though the margins are growing smaller. Ulyett, who came eighth in the averages, scored almost as many runs as Grace. Grace's 105 wickets were many less than were taken by Morley and Shaw; he came eleventh in the bowling averages.

1880	Completed Innings	Runs	Highest Score	Average
W. G. Grace	24	951	152	39
R. T. Ellis	17	569	103	33
Lord Harris	22	722	123	32

The 152 was made in the first English Test. So he ended the decade still on top, though not by very much. Bligh, Barnes of Nottinghamshire, and Lockwood scored more runs, and he only took 85 wickets, though he bowled more than a thousand (four-ball) overs.

So when W.G. began Test cricket, his best years were behind him. But what years they had been! Methven Brownlee compiled a table of the leading batsmen of the decade 1871–80 inclusive. It is an arbitrary choice of period, no doubt intended to flatter his subject, but it makes his point. Here are the first ten in his batting list.

	Completed Innings	Runs	Average
W. G. Grace	342	16,877	49
J. M. Cotterill	50	1,563	31
W. W. Read	71	2,011	28
Hon. A. Lyttelton	92	2,536	27
A. N. Hornby	214	5,827	27
A. J. Webbe	142	3,850	27
W. Yardley	96	2,592	27
F. Penn	144	3,826	26
G. F. Grace	241	6,312	26
Lord Harris	181	4,630	25

The others who scored more than 5,000 runs were Lockwood, Jupp, I. D. Walker, and Ulyett, all with averages below 25. Lockwood's 8,720 was the highest, just over half Grace's total. In this same period Grace took 1,174 wickets, more than anyone except Alfred Shaw. His average of 14 left him fifteenth in the list. The lists, incidentally, confirm the supremacy at this time of amateur batting and professional bowling. In the top 20 batsmen there are 16 amateurs; in the top 20 bowlers there are five.

Brownlee provides similar tables for the following decade. Grace is now *primus inter pares*, no more. He still scored the most runs (14,541 at 35), but not so very many more than Read (12,853 at 34), and Ulyett (11,847 at 25); and Shrewsbury, though with 6,000 runs fewer, had a higher average by five points. In the bowling list, Grace is down to forty-first.

If he was past his prime when he played in Test cricket, Grace was therefore even more so when he came to the captaincy in that second Test of 1888. England won the match in two days, by an innings, and the same thing happened in the third Test, at Manchester. This was a freak summer, one of the wettest remembered. The Australians had no batsmen who could cope with English pitches in such conditions, though they did have a splendidly suited pair of bowlers in Turner and Ferris, who took 534 wickets between them during the tour, 405 more than all the rest put together.

Grace remained captain of England in home Tests until 1899, apart from one match in 1893, when he was unfit. He was also captain of Lord Sheffield's side to Australia, in 1891–2. Altogether he was captain in 13 Tests, winning eight and losing three, although he only won four tosses. In 1890, England won by seven wickets at Lord's and two wickets at the Oval. The Manchester match was washed out. The Oval match provided one of the tense finishes. England needed only 95, but lost eight wickets against Turner and Ferris before they got them. In both these matches W.G. scored 0 in the first innings. He did, however, make 75 not out, the highest score and a match-winning one, in the second innings at Lord's. Eighteen-ninety was another wet summer, though not as bad as 1888. The Australians, though still without several of their best players, were still a good side.

In 1893, the next Australian tour of England, two matches were drawn, and England won the third. W.G., though he had to miss the Lord's match, was captain in the second, at the Oval, when England won by an innings and 43. In his Test innings this season, he scored 68, 40, and 45, acceptable enough, but domestically he had suffered several poor seasons, and there were those who said his days, at Test level, should be drawn to a close. But then there came his astonishing revival in 1895, of which more later, and the following season he was, inevitably, in charge against Australia again. This was a well-contested rubber, one of the best in England, between two strong sides. England won, 2–1. The Manchester match, which Australia won, was one of the memorable ones. It was Ranjitsinhji's first Test. He had not been chosen at Lord's, although his form had clearly warranted it. M.C.C. were responsible for the choice at Lord's, and took the view that an Indian prince had no business playing in a Test match for England. Harris was always a stickler for qualifications, as we shall see later in the case of Hammond. But the argument about Ranjitsinhji arose from his colour, rather than the fact that he was not an Englishman. After all, Sam Woods had been asked to play for England at home in 1888, though he preferred to play for Australia, the land of his birth. Midwinter had already achieved his unique double, if such a phrase is permissible, by playing for both England and Australia in Test matches. Murdoch, Ferris and Woods had all played for English teams in South Africa – though I must repeat that it occurred to no Englishman, certainly no Englishman at Lord's, that the South African matches were 'Tests'.

However, the Lancashire committee invited Ranjitsinhji to play, after consulting the Australian captain, Harry Trott, who said they would be delighted to play against him. Grace had never had any doubts on the subject. He was taken a little aback by Ranji, whose style was so different from his own, but saw the runs mount, and wanted the best team. Ranji marked the occasion with scores of 62 and 154, not out. The second innings was described by George Giffen, who was bowling, as 'absolutely the finest innings I have seen'. I have never known of anyone else who saw that innings, who did not speak of it in similar terms. After England had followed on, Australia needed 125 to win, and now came another historic performance, from the fast bowler, Tom Richardson. He bowled unchanged, with figures of

O	M	R	W
42·3	16	76	6

It was not enough, though it might have been, but for a dropped catch at the wicket. Australia won by three wickets. Sir Neville Cardus wrote one of his most memorable pieces of prose about this match, in his essay on Richardson in *Days in the Sun*. When Australia scored the winning run, he says of Richardson, 'He stood at the bowling crease, dazed. *Could* the match have been lost? His spirit protested . . . He stood there like some fine animal baffled at the uselessness of great strength and effort in this world. . . . A companion led him to the pavilion, and there he fell wearily upon a seat.' James Agate later said this was not true, far from it, for Richardson was first man off the field, and halfway through his second pint by the time the others had reached the bar. Neither of the critics was very old at the time, and it is not a point upon which statistical research is necessary.

It was Agate who said, of his numerous large volumes of *Ego*, his prolonged autobiography, that these were the books by which he would live: 'Sheer bulk will do it'. It is a remark which might have been applied to W.G. In fact, much the same thing was said by one of the old professionals (authorities differ as to which): 'There's lots can do it now and again, but the Doctor, he just keeps *on* doing it.' Bradman again comes to mind.

Before we reach the 1899 season in England, let us glance back at what had been going on in Australia, starting from Sheffield's tour of 1891–2, with Alfred Shaw as manager, and Grace as captain. This tour was more lavish, and better organized, than any which had preceded it. Although England lost the rubber 2–1, it was in almost every other way a successful tour, even from the English point of view. Australian cricket gained much from it. The rifts between their factions began to heal, at least for the time being, and at the end Lord Sheffield presented a shield, for competition between the states.

Sheffield had made himself popular in Australia, and so, once again, with the usual touches of controversy, had W.G. He did not always agree with the umpires, and sometimes said so: but, as A. A. Thomson has pleasingly written, 'He never let the sun go down upon his wrath, though there were some colourful sunsets while it lasted.' It was a pity that the younger generation of Australians saw him only at this stage of his career. In England he had failed, in 1891, to score a century. Nor had he scored a thousand runs. The same thing was to happen in the English season of 1892. On tour, he scored 159, not out, against Victoria at Melbourne, and finished at the head of the averages for all matches, both 11-a-side and those against odds. But he was no longer able to justify the legend. His scores in Tests were 50, 25, 26, 5, and 58. Turner got him out three times, and McLeod, one of the up-and-coming Australians to whom this tour drew attention, twice. The Australians were always relieved to see him out, especially George Giffen, who stresses how much the England teams of this period owed to the solid starts which W.G. often helped to provide, even if he did not himself make an outstanding score.

Lord Sheffield spent £16,000 on the tour, and finished with a loss of £2,000. He did not worry too much about that, as it had not been his principal object to make a profit. You might say that the loss would have been turned into a profit, had W.G. really been an amateur. He was, it was reported, paid £3,000 for the tour, with sundry expenses. There have been arguments about the exact amounts, but it is not to be denied – W.G. did not deny it himself – that he made quite a good thing out of it. This did nothing to enhance his popularity at Lord's, where there were still many amateurs about of true and blue blood. Sheffield, though the third (and last) Earl of that place, came from a Yorkshire family, and his grandfather, the first Earl, had become a peer (only an Irish one, to begin with) because of some stout work in the Gordon Riots. Not one of the top nobs.

Nor did W.G.'s financial success help to increase his popularity with the professionals. This had, ultimately, severe consequences. Before the last Test match of 1896, at the Oval (the rubber depending upon it), five leading English professionals refused to play unless they were paid £20 for the match, twice the going rate. What irritated them was less their own poverty (for they were not so poor as working-men then went) than that an amateur was making so much money out of the game. They may have had Walter Read at the back of their minds, the Surrey secretary who had taken his benefit the year before, but there is no doubt that they were chiefly cross with Grace.

The five professionals were Lohmann, Abel, Richardson and Hayward, all of Surrey, and William Gunn of Nottinghamshire. The Surrey committee would not yield, and three of the professionals withdrew their demand, but Lohmann and Gunn stood out and did not play. Lohmann never played for England again, though in any case he could hardly have done so, because of declining health. Gunn did play once more, at Trent Bridge three years later. The Surrey committee felt it necessary to issue this statement:

During many years, on the occasions of Dr. W. G. Grace playing at the Oval, at the request of the Surrey County Committee, in the matches Gentlemen v. Players and England v. Australia, Dr. Grace has received the sum of £10 a match to cover his expenses in coming to and remaining in London during the three days. Beyond this amount Dr. Grace has not received, directly or indirectly, one farthing for playing in a match at the Oval.

Grace's 1891–2 side was reckoned a strong one, although only six of them had played in Tests at home in 1890. The bowling was up to England standard, but the batting lacked depth. Australia won the first Test by 54 runs and the second by 74 – a notable victory, for England had led by 307 to 145 on the first innings. Australia then made 391, so England needed 230. This was an occasion when Grace's tactics were criticized. Despite poor light, he stuck to his usual batting order, and he, Abel and Bean were out for 11 runs. He expected the pitch to deteriorate. In fact it rolled out well the next day. Had he sacrificed the tail, England might have won. However, as Giffen points out, these criticisms were made with hindsight. W.G. never liked altering the order. 'If there's any trouble out there', he would say, 'who's more likely to deal with it than me?' Generally he was reckoned a sound and shrewd captain, if not one of the more imaginative ones.

The next two tours to Australia were led by A. E. Stoddart. The first, in 1894–5, was won 3–2; the second, in 1897–8, was lost 4–1. It was known that the Australian side to visit England in 1899 would be a very strong one. For the first time, at home, five Tests were to be played. For the first time, too, a selection committee was appointed. The first selectors were Hawke, Grace, and H. W. Bainbridge, the Warwickshire captain. It is clear from various references that the activities of the committee were, and continued to be for some time, a good deal less formal than they are today. Co-option was frequent and casual. Since the selectors were active players, they had to rely much on hearsay. The amount of say the captains had in the choice depended much upon the personality of the captain (though I dare say this is still true). In one year when he was chairman, Hawke was not even in the country for part of the season. Sometimes there were more or less regular meetings, sometimes sides were chosen by correspondence. Still, if it was all a little haphazard, it did represent an advance on the old system, which made it difficult to build a side, and frequently led to inter-county ill-feeling.

So the side was chosen to play Australia at Trent Bridge, the first Test there, and W.G. was once more captain. The match was drawn, and Australia had rather the better of it. In their second innings England needed 290 to win, after an Australian declaration, and had lost seven wickets for 155 at the end. Grace scored 28 and 1. In the first innings he had taken part in a first-wicket stand of 75 with a relative newcomer, C. B. Fry. That was good enough – a solid start. In the second innings he was quickly bowled by Howell. Since in the same innings Fry scored 9, F. S. Jackson 0, Gunn 1, Tyldesley 1, this was nothing of which to be ashamed. He was still worth his place as a batsman, as likely to give England a good start as anyone. But he could not field any more. He could catch them if they came to him, but he could not bend. In the Australian second innings, when Noble and Hill were cutting them past him at point, the Nottinghamshire crowd began to jeer. Thus when the team was to be chosen for the second Test at Lord's, W.G. had accepted the thought that perhaps he should be dropped, and put it to the committee.

Fry, with all the experience of one Australian Test behind him, turned up at the committee meeting, late, and was immediately confronted with the question, 'Do you think MacLaren should play?' He agreed that MacLaren would be a good choice. 'That's it, then,' said W.G. It had already been decided, one presumes, that if MacLaren played, W.G. would not. Fry asserts that he had no idea, when he made this quick answer, of its immense consequence. But this account cannot be quite complete. Of the English batsmen in the first Test, Gunn was also dropped, and replaced by C. L. Townsend (who only played in one more Test, the fifth of the same rubber). Grace had possibly been pushing the claims of his fellow Gloucestrian, Townsend, and found himself caught in his own snare. If Townsend was to be picked, and MacLaren was to be picked, then another batsman had to be dropped, and you could not really, at that stage of his career, choose Grace ahead of Fry, Jackson, Ranji, Hayward and Tyldesley.

So MacLaren became captain, for the first time at home, and marked the occasion at Lord's with a characteristic double: that is to say he played a magnificent innings of 88 not out, and lost the match by ten wickets. Jackson ought to have been chosen captain. Fry says that the matter of Jackson's seniority, from their days at Harrow to their appearences in the England side, somehow came to be 'overlooked'. MacLaren was, however, captain of his county, and had been Stoddart's deputy in Australia. Jackson only captained Yorkshire when Hawke was away. It is difficult to be sure just what happened: and Jackson was not the man to fuss or intrigue. As far back as 1893, he had scored a century for England at the Oval (batting No. 7) but had then declined to play in the third Test because Yorkshire had an important match. This was not, you understand, because Jackson had to do what he was told, as some of the professionals did. He was an Honourable, a member of a noble family, and the noble families of the north did not bother much about what the noble families of Lord's thought. They played for whom they thought fit, when they thought fit. Still, it was a pity that Jackson was not chosen as the successor to W.G., instead of MacLaren. England would have won a few more Test matches.

W.G.'s departure was greeted with some dismay. 'England without the Champion!', thought 'Country Vicar', 'That's asking for it!' But it was time he went. He was mistaken in playing Tests at the age of 51. I wish he had been spared that booing Nottinghamshire crowd. He ought to have retired at the end of his successful 1896 series, which would have given England a little more time to contemplate the succession.

To say that W. G. Grace was a cricketer is to say everything about him, and yet nothing about him. It was only through cricket that he became famous. He never aspired to any other form of glory. Yet his was much more than the customary fame of a leading player of games. I cannot think of any parallel to it, in his time. Remember he lived before the age of ballyhoo in sport. Perhaps some of the old boxing heavyweight champions came nearest, particularly John L. Sullivan, whose fame, like Grace's, remained undiminished long after his finest hours had passed. But the parallel cannot be pressed too far. Sullivan shook hands with the Prince of Wales, and boasted about it for the rest of his life. I do not think anybody bothered to record whether Grace did. Had he done so, it would have been unremarkable. If he did not, who cared? Well, the Prince of Wales, perhaps.

Grace's contribution to cricket was far greater than the runs he scored and the wickets he took. It was his example, his commanding presence, which changed cricket from an occasional, mostly provincial, sometimes rather shady pursuit, into the National Game. I am not suggesting it is the national game now, but it was, in most senses, for more than half a century, and it still flourishes in many parts of the world. If Hawke was the principal exporter of the product, Grace was the manufacturer. This transformation would not have happened, in any comparable way, without him. It was said that he was by far the best-known man by sight in England, which was something to say then. When, in 1932, H. J. and Hugh Massingham produced *The Great Victorians*, a collection of essays, there was Grace among them, taking his alphabetical place just behind William Ewart Gladstone and just before Thomas Hardy. R. A. Knox once wrote an essay purporting to show that Grace and Gladstone were one and the same person. It was no more than a light satire, yet it tells you something that it should be written at all. It was said seriously by a bishop, and repeated by Altham, himself a classicist and historian, that 'if Grace had been born in Ancient Greece, the Iliad would have been a different book'.

If you think that a little high-flown, I can at least assure you, as one who has lived for years in or near Bristol, that if Grace had not been born in what is now the suburb of Downend, Bristol would have been a different city, physically different for one thing. The area round the county Ground, where all the roads are named after cricketing counties, is in a sense his memorial. The County Ground Hotel, large and labyrinthine, echoing with memories of the past, was built for those who came to watch him.

He was born in 1848, the year of revolutions. He died in 1915, driving the war for a day from the headlines. He wrote four books about himself: that is to say, four books appeared under his name, for he was no writer. They were edited by H. Methven Brownlee, William Yardley, Arthur Porritt, and E. H. D. Sewell. He was fortunate in his ghosts. His character often comes through them, so that one seems sometimes to hear him talking, in that high-pitched voice which comported so oddly with his massive figure. Although a good and constant talker, he was no public speaker. The after-dinner speeches he made on the tour of North America, under Fitzgerald, were recorded by his captain. At Montreal:

> Gentlemen: I beg to thank you for the honour you have done me. I never saw better bowling than I have seen today, and I hope to see as good wherever I go.

At Ottawa:

> Gentlemen: I beg to thank you for the honour you have done me. I never saw a better ground than I did today, and I hope to see as good wherever I go.

At Toronto:

> Gentlemen: I beg to thank you for the honour you have done me. I never saw better batting than I did today, and I hope to see as good wherever I go.

And, again, at Toronto:

> Gentlemen: I beg to thank you for the honour you have done me. I never met better fellows than I have met today, and I hope I shall meet as good wherever I go.

A daring variation, at Hamilton:

> Gentlemen: I beg to thank you for the honour you have done me. I have never seen prettier ladies than I have seen today, and I hope I shall see as pretty wherever I go.

At New York, with a touch of desperation:

> Gentlemen: I beg to thank you for the honour you have done me. I never tasted better oysters than I have today, and I hope I shall get as good wherever I go.

Fitzgerald reports these speeches in *Wickets in the West*, and in *Cricketing Reminiscences* Grace quotes them, or allows Porritt to quote them, against himself, adding

> I think it is rather too bad of Fitz to have perpetuated my first utterances in this way, but I dare say the reports are not libellous. I make no pretensions to oratory, and I would any day as soon make a duck as a speech.

Arthur Porritt was then a young man who reported cricket, amongst other things, for the *Manchester Examiner*. Later he became, for many years, the editor of an influential religious paper, the *Christian World*. The *Christian World* has symbolically vanished since then, but editors of Dissenting religious papers were important people in the first quarter of this century, and Arthur Porritt became famous enough to write his own reminiscences, *The Best I Remember*, published in 1922. A very entertaining book it is, too. He gives a chapter to his collaboration with the great man. 'Grace', he says,

> was choke full of cricketing history, experience and reminiscences, but he was a singularly inarticulate man, and had he been left to write his own cricketing biography it would never have seen the light. [A friend] sought my co-operation with Grace, who had entered into an agreement with him to produce a volume of reminiscences for publication in his jubilee year. It had seemed that the contract would expire without a line of the book having been written.

So Porritt took on the job, and spent three half-days a week for 12 months, trying to lure Grace into producing autobiographical material. He found that

> his mind functioned oddly. He never stuck to any train of recollection, but would jump from an event in the 'sixties to something that happened in, say, the last Test match. Often I left his house in absolute despair. . . . I remember very distinctly one age-long afternoon when I was trying to get out of W.G. something of the psychology of a batsman making a big score in a great match. All that he wanted to say regarding some dazzling batting feat of his own was, 'Then I went in and made 224'. 'Yes,' I would reply, 'but that is not good enough! People want to know what W. G. Grace felt like when he was doing it; what thoughts he had, and what the whole experience of a big innings must mean to a batsman.'

Grace would reply,

> I did not *feel* anything. I had too much to do, to watch the bowling, and see how the fieldsmen were moved about, to *think* anything.

The best Porritt could get from him was this laboured witticism:

51

Some days a batsman's eye is *in* and other days it is not. When his eye is in, the cricket ball seems the size of a football and he can't miss it. When his eye isn't in, then *he* isn't in, long, because he's soon bowled out!

No boaster was Grace, though he took it for granted, as did everybody else, that he was the best cricketer in the world. He was conscious of his lack of literary skills, and was anxious lest Porritt should put into the book words that were not in his accustomed vocabulary. One day, while they were running through a chapter for revision, W.G. pulled up at the word 'inimical'. 'No', he said, 'that word can't go in. Why, if that went into the book I should have the fellows at Lord's coming to me in the pavilion and saying, "Look here, W.G., where did you get that word from?".' The reference to the fellows at Lord's is interesting.

About W. G. Grace, Porritt concludes, there was

something indefinable – like the simple faith of a child – which arrested and fascinated me. He was a big grown-up boy, just what a man who only lived when he was in the open air might be expected to be. A wonderful kindliness ran through his nature, mingling strangely with the arbitrary temper of a man who had been accustomed to be dominant over other men. . . . We were good friends to the end of the partnership, and afterwards. . . . I think I did once make him really cross. It was when I flatly refused to believe his statement that he had only one lung, and had, in fact, had only one lung since his childhood. 'Now who,' I asked him incredulously, 'is going to believe that?' Grace was, for the moment, nettled, and then he said rather testily, 'I'm not going to have you doubting what I say; I'll call my wife, and she'll confirm it.' He called Mrs. Grace, who corroborated W.G.'s story. I apologized and we made peace.

All the same, I do not think that this story has ever been substantiated, and clearly Porritt, though tactfully 'making his peace', did not believe it. Grace had suffered from a severe attack of pneumonia when a child, and possibly thereafter one lung did not function so well as the other. But that is some way from saying that one of the broadest chests in England had only one lung behind it.

W.G., coming from a medical family, qualified as a doctor himself, though it took him a long time, and much effort. He was 31 when the University of Edinburgh granted him his L.R.C.P. Soon afterwards he met the old Yorkshire professional, Tom Emmett, in the St John's Wood Road, on their way to Lord's. 'Is it all right, sir?' asked Tom, knowing what was at stake. 'Yes,' said W.G., beaming, 'I've got my diploma.' They started play, and quite soon Emmett, fielding in the covers on a damp day, was sent rolling over by a fierce drive from W.G., which he somehow managed to stop. He lay there prone for a moment or two, and the batsman solicitously enquired, 'All right, Tom?' 'Ay,' said Emmett, picking himself up, and turning round to display a large green splotch on the seat of his flannels – 'and I've got me bluidy diploma.' The story comes in various versions, but something like this must have happened, though both the participants were great ones for polishing and elaborating stories afterwards.

Grace kept up his medical practice in Downend for a long time, though he had an assistant once he became established, and during the cricket season would employ a locum. The nature of his doctoring is reputed to have been rough-and-ready. An anxious mother of young twins was worried that her children, with high temperatures, might have measles. Grace reassured her, told her to put them to bed, and said, 'No need to call me unless they get up to 200 for 2 before lunch.' And then he had a difficult maternity case, and told his friends, 'Well, the baby's dead, and I don't think there's much hope for the mother, but I do believe I shall pull the father through.' Neither of these stories – which he loved to tell against himself – should be taken seriously. There are many testimonies from his patients, some of whom I have spoken to myself, that he was a splendid doctor, in his brusque but jovial way. Poor families did not need to worry about calling him in, when there was need. The bills had a habit of not arriving.

Sometimes his medical skills were required on the field of play: a finger or a shoulder to be put back to joint, perhaps. His methods in these cases were drastic and sometimes successful, though H. D. G. Leveson-Gower once said to him, after some immediate treatment for a bruised thumb, which was feeling much worse, 'I can't pay you for this treatment, Doctor. I shall want some money from you.' 'But,' says Leveson-Gower, 'he only laughed.'

On the other hand, there was a time when a fieldsman had spiked his throat on a boundary fence. W.G. held the wound together with a steady hand for half an hour, until a doctor with a surgical needle could be found. 'And he had been fielding out for 400 runs,' said the fieldsman, 'and if his hand had ever wavered I would not be here to tell you the story.' As the fieldsman was A. C. M. Croome, who later became cricket correspondent of *The Times*, we may take this as one of the more carefully observed and recorded stories.

Gradually, however, cricket and not doctoring became W.G.'s life. When all allowances have been made, the protesting professionals of 1896 had some justice on their side. The amateur–professional relationship, which endured in cricket for so long, caused some bitterness, and had some merits. Since its formal abolition, the game has not noticeably become more harmonious. The regulations in Grace's time were so vague that he can never have been strictly said to have transgressed them. He never became a rich man, nor was he ever a greedy man, except for runs. Sometimes, from goodwill, he *lost* money on cricket. 'Somehow', he wrote,

. . . I seemed to invariably make a century when I played in a professional's benefit match. One outcome of this was that I was always being asked to play in benefit matches. When John Lillywhite was having a benefit at the old Hove ground at Brighton he asked me to come and play for him. I went down, and when my innings began took up my place at the wicket to bat. It was a very bright sunny day, and the glare dazzled my eyes.

He did not much like to admit that he was ever got out except by some such circumstance.

Anyway I was bowled by the first ball. I went to Lillywhite and told him how sorry I was. . . . 'Never mind', he said. 'Here's a couple of sovereigns. You can have them, if you agree to give me sixpence for every run you make in the second innings.' I accepted his condition, put the money in my pocket, and on the next day went in to bat again. Before stumps were drawn I had made 200 not out, so I went up to Lillywhite and said, 'I owe you five pounds. Here it is, but if you don't let me off any further liability I shall knock my wicket down with the first ball tomorrow morning.' Lillywhite laughed and said, 'All right, we'll cry quits!'

I have sometimes wondered if Grace's first-innings 0 was connected with the lack of a *douceur*, but if so it only improves the story, which makes us like both men.

There were altogether five Grace brothers, all cricketers. Indeed the whole family had a passion for the game. E.M. was the third son, W.G. the fourth, G.F. the fifth. E.M. was a brilliant, unconventional batsman, who liked to hit across the line (W.G. was not usually unconventional: he did the orthodox things, but better than anyone else). E.M. was known as 'The Coroner', an office which he held at Thornbury for many years. Once Gloucestershire were playing away, and a reply-paid telegram summoned E.M. home for an inquest. It was handed to W.G., as captain. He made what Leveson-Gower calls 'the Napoleonic decision' to spend the cost of the reply in backing a horse, instructing his brother to send, at his own expense, the message 'IMPOSSIBLE TO COME TODAY PLEASE PUT CORPSE ON ICE'. E.M. scored 36 and 0 in the 1880 Test, his only one. G.F. scored 0 and 0, so the family contributed three noughts to the occasion. However W.G., with 152 and 9, improved the average.

G.F. was nevertheless, as we have seen from his performances in the 1870s, a fine player. He was another whose true amateurism was in some doubt. Indeed, at one time he was excluded from the Gentlemen *v.* Players match. He had, probably, taken fees (and very likely W.G. had too) in early days with the United South of England XI. One is always a little cautious about accepting at their face value encomiums on those who die young, but Fred Grace was a very popular man, quieter and gentler than his boisterous brothers. Although his Test batting record could not have been worse, in the same match he made a famous catch. The batsman was again the huge Australian, Bonnor. W.G. thus describes it:

> Bonnor got hold of a ball from Shaw, and sent a tremendous skier into the long field, which G.F. judged in a wonderful way. Mr. Frederick Gale, who chained the distance himself, with two of the Oval ground men, stated that the hit measured 115 yards as a minimum. When at its greatest height the ball seemed to hang in the air, and two runs were finished before it dropped into G.F.'s hands.

After the Test, G.F. went to Stroud to play for the United South of England XI, returned to Downend, and set off for a match at Winchester. He was taken so ill that he had to stop at Basingstoke. A chill turned to congestion of the lungs, and he was dead in a few days. It was always said in the family that he either caught or exacerbated the chill by sleeping in damp sheets, whether at Stroud or Basingstoke is not clear.

E.M. and W.G. both continued playing into their sixties, indeed W.G. actually played first-class cricket in his sixtieth year. There was another exceptionally good player in the family, whom we have met in passing, a cousin William Gilbert, after whom W.G. was named. William Gilbert was, I am afraid, the black sheep. He was found stealing in the dressing-room, and despatched to America, which was then standard treatment for a black sheep of respectable family. He does not seem to have been too abashed, and became a leading figure in cricket over there.

Even in such a family, nobody doubted, from an early stage, that W.G. was best. When he was only just in his 'teens, his mother wrote that he would make a better batsman than any of the others, 'for his back play is superior to theirs'. It was she, and her brother, known to the family as Uncle Pocock, who were his earliest coaches, in the orchard at Downend. Mrs Grace was as keen as any of them, and an acute judge. Her name is recorded amongst the 'Births and Deaths of Cricketers' in *Wisden*, the only woman in the list. Even in his great days, if he made a foolish stroke, she would admonish him: '*How* many times, Gilbert, have I *told* you how to play that ball?' She lived until 1884.

'The shire of the Graces' was often the leading county in the early days of county cricket. Roy Webber, in his *County Cricket Championship*, ranks Gloucestershire joint champions in 1873 and 1880, and sole champions in 1876 and 1877. The *Wisden* list is slightly different. There was then no official championship, and the press, who took it upon themselves to name the victors, did not always use the same methods of working it out. Most of W.G.'s greatest feats were achieved for Gloucestershire, though he played for many other sides, for there was much less county cricket then, and he never liked turning down a match. It was for Gloucestershire at Bristol, in 1895, that he scored his hundredth century, when he was nearly 47 years old. To realize how staggering this seemed to his contemporaries, remember that no other batsman had then made half as many. He reached his century on the second morning of the match against Somerset. Sam Woods, who was more nervous than the Doctor himself, in case he got him out, provided a full toss to leg when his score was 98. At lunch, amid much jubilation, his health was proposed. His terse speech in reply has a familiar ring:

Gentlemen: I sincerely thank you. I hope you will excuse me from saying more, as I have a long afternoon before me.

He scored 288 before he was out.

This was the year of his Indian summer, as it has often been called. Not only did he make the hundredth 100, not only did he score 2,346 runs in the season, at an average of 51 – the last time he scored more runs than anybody else, though MacLaren, with half the runs, had slightly the better average: not only did he do these things, but he scored a thousand runs in May.

It is an odd thing that this statistic has come to occupy so large a part in the minds of cricketers. Nobody much cares who has scored a thousand runs in June, or July, or August. As I write, only three batsmen have scored their thousand in May, though four others have done it before the beginning of June. The three are Grace in 1895, Hammond in 1927, and Hallows of Lancashire in 1928 (although he was a fine batsman, it was an improbable feat for him). Counting matches in the last days of April, Bradman has done it twice, Hayward, W. J. Edrich and G. M. Turner once. Bradman's averages were the highest. Grace's time was the shortest – May 9 to May 30; though if you count the actual playing days, 22, Hammond did it as quickly. Not that this really matters. I happened to see Turner reach his thousand, at Northampton, in unexciting circumstances on the third morning. Turner scored 1,018 runs from April 24 to May 31, average 78·30: an excellent month's batting, but nothing to marvel at. A statistician had rushed up from town to gaze upon the event, and rushed away immediately it was concluded. The statisticians would scarcely have bothered about it, had not the Champion startled everyone into attention in 1895 (1,016 runs, average 112).

These were his scores:

For M.C.C. *v.* Sussex 13, 103
For Gloucestershire *v.* Yorkshire 18, 25
For Gloucestershire *v.* Somerset 288
For the Gentlemen *v.* Cambridge 52
For M.C.C. *v.* Kent 257, 73*

For England *v.* Surrey 18
For Gloucestershire *v.* Middlesex 169
Not out

In 1899, the same year as he had lost the captaincy of England, Grace fell out with Gloucestershire. This was not altogether unexpected. There had been rumpuses before. No doubt he had become something of a dictator in the county. A new cricket club had been formed to play matches at the Crystal Palace. It was to be called London County, and W.G. was offered the post of secretary and manager. He ought not to have been hard up. After his 1895 season, three separate testimonial funds had been opened for him – by M.C.C., Gloucestershire, and the *Daily Telegraph*. Together they raised nearly £10,000. But W.G. decided he would like the job. London County did not compete in the championship, though some of its matches were ranked first-class. He saw no reason why this new post should interfere with his cricket for Gloucestershire. But the Gloucestershire committee were not pleased, and passed a resolution enquiring about the future intentions of their captain. The reply was predictable, and this we may take to be one of the pieces of prose that came from the master's own hand:

> Gentlemen, in answer to yours of the 26, re resolution passed on the 16th and kept back from me for reasons best known to yourselves, I beg to state that I had intended to play in all our matches, but in consequence of the resolution passed and other actions of some of the committee, I sent in my resignation as captain, and must ask the Committee to choose the teams for future games as I shall not get them up.
>
> I have always tried my very best to promote the interests of the Gloucestershire County Club, and it is with deep regret that I resign the captaincy. I have the greatest affection for the county of my birth but for the committee as a body, the greatest contempt.

He never played for Gloucestershire again, though there was a partial reconciliation, and he did play in a match at Bristol (for the opposition) some years later.

Even today, many of you who read this will have some idea of what W.G. looked like, but you will probably think of him as the vast man with the long grey beard and the red and yellow cap. The red and yellow cap of the M.C.C. was his favourite, and in latter days he hardly wore any other, which is slightly surprising in view of his ambivalent relations with M.C.C. The establishment was always made a little uneasy by this large, boisterous, rollicking, squeaky provincial doctor. Yet it is rare today to see anyone wearing an M.C.C. cap. It gradually seemed to be accepted that nobody else was worthy of it.

Action photography in cricket came too late for Grace. Just think what Patrick Eagar would have made of him! G. W. Beldam took some photographs of him well into his middle age which give us some clues, but we have nothing except unsatisfactory posed pictures to suggest what he looked like, in action, in his prime. It is a mistake to think of him as a heavy, lumbering man. In his youth he was a sprinter and jumper, one of the fastest men over hurdles in England. The patriarchal figure you remember was the result of the growing midriff and grey hairs of the years.

I return to Arthur Porritt's description of him: a simple man, with a simple, schoolboyish sense of humour. He never quite grew out of the joys of the apple-pie bed, and the booby-trap on the door-jamb. Bernard Darwin considers this his best joke.

Mr. C. L. Townsend came to stay a night, and W.G. at once led him out into the garden, saying that on such an occasion they must have some asparagus for dinner. The asparagus beds were inspected and found rather disappointing. W.G. appeared a little depressed, but gathered a few heads of asparagus, said they must do as best they could, and led the way indoors. Dinner duly came, and with it the most resplendent dish of asparagus ever seen. The Old Man had carefully picked them before his guest's arrival, and plotted his joke accordingly.

Even if the W.G. stories *were* elaborated, or attributed, you learn much of a man's character from the stories that gather about him. I think my favourite W.G. story of all is how, when he had scored 99, he hit an easy catch towards a safe cover-point, and while the ball was in the air, cried out, 'I declare the innings closed!' This is obviously untrue, unless it was a carnival match. It *is* true, however, by his own account, that he once gave away his wicket when he had scored 93, because 93 was the only score from 0 to 100 which he had never made in a first-class match.

In his last months, during the First World War, he was living at Eltham (the last club for which he played) and was much troubled by the Zeppelin raids. How is it, asked his friends, who often visited him, that you, who tamed all the great fast bowlers of your period, even in your earliest days on the fieriest of pitches, so much so that the bowlers themselves said it was a miracle that you were not maimed, or killed outright? – how is it that you, of all people, are worried by a few bangs in the night? And he would reply, clenching his fist at the sky, 'Ah, but I could see those other fellows. I could take a bat to them. How can you take a bat to these, eh?'

He played his last match, for Eltham against Grove Park, a week after his sixty-sixth birthday, a month before the war began. He scored 69 not out, so the last bowlers who bowled to him could not take his wicket. He died after a heart attack in his garden. I like to think he was contemplating the asparagus beds. Of all the tributes to him, then and since, one of the pleasantest is by a fellow cricketer, D. L. A. Jephson, who was a poet of sorts. It begins

> With what great zest through all your merry years
> Did you not cast into a million hearts
> The golden spirit of our England's game,
> To hearts that otherwise had passed it by . . .

Zest was a good word, and so was *simple*. Simple zest was what W.G. brought to cricket. Not all subsequent captains of England have done the same. But those who have, win or lose, are the ones we like the best.

3

DEAR DEFEATED STOD

Yet still between his Darkness and his Brightness
There pass'd a mutual glance of great politeness
Byron, *Vision of Judgement*

Grace, then, was a simple man. Stoddart was a complex one. His career touched heights of glory, and depths of disappointment, His life ended in tragedy, as his friends had long feared. Of all the England captains, he might be the most rewarding study for a psychologist (though I respect the claims of Lord Harris, and A. P. F. Chapman, and W. R. Hammond, and Geoffrey Boycott). I am not qualified to attempt such a study, but the basic material for it is to be found in David Frith's biography, *My Dear Victorious Stod*. He takes his title from a poem in *Melbourne Punch*, written after Stoddart's triumphant 1894–5 tour of Australia:

> Then wrote the Queen of England,
> Whose hand is blessed by God,
> 'I must do something handsome
> For my dear victorious Stod' . . .

But even if it had then been the custom to award royal honours to sportsmen – and a poor custom it is too – even had it been customary, it is improbable that Victoria's eye, always watchful in such matters, would have fallen upon Andrew Ernest Stoddart, who was known, at least by his family, as 'Drewy'. Stoddart was too much the Victorian masher – the kind of young man who had led the Prince of Wales so unfortunately astray.

'Masher': the *Shorter Oxford* defines it as, 'A fop of affected manners and

60

"loud"-styled dress who frequented music-halls, etc., and posed as a lady-killer. A man who thrusts himself on women'. This was American slang in 1882, and the term survives there to this day. Brewer's *Dictionary of Phrase and Fable*, rather later, gives what I feel to be more the English version:

> Masher: an old-fashioned term for 'nut', or 'dude'; an exquisite; a lardy-dardy swell, who dresses aesthetically, behaves killingly, and thinks himself a Romeo. This sort of thing used to be called 'crushing', or killing, and as mashing is crushing, the synonym was substituted about 1880.

I am not suggesting that Stoddart lived a life of exceptional immorality – there is little evidence of such a thing – but he certainly did his best to look the masher's part. This in itself is curious, because he did not have the appropriate background for it. He was the son of a fairly prosperous Tyneside merchant, born in Westoe, South Shields. Westoe was one of the best districts of Shields, or so my mother assured me, but then mother was born in Westoe herself, so cannot be regarded as an entirely dispassionate witness. When Drewy was nine, the Stoddart family moved to London, and lived in Ormonde Terrace, by Primrose Hill, near Lord's. The boy was sent to a private school, St John's Wood School, in Acacia Road. It was a preparatory school, and also (I quote David Frith) a school where 'if the boys were not to have a public school education, they could continue until they were 18 or 19. Stoddart was one of these'.

In other words, it was a school of no particular merit, which catered for large boys who had insufficient talent, or whose parents were insufficiently wealthy, to take them somewhere better. Such schools were not uncommon at the time (and are still not quite unknown). So Stoddart, like Grace, had no public school or university education, and no aristocratic connections. This did not make it too easy to be a masher. However, his exceptional skill at games was of considerable assistance.

His first-class career began in 1885, when he was 22 years old, rather late, it seemed to his admirers in the Hampstead club, and ended in 1900 – an early retirement for those days. He scored 17,000 runs at an average of 33. He visited Australia in 1887–8 and again in 1891–2, before the tours he made as captain. He played for England at home in 1893 and 1896. That made 16 matches altogether, all against Australia, during which he scored almost a thousand runs at an average of 35. It is always unusual for a man's Test average to be higher than his average for all matches. He captained England eight times, winning three and losing four matches.

In the first Test of 1893, when Grace had a damaged finger and Stoddart was captain for the first time, Stoddart scored 24 and 13, and led the side acceptably enough. England had rather the better of the play, but rain prevented a finish. His 1894–5 tour is among the historic ones. From it many writers have dated the intense interest of the English public in tours to Australia. W.G. had done much by his visit three years earlier, but this time the English press, without going so far as to send special correspondents, gave more space to the Australian cables than ever before.

There is a case for saying that the first Test match of this tour was the best played so far, though that is a phrase I shall find myself repeating. Englishmen were inclined to think so, but then England had won, by 10 runs. Australians still urged the claims of their even narrower win, at the Oval in 1882. The Oval match was low-scoring: 363 runs for 40 wickets, which was not uncharacteristic of English pitches of the period. At Sydney, in 1894, 1,514 runs were scored for 40 wickets, which was not uncharacteristic of Australian pitches of the period. The Sydney match went on into the sixth day, the first time this had happened: by now it was agreed that all Tests in Australia were to be played to a finish, and this remained the rule until after the Second World War. Australia won the toss and scored 586, which was the highest score anybody had then made in a Test match; and remained the highest score Australia made against England for 30 years. England scored 325, followed on, and then scored 437. Australia needed 177 to win, the pitch still playing well, and at the close on the fifth evening had reached a comfortable 113 for 2. It rained in the night, and on the last morning Peel and Briggs (imagine having *two* slow left-hand bowlers in an English side at Sydney today!) bowled Australia out. Blackham, the Australian captain and wicket-keeper, who had damaged a hand – an injury which, as it proved, ended this long and distinguished Test career – came in last, and batted one-handed in a vain effort to secure the last few runs. England had been lucky in the change in the weather, yet it was in any circumstances an extraordinary feat to win, after fielding to a score of 586.

Bobby Peel, who had bowled 53 overs in the first innings, had the previous night looked upon the malt when it was brown. Play started late on the last day, because he and Lockwood were late on the ground. It was a generous action on the part of the Australian captain to allow this, and the delay of 20 minutes may have cost Australia the match, because the pitch was becoming steadily more difficult as the sun beat down. but Blackham was a generous man, and liked Stoddart, as nearly all Australians did, at least at this stage of his career. Stoddart pushed Peel under a cold shower, and got him out to the middle. Peel had not known of the storm. When he looked at the blackened pitch, he thought somebody had been 'watterin' t'wicket'. He then requested the ball, assuring Stoddart that he would have them out by lunch. Peel took 6 for 67, Briggs 3 for 25, and the last wicket fell on the brink of the interval.

When the captains were tossing at the beginning of this match, Stoddart said to Blackham, 'Someone will be swearing directly, Jack. I hope it's you!' During the celebrations afterwards, he said, 'There'll be a good deal said about this match', which was a notable understatement. Of the more modern reports, I know of none better than David Frith's, and one by Richard Binns in his attractive book, *Cricket in Firelight*.

England won the second Test as well, after losing the toss and being put in. They scored only 75, but Australia did little better, and a score of 475 in the second innings gave England 94 runs to spare. Stoddart scored 173, his second Test century, and his highest (the first had been in the third Test of Grace's tour). But Australia won the third by 382, and the fourth by an innings and 147 (this after Stoddart, winning the toss for the only time in the series, had put Australia in). The luck with the weather had evened itself out by now. The fifth Test was another of the classics, if it did not have quite the astonishing fluctuations of the first. Australia led on the first innings by 414 to 385, and scored 267 in their second innings. Two-hundred-and-ninety-seven was a great many in a fourth innings, but the Melbourne pitch was still playing truly. England lost two wickets for 28 runs, and then a partnership of 210 between J. T. Brown (140) and Albert Ward (93) settled the match. They were both Yorkshire-born, though Ward played almost all his first-class cricket for Lancashire. Brown reached his first 50 in 28 minutes, which *Wisden* of 1976 reports to be still the fastest recorded 50 in a Test match. He did not keep up this rate throughout, but his whole innings lasted only 145 minutes and effectively won the match and the rubber. He never did anything comparable in Test cricket before, or afterwards.

J. T. Brown had been the last choice for the tour, after Abel had withdrawn. F. S. Jackson, who never went to Australia, was another notable absentee. But Stoddart's was a strong side: seven of them had played at home against Australia in 1893, and two more were to do so in 1896. MacLaren ought to have been the leading batsman, and looked very impressive in lesser matches, although it was only with a century in the first innings of the last Test that he justified himself at the highest level. On the next two tours, the Australians were rating him the best batsman England had ever sent to them. In Richardson and Lockwood, Stoddart had two splendid fast bowlers: or, one must make the reservation again, ought to have had. In practice, he had only one. For though Richardson did all that could be expected of him and more, with 32 Test wickets at 26, Lockwood took only 5 at 68. He was always an awkward customer for his captain, was Lockwood. Despite his convivial habits he was not the man to settle down in a touring party. He never toured again, although he played for England at home, and his career still had a decade to run. Stoddart, whose mixture of coaxing and firmness was so effective with Peel, found Lockwood a harder nut to crack.

But Lockwood, in no sort of form, had to play in all the Tests, for there were only 13 in the party, including a spare wicket-keeper, and Walter Humphreys. Humphreys was a lob bowler, the last to tour Australia (though another lob bowler, Simpson-Hayward, toured South Africa in 1909–10, played in all five

Tests, and took 23 wickets at 18 apiece, including 5 for 69 on the matting at Johannesburg). Humphreys was useful to Stoddart's side, because he could polish off up-country matches quickly, but the principal Australian batsmen played him so easily that he could not be risked in Tests. It is odd that he was chosen for the tour at all. He was aged 45 at the time, had never played for England, and never was to do so. Frith says he was 'apparently requested by the Melbourne Club, and fairly fit at 45 because he rode a tricycle'. He was naturally a man of some seniority in the side, and carved the beef on Christmas Day.

Wicket-keeping was another problem. Gregor MacGregor, he who shared the rooms and the lobsters with Sam Woods, had been England's wicket-keeper in 1893, but could not make the trip; Lilley of Warwickshire was to take over in 1896, but not much was known of him in 1894, and Warwickshire was hardly established as a first-class county. Those chosen were Gay, a Cambridge Blue who had appeared for Hampshire and Somerset; and Philipson, five years older, an Oxford Blue who played for Northumberland and Middlesex. Gay was supposed to be the first choice, but did not keep well in the first Test, and was replaced by Philipson in the rest. Philipson had toured Australia under W.G. as reserve to MacGregor, and had played in the last Test, when MacGregor was injured. Neither would seriously have been considered for a Test match at home. Philipson was a Tynesider, like his captain, and some years later it was reported – though the event did not occur – that Stoddart was going to marry his sister. He was a man of some private means; so, it was supposed, was Stoddart.

There was also F. G. J. Ford, another Cambridge hitter, who averaged 18 in the Tests, the only ones he ever played in. Thus with MacLaren, Ford, Gay, Philipson, and the captain, five amateurs out of 13, the Melbourne Club might have reasonably hoped that the tour would not cost them too much money. In this hope they may have been slightly disappointed, so far as the expenses went, but the public enthusiasm shown was so great that they must have made a handsome overall profit.

This triumphant team of Stoddart's does seem, in retrospect, to have been cast for tragedy. The captain killed himself at the age of 52. Richardson, the great bowler, 24 years old at the time of the tour, was retired by Surrey in 1904 and died only eight years later. He had grown fat and begun to see the world through an alcoholic haze. In the four English seasons 1894 to 1897, Richardson captured over a thousand wickets, a staggering feat for any bowler, let alone the fastest of his time, with a long, pounding run: enough to take the steam out of any engine. The Gentlemen v. Players match was interrupted for 20 minutes on the news of his death, as a mark of respect, and I like to think that some of his old colleagues took the opportunity of a respectful memorial pint. J. T. Brown died at 35, of heart trouble and asthma. He was a nervous man beneath that cool, tough exterior. Briggs had a fit during the Leeds Test of 1899, and was taken to an asylum. He recovered, and played another season for Lancashire, but it was only a temporary recovery, and he died in 1902. Brockwell lived to a good age, but fell on hard times. When Hawke and Sir Home Gordon were playing golf one day at Sundridge Park, a caddy pointed out to them a partially roofless hovel where Brockwell slept. Brockwell, Sir Home points out, 'had been one of the smartest in appearance, highly self-respecting as well as deservedly popular when playing, his benefit having been one of the most lucrative ever held at the Oval'. They did what they could for him, and it would not have been little. Peel was publicly dismissed from the field, and from cricket, by Lord Hawke in 1897. He had arrived on the field drunk, and endeavoured to demonstrate his sobriety by bowling, but unfortunately aimed at the sightscreen at the bowler's end. It is a story with its funny side (beautifully described by A. A. Thomson in *Hirst and Rhodes*), and perhaps it is wrong to describe it as tragic, for Peel was a resilient character, made a career in the Leagues, and did not die until 1941, when he was 84. But still, that makes up rather a doleful list from the heroes who were so triumphantly welcomed home with Stoddart. And in the Australian side was Albert Trott, an exceptional success both with bat and ball in the third and fourth Tests (his first two), then aged only 22, the brightest prospect, you might have guessed, in either of those talented sides. He never played for Australia again, and killed himself in 1914. His brother Harry, the Australian captain, also suffered a series of mental breakdowns later in life.

But there was at least a truce of gloom when they came back. At a swish dinner at the Del Monico, Piccadilly, the victory was celebrated, with much champagne. Stoddart's speech was 'modest, and very happy'. W.G. also spoke, fresh from his hundredth century. He must on this occasion have managed at least three sentences. The members of the House of Commons raised £100 to be shared equally between Brown, Peel, Richardson and Ward. Stoddart, as an amateur, naturally could not share in this bounty, but I dare say he had a few drinks on the Terrace.

In 1895, Stoddart scored over 1,600 runs at an average of 38, one of the best of his domestic seasons. In 1896 he scored a few more runs at a slightly lower average. This year was slightly shadowed for him, as it was for Grace, by questions concerning his amateur status. He had some private means – an Australian journalist had estimated £500 or £600 a year – but not enough to tour the world on. He had no 'expectations', of the kind which enabled many a young blood to live on credit for years. When rumour was flying free, it was inevitable it should rest on him. *The Morning Leader* and its correspondent 'Rover' were particularly severe, and malicious. ('Rover's real name was Alfred Gibson, no relation, I am relieved to say.) Stoddart withdrew from the Oval Test (the 'strike' Test) just before the start. There were various explanations of this: he had a cold, he wanted to let MacLaren play (for owing to the threatened strike, there were more potential players present than could be fitted in). I once heard that Stoddart said, bitterly, 'Archie needs the money'. Whilst it is not possible to read a man's mind in these things, Mr Frith, who has studied the evidence more carefully than anyone else, concludes that 'he withdrew chiefly because of his vilification by some of the popular papers'. Grace played, made Surrey issue that statement on his behalf, cocked a snook at the press, the parson and the squire, won the rubber, and passed genially on his way. Stoddart withdrew, hurt and depressed. Years later, after his retirement, he wrote a letter to the press in defence of his amateur status, more spiritedly. Of his Australian tours, he said, the authorities – that is to say, the Melbourne Cricket Club and the Trustees of the Sydney Cricket Ground – had paid all travelling expenses and hotel bills, and he was left a discretion in the matter of ordering champagne. 'With the weather we experienced there this was almost a necessity, and the discretion was exercised by me freely, but wisely, in the best interests of our health and cricket.'

Curious, this contemporary belief in the merits of champagne, whether as a drink or an elixir. Even W. G. Grace shared it ('It's in the well! It's in the well!' he would cry on the morning of a match to those friends who were going to dine with him in the evening). A taste for champagne was one of the marks of the amateur. I doubt if it was the favourite tipple of Peel and Lockwood. Many years later the austere Jardine – at the crisis of a Test match which was so fierce that police were on the ground to guard against a riot – during the lunch interval nursed Larwood through, in the privacy of the dressing-room, with sips of champagne. I have often wondered what Tom Richardson would have said in similar circumstances; and I have no doubt what Larwood, one of the many great fast bowlers who trained on beer, thought.

Still, champagne was unquestionably an amateur habit. And shooting was an amateur habit: in the season of 1896 Stoddart vanished from the cricketing scene for a week or two in order to take a 'shooting holiday'. He had no grouse-moor background, but it was a very proper thing for an amateur to do.

There was also his football, which demands a little deeper consideration than we have given it so far. Stoddart played in 11 Rugby Union internationals between the years of 1885 and 1893: twice against Scotland, three times against Ireland, five times against Wales, and once against the 'Maoris', a New Zealand side which in fact had more white men than brown, and played an enormous number of matches all over the British Isles, including games against England, Wales, and Ireland (subsequently recognized as internationals). Stoddart's matches with Shaw and Shrewsbury's team in Australia have never been recognized as international matches by the Rugby Football Union, though in terms of quality they had as much right to be as many of the early Rugby tours. So Stoddart cannot, technically, be counted as the second man (Hornby, you remember, was the first) to have captained England at both cricket and Rugby, since in none of his home internationals was he captain. He must, however, be the only man to have captained England in major international contests against Australia at cricket, Rugby, and Victorian Rules. This is a record unlikely to be beaten.

Stoddart played Rugby for Blackheath, Harlequins, the Barbarians, and Middlesex. He was, beyond doubt, one of the outstanding players of his brief period. In the 1892 edition of *Marshall*, Arthur Budd, a calm judge, declared that he was

> without doubt the most agile and finished wing-three-quarter who has done service for England. This athlete, by his performances in the cricket field, and as a Rugby Union player, has earned for himself a fame that has fallen to the lot of no other man, and his deeds have even equalled those of the renowned A. N. Hornby. Of great speed, and possessed of wonderful dodging powers, Stoddart has left behind him a unique record of achievements on the football field. These qualities, combined with great powers both as a drop and place-kicker, have caused him to be regarded as one of the best men who have filled the position of wing-three-quarter. Unfortunately for him absence from England, and the discontinuance of International matches in 1888 and 1889 as far as England was concerned, prevented him displaying his unrivalled powers in the great matches as often as he would have liked; and thus his record of appearances in the classic fixtures has suffered in comparison with others whose playing days fell in more propitious times. But by general consensus Stoddart is regarded as *the* wing-three-quarter during the middle and latter part of the decade.

This was not a routine tribute. It is reinforced by a picture of Stoddart, left hand on hip, right hand clutching Rugby ball, every inch the masher in mufti. All those who saw him play Rugby believed they had seen one of the great ones; all those who saw him play cricket believed, often, that they had seen the nearest English approach to Grace. And yet, when you look back on his career in either sport, for one reason or another the figures do not quite match the ability . . . for one reason, or another.

At the end of the 1894–5 tour, Stoddart was one of the most popular men in Australia. At the end of the 1897–8 tour – well, it would be wrong to say that he had fallen from favour, but his public popularity was sensibly diminished. This in itself was strange, because on the first tour he had won, and on the second he lost, and defeated captains on tour are usually more popular than victorious ones, understandably.

It was not a fortunate tour. For Stoddart, with his increasingly melancholic turn of mind, it became almost a tragedy. Yet the omens were hopeful. Afterwards it was clear that the side was not strong enough, but it did not look so

67

bad a one when it was chosen. Most importantly, Ranji was going. The news of his visit raised tremendous interest in Australia, and at least guaranteed a financial success. MacLaren was going again. With the captain, this made an impressive nucleus of amateur batsmen. Two more young amateurs made the trip, J. R. Mason and N. F. Druce. Druce was 22, from Marlborough and Cambridge, and had headed the first-class averages the previous season, a proper enough choice. He scored 252 runs at an average of 28, a respectable start. He never played Test cricket again; indeed, hardly any first-class cricket again. No tragedy here, I think; he just found other things more interesting. Had he stayed in the game he might well have been an England captain.

Mason was 23, a much admired batsman for Kent for many years to come. He too did not play Test cricket outside this tour. Altham says 'it is arguable that no better cricketer has ever missed the honour of playing in a Test match in England', but perhaps for once the sage – a Wykehamist writing of a Wykehamist – pitched it too highly. Certainly on this tour Mason did nothing to advance himself as a Test player, scoring only 129 in 10 innings, and taking 2 wickets at 75.

The professionals were Hayward, J. T. Hearne, Richardson, Briggs, Wainwright, Hirst, and – the wicket-keepers – Board and Storer. What on earth, you might say, is wrong with that? Some of the most famous names of history are there. But Richardson, after his tremendous efforts of the past few seasons, was burning low: only rarely could the smoking flax be fanned into a flame. He tried as hard as ever, and got through an immense amount of work, but his 22 Test wickets cost 35 runs apiece. Hearne was steady, but no more, in Australian conditions: it was his only visit. Indeed, it is a curious thing about Hearne that, though the fourth-highest wicket-taker in the history of the game, he played in only a dozen Tests. Eight other bowlers who were tried in the Tests took 20 wickets between them. Briggs, on his sixth consecutive tour to Australia, was nearer to twilight than noon. Hirst was a strong young man who bowled fastish left-hand stuff, of no particular skills. He had not yet learned to swerve the ball. Wainwright, and, at this stage of his career, Hayward, could get plenty of wickets in England, but found the Australian pitches beyond them. Two Test wickets were taken by Storer, handing his pads and gloves to Druce, and one by Stoddart himself. He always liked a little bowl, with his little spinners.

Thirteen players was not really enough. It is true, if I may offer a variation upon a theme of Professor Parkinson, that the fewer players you take upon a tour, the smaller will be the proportion of the injuries (or at least it was true then, before spare parts could be whisked across the world in a day). But this team did suffer exceptionally from injuries and illness, and an extra man might have made a big difference, by taking some of the weight off the others. The terms of Stoddart's agreement did not allow it. He said before he left that he was sorry to leave Brown and Ward behind. But he did not really need an extra batsman. Another hardy bowler might have made a big difference: Peel would have been the man, and there are hints in Stoddart's notes that Peel was the man he would have liked. Nor can there have been, I think, any legal reason for not choosing him: but had he done so, Stoddart would have risked much high-powered disapproval. Mold of Lancashire, a very fast bowler, would have helped Richardson: but Mold was suspected of being a thrower, and at this time throwing was a touchy subject. Walter Mead of Essex would have given Hearne some relief. But there it was. The English side ought to have had enough bowlers. It was a case of many chosen, but few called. England batted well enough, on the whole, but could not get the Australians out.

England won the first match. MacLaren scored one of his many Sydney hundreds, and Ranji, going in at No. 7 because he had been unwell, materialized the oriental magic of which so much had been written. He scored 175 and was last out. It was the first time England had passed 500 against Australia. Australia, however, battled ominously well in their second innings. Darling scored a century, and Hill 96. These two left-handers were to be an English bane for the whole series, and years to come.

Australia won the next three Tests, and the rubber, easily: winning the toss each time and making England follow-on. In the last match England made a better fight, leading by 96 on the first innings, but once again could not bowl Australia out (Darling 160) and lost by six wickets.

Yet it was not the defeats which made it an unhappy tour. Nothing seemed to go well from the start. Stoddart was down with influenza after a few days, and Ranji suffered throughout the tour from a quinsy, an inflammation of the throat which is nowadays called tonsillitis. The bad news came on December 8, five days before the first Test was due to start, when Stoddart heard by cable that his mother had died. He had been devoted to her, as many men of his type were. It put an end to his cricket for weeks.

There were other troubles. Ranji had undertaken to write articles for the press on the tour (and may even have written parts of them). He was critical of the bowling action of Ernest Jones, the Australian fast bowler. Jim Phillips, who had gone out as a kind of general factotum, assistant manager to Stoddart, newspaper correspondent, and umpire, had no-balled Jones. Phillips, and it was a fortunate circumstance, was an Australian. The Sydney committee postponed the first Test for a few days, no doubt in the hope that Ranji would be fit, and even Stoddart. They took this step without consulting either captain. Stoddart made a protest, which was never acknowledged, though there were courteous condolences upon his bereavement. He did not play. None of this mattered much: the Australians were obviously anxious not to embarrass him at a time when he hardly seemed to know where he was. But it did not make for a friendly atmosphere. MacLaren was captain in the first Test. There was a deplorable incident when C. E. McLeod, who was slightly deaf, did not hear a call of 'no ball'. Richardson hit his stumps. McLeod innocently walked away, out of his crease, Storer pulled up a stump and appealed for a run out, and Phillips – who, one recognizes, had no choice – gave him out. A strong, quick-thinking, generous captain could still have put things right, as similar incidents over the years have demonstrated. MacLaren, in his first Test as captain, did nothing.

Stoddart became less bemused, picked himself for the second Test, and withdrew when he learnt that Ranji would be fit to play. He watched the match from a high window in the pavilion, ogled by the girls below. It was widely suggested for the rest of this Australian summer that he was looking for a wife: 'Whose wife?' was one mordant reply.

He played in the third and fourth matches, but without doing any noticeable good to the side. Ranjitsinhji was writing rudely about the Australian crowds, who certainly were not at this period in one of their more genial moods. Stoddart was unwise enough to join in this criticism. When you have just lost the Ashes is no time to pick a bone with the opposing spectators. What he said was probably true enough, and most of the leading Australian cricketers supported him – he was still held in high affection by them – but it was a little embarrassing all round.

He stood down from the last Test, though fit to play, MacLaren again taking over. His Test scores had been 15, 24, 17, and 25, batting low in the order. This was not sufficient evidence for him to drop himself on, in the circumstances. Nor could it have been the feeling that, with the rubber settled, it would be generous to 'give the other chaps a crack', as happened with commanders of more numerous parties in later days. He was just sick and sorry, and wanted to go home, except that he no longer had a proper home to go to.

Iredale, one of the Australian successes of the series, a considerable cricketer, a shrewd judge and later a selector, said of Stoddart, 'We looked upon him as the beau ideal of a skipper, and as fine a sportsman as ever went into a field'. He was sorry that Stoddart took so much notice of the crowd. David Frith, following Iredale's view, makes this comparison between Stoddart and MacLaren as captains. 'Where Stoddart would coax a cricketer by playing upon his feelings, MacLaren would drive him, in the manner of W.G.' (I am not quite sure about the last bit: W.G. could coax as well as drive.) 'Stoddart lived for his team and always commanded their respect; MacLaren's men admired him but feared him. Stoddart was often impulsive, but MacLaren was quick-tempered, easily angered. A moody player always chafed under MacLaren, but not so under Stoddart, who generally humoured him.' This is a judgment worth bearing in mind as we approach a consideration of MacLaren.

What then had Stoddart said to cause the upset? He gave the gist of his views in an interview with the *Sydney Referee*, which Mr Frith reprints at some length, but of which I reproduce only a few, I hope fairly chosen, extracts. He began foolishly: 'My remarks are intended for the people of this country, otherwise I would have no object in speaking. When I return home I will not mention a word on the subject.' Did he imagine that his words would remain unread in England?

I shall, in all probability, never visit this country again with a cricket team, and what I have said has been purely for the good of the game, for the sake of the players in this country, and of English teams coming out here in future.

This system of barracking, if allowed to go on, will inevitably reduce cricket to a low level. . . . The jeering by the crowd has occurred on all the grounds, and in all our big matches.

Our first experience was at Adelaide, where we were advised to take no notice of it. The same thing occurred at Melbourne, and we were similarly advised, whilst our Sydney experiences were no different. We did not take any notice of it, but when the thing is repeated in every match, and on every ground, I feel it my duty to speak, and to deplore that those in authority do not take steps to prevent it.

I don't mean that those who jeer and hoot should be turned out of the ground. I would suggest that an appeal be made to their better feelings. If some of your influential men were to walk round the ground, speak to the people, reason with them, quietly and rationally, I am sure a great deal of good in the direction of preventing these scenes would be achieved.

To show that moral suasion is useful in a matter of this kind, I will quote an incident of my own experience: At Brisbane, the day we played the Combined Team, it was wet, and owing to a shower a cessation in play took place for a little time. The Combined Team had been in the field in the morning. When they went out again in the afternoon they were hooted by a certain section.

I saw one man who had hooted, and went up to him and said, 'Now, why did you hoot your own side?' He replied: 'Because they fielded badly.' Then I said, 'Do you consider that hooting them will make them field better?' He replied: 'I don't know.'

I talked to him very quietly and seriously for about ten minutes during which he gazed at me and seemed to wonder what sort of person I was. At the end of that time he said he was damned if he would ever hoot them again. Every man has a generous spot in him; most of those who jeer and hoot have good points, and, if you appeal to their better nature, I am sure they will give it over. . . . If you can successfully appeal to one man, you can do so to a body of men.

David Frith calls the last sentence 'an idealistic summing up', and well he might. I doubt if Stoddart can have been so naïve. After all, he must have encountered a few Newcastle United football supporters in his time. No doubt it

71

was his way of trying to soften his criticism. That he was deeply upset there is no doubt. He returned to the subject in a public speech, when replying to a toast, no less:

> If you will excuse me, I would like to make a few remarks which may, however, not be pleasant. . . . I have a right, as an English cricketer who has been out here so often, to make reference to the insults which have been poured upon me and my team during our journey through this country.

This was surely going too far. Not Jardine himself in the 'bodyline' season could have said as much. Harry Trott, the Australian captain, showing a good deal more tact and generosity than his guest, rose to say:

> I quite agree with Mr. Stoddart's remarks about the crowd. They are a perfect nuisance. (Cheers) And yet we can't do without them. (Laughter)

Whether the Australian crowds were particularly troublesome on this tour, or the English captain unduly sensitive, it is not easy to say. Certainly there were those, including some Englishmen, who thought Stoddart's protests were overdone, and criticized his sportsmanship. On the other hand, Ranjitsinhji, summing up the tour in his book *With Stoddart in Australia*, does repeat the complaint. It was not, he says, a condemnation of the Australian crowds, but 'the rebuke of an evil which visitors and local players alike suffer from'. Even if this was the case – and it was not exactly the impression most Australians had – it leaves us with a slightly uncomfortable feeling.

Ranji himself retained much of his popularity, although his batting was less successful after the first Test, and at the tour's end he sent, in the grand manner of princes, a letter of thanks to the Australian public. But it was in a general air of disappointment and gloom that the team returned.

Stoddart's subsequent form did not seem affected. He played only 15 matches in 1898 but reached his 1,000 runs. But he declined the captaincy of Middlesex for 1899 and in the spring of that year announced his retirement. He played just a few times in that and the following season, made a short tour of America, and that was all.

He had been articled to an architect, but nothing came of that. He was a member of the Stock Exchange, but his financial fortunes at best fluctuated. He had other jobs from time to time, for a while being secretary of Neasden Golf Club. In 1906, he became secretary of Queen's Club in Barons' Court. This was sufficiently important a post for the secretary to be paid £300 a year, though the duties were not arduous. The University Rugby match was played at Queen's in those days, and it was a leading centre for lawn tennis and other racquet games.

Stoddart needed the money, for he had, at last, decided to marry. Now in the tradition of the Victorian novel, one of two things happened to a masher. He went to seed, or he was saved by the love of a good woman. His bride was an Australian, Ethel Luckham, née Von Simbech. He had met her on his first trip to Australia, 19 years earlier. They had renewed friendship during his last tour, about which time she moved to England. The wedding was a crowded and cheerful occasion. The marriage, however, was not a success. Small blame to Mrs Stoddart. Melancholia increasingly had her husband in its grip: he went to seed steadily over the next few years.

On Easter Saturday, 1915, Stoddart came home in the evening, took a pistol from his pocket, put it on the table, and told his wife he was tired of everything and going to end it all. His wife picked up the pistol but he wrested it from her. She did, however, keep the box of cartridges, knowing the pistol to be empty. He said good-night to his wife and her companion and went to bed. Just before midnight his wife found him dead. They had heard no shot, but he had had another box of cartridges. He had shot himself through the head. The Marylebone jury found that it was suicide, and the addition 'while of unsound mind' had plenty of evidence to support it. W. G. Grace still had six months to live.

4

FOUR EDWARDIANS

They four had one likeness, as if a wheel had been
in the midst of a wheel . . . and every one had four
faces: the first face was the face of a cherub, and
the second face was the face of a man, and the third
the face of a lion, and the fourth the face of an
eagle

Ezekiel x, 10–14

From the second Test of 1899 until the outbreak of the First World War, four
men dominated the English captaincy – four great men, or anyway famous men:
A. C. MacLaren, P. F. Warner, F. S. Jackson, and C. B. Fry. Other men
held the office during this period: R. E. Foster, A. O. Jones, F. L. Fane,
H. D. G. Leveson-Gower, and J. W. H. T. Douglas. Of these latter, Foster was
captain in three matches against South Africa at home; Leveson-Gower in three
against South Africa abroad; Jones in two against Australia abroad; Fane in
three in Australia, as deputy to Jones, and two in South Africa, as deputy to
Leveson-Gower. Douglas began as a deputy, when Warner fell ill on the
1911–12 tour, but went on to become an England captain in his own right, his
career spanning the war. They were all good cricketers who added their own
touches of colour to the tapestry, but none of them had the kind of national
recognition – the acceptance as a proper heir of W.G. and Stoddart – which was
achieved by the first four.

It might be as well, before considering the heroes separately, to give an outline
of the course of Test matches in the years of their hegemony. Their records are,
as captains:

	Matches	Won	Lost	Drawn	Tosses won
A. C. MacLaren					
v. Australia	22	4	11	7	11
P. F. Warner					
v. Australia	5	3	2	0	2
v. South Africa	5	1	4	0	3
	10	4	6	0	5
F. S. Jackson					
v. Australia	5	2	0	3	5
C. B. Fry					
v. Australia	3	1	0	2	3
v. South Africa	3	3	0	0	1
	6	4	0	2	4

In all, MacLaren played in 35 Tests, scoring 1,931 runs with a batting average of 33·87; Warner in 15, 622 runs at 23·92; Jackson in 20, 1,415 runs at 48·79; Fry in 26, 1,223 runs at 32·18. Jackson, the only bowler among them, took 24 wickets, average 33·29. MacLaren made 13 scores of over 50 in 61 innings, Warner 4 in 28 innings, Jackson 11 in 33 innings, Fry 9 in 26 innings.

When MacLaren took over from Grace in that Lord's Test of 1899, England lost it, and the remaining three matches of the rubber were drawn. There was no disgrace in losing this series. Australia were a strong side – their best, it was commonly said, since 1882. It was Trumper's first tour. In 1901–2, MacLaren took the next side to Australia, and was beaten 4–1. As in 1897–8, only the first match was won. The England side was again below strength: Hirst and Rhodes would have made a big difference. This was S. F. Barnes's first trip. MacLaren, always a remarkable judge of a cricketer, chose him straight from the Lancashire League, and had he not broken down in the third Test, after taking 19 wickets in the first two, much might have been different. This was also Jessop's only visit to Australia. He did not have much success. Indeed, his Test career generally, with one famous exception, did not match the marvellous feats he performed in county cricket.

So we come to 1902, one of the most memorable of English summers, if also one of the wettest. The Australians did not begin very well. At Leeds, Hirst and Jackson bowled them out for 23, Yorkshire beating them by five wickets. In the first Test at Edgbaston, England scored 376, and Hirst and Rhodes bowled Australia out for 36. Rain saved them in the follow-on. In the second Test at Lord's, England batted first and lost two wickets for no runs, and those the wickets of Fry and Ranjitsinhji. MacLaren and Jackson put on 102 before it rained, and there was no more play. The failures of Fry and Ranjitsinhji, then at their zenith, were not the least astonishing thing about this series. Fry averaged 1·25 and Ranji 4·75.

The third Test, at Sheffield, was comfortably won by Australia. At Manchester they won the fourth, and with it the rubber, by 3 runs. Trumper scored a century before lunch on the first morning. The batting of Trumper this streaming summer made men rub their eyes, accustomed to majesty and brilliance in batsmanship as the spectators of that time were. No Australian batsman had so captured the English public. He scored 2,570 runs, more than anybody else, at an average of 48·49, most of them at a great pace. He scored 11 centuries. Altham's tribute has often been quoted, but let us recollect it as we pause in salute: 'From start to finish of the season, on every sort of wicket, against every sort of bowling, Trumper entranced the eye, inspired his side, demoralized his enemies, and made run-getting appear the easiest thing in the world.'

Then came the fifth Test at the Oval, just as exciting, with England getting home by one wicket. They looked well out of reach when, needing 263 in the last innings, they had 5 down for 48, but there came a dramatic intervention from Jessop, with a hundred in an hour and a quarter, and Hirst and Rhodes got the last 15 runs as the rain was beginning to fall again. We shall have occasion to touch on this historic series of matches again.

That was four consecutive rubbers to Australia, which was one of the reasons why the next tour there, in 1903–4, took place under the auspices of the M.C.C. Such a move had been discussed several times before, but difficulties kept cropping up – over finance, over the readiness of counties to yield their players, over the divided control of Australian cricket between Melbourne and Sydney, between players and administrators. Once again there were some leading players who could not go – no Jackson, no Fry, no Ranji. MacLaren could have gone, it was thought, but the captaincy was offered to Warner. MacLaren thereupon declined to tour. There was an outcry about all this, especially in the north, where there has always been a suspicion that Lord's looks after its own. But a strong side was got together; Warner handled it well, played at least adequately himself, and won the Ashes – helping to make the term common parlance – 3–2. The first Test goes on to the short list of the best ones. Australia scored 285 in the first innings, England 577. R. E. Foster made 287, the record score for England–Australia matches until Bradman beat it in 1930. When Australia went in again, Trumper scored 185 not out, and England needed 194. They got them, by 5 wickets, but only after losing 4 for 82 – and Hirst, who made 60 not out, was dropped before he had scored. The rest of the matches naturally did not quite maintain this standard, but it was a very satisfactory win from the English point of view.

Warner could hardly be expected to carry on as captain at home, if only because he could not in the normal way hope to command a place in the side, and so, in 1905, when the Australians were next here, the honour at last came to Jackson, MacLaren playing under him agreeably enough. This has always been known as 'Jackson's Year'. He scored two centuries, 82 not out and 76, and headed the batting averages. He also headed the bowling averages, with 13 wickets at 15·46, and at a critical moment of the first Test took three wickets – Hill, Noble and Darling – in an over. He also won the toss five times. England won the rubber 2–0, and had the better of all three drawn games. This was England's most decisive win since the days of W.G. Given the strength of the opposition, and even allowing for the luck of the toss, there is a case for regarding it as the best of all wins, at least up till the time of Chapman's tour in 1928–9. (There were special circumstances about the victory of 1911–12, which was nevertheless also a good one.)

But Jackson played no more Test cricket, and little enough cricket of any kind, so the captaincy became an open question again. Here let us take another look at South African cricket, which we left just before the end of the nineteenth century. A South African side had visited England in 1904, and done very well, not playing Tests but winning 13 and losing only three of 26 matches. It was clear that soon they would be entitled to Test status in England. In the meantime, in the winter of 1905–6, an English side was setting out for South Africa. These matches might reasonably be regarded as the first proper Tests between the countries. M.C.C. again took responsibility for the tour, and again, entirely justifiably, appointed Warner as captain. It was the strongest side to visit South Africa yet, with half-a-dozen men of authentic England quality and no passengers: but South Africa won 4–1. The first Test, which South Africa won by a wicket, still has a claim to be considered the most exciting ever played between the two countries, despite some formidable competition since. England scored 184 and 190, South Africa 91 and 287 for 9. The ninth South African wicket in their second innings fell at 239. A. D. Nourse was going well, and their captain and wicket-keeper, P. W. Sherwell, came in at No. 11. These two did not so much score the runs as knock them off, Sherwell hitting the first ball for four, and the last. Warner once described this as the greatest game he had ever played in.

The South African tour of England duly took place in 1907. They were a capable and attractive side, with four googly bowlers (the googly then being almost new, though Bosanquet, its inventor, had won a Test match with it in

1903–4 and another in 1905) and one very fast one. They gave England plenty to think about, though they lost the only one of the three Tests to be finished. Who was to be the England captain? Fry was the obvious choice, but there was some doubt about his fitness, though in fact he played in all three matches; and he was also, as we shall see, something of a controversial figure. R. E. Foster was chosen and performed well enough. He had not played in a home Test before, but nobody doubted that he had the ability: he was another who suffered from business demands. Now there was the question of the tour to Australia in 1907–8, and once again the usual speculation as to which of the leading amateurs would be willing and able to make the trip. In the end the choice fell on the Nottinghamshire captain, A. O. Jones, who had already played for England both in Australia and at home. He did not have a strong side, although Barnes was once again summoned from the Leagues and Staffordshire. Australia won 4–1. Jones himself suffered from poor health on the trip and could play in only two of the Tests. F. L. Fane, who had been the Essex captain until the previous season, took over the captaincy for the first three Tests.

This defeat was not taken too tragically in England. It was clear enough now that only the best, or something very near it, could hope to beat Australia, and the Australian side which came over in 1909 looked on the face of it no stronger than the one of 1905 which Jackson had dealt with. Nor did this side, under M. A. Noble, make a good start. Bad weather and injury and illness led to some early defeats.

MacLaren was recalled to captain England. It was a strange decision, for Fry, Jones and Warner all played in the Tests. The selectors this season came in for much criticism, which seems in retrospect well deserved. It must be said, though, that MacLaren did not wish to return to the captaincy. He was 37, and considered himself too old. England won the first Test, lost the next two, and the last two were drawn.

There had been a proposal, originating with the South African magnate Sir Abe Bailey, that the Tests of 1909 should take the form of a triangular contest between the three countries. Insufficient thought had been given to it, the Australian reaction was unfavourable, and at one moment it had looked as if there might be no 1909 Tests at all. However, matters were smoothed over – a letter from F. S. Jackson to *The Times* having a salutary effect – and it was decided that England should visit South Africa in 1909–10; that South Africa should visit Australia in 1910–11; that England should go to Australia in 1911–12; and that the triangular tournament should take place in England in 1912. All this duly happened.

South Africa beat the 1909–10 tourists by three matches to two. The English captain was H. D. G. Leveson-Gower. Fane deputized for him in the last two matches. It was a side of uneven merit. It contained Blythe, Woolley and Rhodes, who must surely have been the three best slow left-arm bowlers ever to appear in the same side, though Rhodes was doing little bowling at this stage of his career – in fact, it was on this tour that he began his series of opening partnerships with Hobbs. The most successful bowler was G. H. Simpson-Hayward, the last of the lobsters. The supporting cast was not so strong, as may be judged from the fact that Hobbs opened the bowling in three of the Tests; and though he could bowl a bit in those days, it was never his strong point. Most of the leading members of the 1907 South African team were still available, and they had the rubber won by the fourth Test.

South Africa were beaten 4–1 in Australia a year later, but not disgraced in a high-scoring rubber. Then there came the English tour of Australia in 1911–12. It was hoped that Fry would be able to captain the side, and R. H. Spooner was a possibility if Fry could not manage it. Spooner, an outstandingly elegant batsman even in an age of elegance, was well liked by his fellow-cricketers, both amateur and professional, and had first played for England under Jackson in 1905. He was often considered for the captaincy, but for one reason and another never achieved it. He might well have had it, one feels – barring some prohibitive reason not apparent over the years – in 1909. Spooner was a good enough player. He had ten Tests, all at home, and averaged 32, with a century and four 50s. Jessop, who had had an excellent season with Gloucestershire, was also approached. But when all these decided they could not go, it fell to Warner. After all, in the last four visits to Australia, Warner had been the only man to come home a winner. And in 1911 he had been in his best form, scoring over 2,000 runs at 46, seventh in the averages.

Great care was taken in choosing the side, and though there were only three amateurs amongst it, there were no other obvious amateur contestants. There were Yorkshiremen who felt that Denton, undoubtedly a player of England quality who did not have much luck in his limited opportunities, ought to have been chosen ahead of Kinneir, of Warwickshire. Who now remembers Kinneir? Kinneir was 38, Denton 37. But Kinneir had averaged 49 in 1911 to Denton's 42. Furthermore, Warwickshire had just won the county championship, the first time any of the less ancient counties had done so (we had to wait until 1936 for the next time this happened, when Derbyshire won it). It was felt that the county champions of England deserved a good show in the England side, and that this was especially true when the champions were, very unexpectedly, so unfashionable. F. R. Foster, who had just taken over the Warwickshire captaincy, made one; E. J. Smith, 'Tiger' Smith, their wicket-keeper, made a second; Kinneir made a third.

I must not be drawn into these aged disputes. The amateurs, apart from the captain, were F. R. Foster and J. W. H. T. Douglas, Douglas had taken over the captaincy of Essex in the same season as Foster had taken over that of

Warwickshire, but was seven years older, 29 to 22. I am not just filling up the book by throwing these figures at you. They became important.

This was certainly the most representative English side, and almost certainly the strongest up to that point, to tour Australia. It won 4–1, which had not been done before. I only put in the qualifying 'almost' before 'certainly', because, unluckily, they caught Australian cricket in a miserable season. Most of the great Australian names were still there: Trumper, Hill, Armstrong, Bardsley, Ransford, Carter, Cotter, along with a formidable new one, the googly bowler H. V. Hordern. It ought to have been a classic series: but Australian cricket was riven.

They had had rows over there before, as we have noticed. So had English cricket been troubled from time to time. But over the history of cricket (and some other things as well) English rumpuses have usually been more discreetly conducted than Australian. It is arguable, and once was cogently argued to me by Jack Fingleton (as knowledgeable about Australian politics as about cricket), that this is really a point to Australia, because once they have had a public, healthy blow-up they all feel better about it, and are soon friends again: whereas in English feuds the suppressed venom poisons the system. There may be something in this, but I doubt if it applied to Australian cricket at this period.

The trouble was partly the old Melbourne–Sydney rivalry, complicated by the advance of Adelaide, but mostly it was a dispute between the leading players and the Board of Control. Australian players had for many years been accustomed to run their overseas tours, and could not help feeling that the Board of Control was a bit of new-fangled, bureaucratic nonsense. But there was more to it even than that: there were intense clashes of personality, to put it mildly. Hill, the Australian captain, and McAlister, one of the selectors, had a stand-up fight at a committee meeting, of which full (though somewhat contradictory) details appeared in the press. The actual points at stake, stemming from a dispute over the proper presentation of the accounts for the 1909 tour of England, seem trivial enough over the years, and a little goodwill on both sides could surely have settled them. Those who are interested may find them set out in Warner's account of the tour, *England v. Australia, 1911–12*. The goodwill was not forthcoming, with the result that Australia were an unhappy side throughout the series, and the further, even more disastrous result that the team which they sent to England for the triangular tournament was only at about half-strength.

This was wretched luck for England as well as Australia. Warner's side, with Barnes and Foster bowling, and Hobbs and Rhodes to open the batting, was good enough to have won in any circumstances, but was not fully tested. However, England had their own misfortune. Warner himself, after scoring 151 against South Australia in the opening first-class match, was taken ill and could not play again (he suffered from intermittent ill-health throughout his career, something that always has to be taken into account in assessing his merits as a batsman). This may not have made much difference to the technical merit of the side, because there were plenty of good batsmen, but it certainly did to their effectiveness as a unit. Foster would probably have been the best substitute, but Douglas was the senior and more experienced, and led the side in all the Tests. Errors of captaincy contributed to defeat in the first match. But as Warner's health improved he began to make his influence felt even from off the field, and Douglas gradually got the side in hand. It was widely and justly felt that Warner, for all his inactivity as a cricketer, had a lot to do with the side's success.

There now arose the question of the captaincy at home in 1912. Warner was fit again, and scored a century for his team when he played for them against the Rest of England, a match which they handsomely won. He was an obvious candidate. Douglas had just won four Tests in a row, and could not be ruled out. Spooner was available. So was Fry, who had after all been the first man asked to take the team to Australia. As Altham wrote, 'it has always been a matter of regretful conjecture what he might not have done in Australia had he settled down to the business of run-getting'. Yet for 1912 M.C.C. were reluctant to choose Fry. Warner had his advocates in the south, Spooner in the north. Fry had no geographical base, no party, and had alienated, or at least irritated, lesser men by his Asquithian self-assurance.

They asked Fry, but grudgingly. He was offered the job not for the series, but only for the first match. This had not happened since the old days when the county authorities used to choose their own teams (W.G., you will remember, discharged himself). Fry replied to Lord Harris, who was at this time Chairman of the Board of Control for Test Matches at Home (a grandiose title which meant that it was an important sub-committee of M.C.C., in practice) that he would accept the invitation only if he was made captain for all matches; adding that there should be a selection committee of three, of whom the captain would be one, with no other members to be co-opted. This last bit was a little cool, considering how often Fry had been a co-optee. Fry might not have been altogether surprised if this ultimatum was turned down. Lord Harris read it out to the board, and then, rising to the occasion, said 'I think this fellow Fry is right'. So C.B. was captain for all six matches. The other members of the selection committee were H. K. Foster, of Warwickshire, and John Shuter, who had been captain of Surrey some years before. They were not an especially formidable couple. They agreed with Fry about the best side, and the best replacements in any emergencies, and never met again. This is what Fry liked to say, and though it must be, from other stray references one finds, something of an exaggeration, there is no reason to doubt that he was in command of the England side, selection and all, for the rest of the season.

Fry's captaincy of England was successful enough, but must have been a little disappointing to him, for he did not have much to beat. The Australians were without Hill, Trumper, Armstrong, Cotter, Carter and Ransford, all of whom had refused to come, unless the players could appoint their own manager. This the Board would not permit. Warner's efforts at making peace, spurred on by the anxious authorities at home, had been in vain. Noble, who had not played in the winter but might well have been recalled in the emergency, had also fallen out with the Board. Hordern was another absentee. His heart was never in cricket, nor even in Australia. The captain in the end was Sydney Gregory, who had first played in Tests 22 years earlier. He had served Australia well, but naturally was past his best. The rest made by no means a bad side, and it was this tour which gave Macartney the chance to establish himself as one of the great batsmen – hitherto he had been regarded chiefly as a bowler – but there was a feeling of anticlimax.

To make matters worse, the South Africans were not a strong side, nothing like so formidable as they had been in 1907. The googly bowlers were past their peak, and some other key men had retired. One of the reasons why Sir Abe Bailey had been anxious for the tournament to take place as soon as possible was the knowledge that the players of 1905–10 (South Africa's best period, as it turned out, until the 'thirties) could not go on much longer. And then it was a wet summer, which did not help either set of visitors to make the most of what talents they had.

The eagerly-awaited triangular tournament was therefore not a success. Although it was originally intended to be the first of a series, it was never tried again. This was perhaps a pity. It would have been interesting in, say, the 1930s, on English pitches – and provided that it was limited, as in 1912, to nine Tests of three days each. In 1975 I would have enjoyed a triangular tournament under such conditions between England, Australia, and West Indies (or, come to that, Pakistan) much more than the 'World Cup'. I suppose that nowadays, when we often have two touring sides here in the summer, a revival of the idea is not impossible, though their visits would have to be mingled, rather than divided as at present.

England beat South Africa three times, easily. The first two matches against Australia were drawn, both ruined by the weather. Australia beat South Africa twice, though the South Africans had the better of the draw in the third match. Victory in the tournament therefore depended on the last match, between England and Australia at the Oval. This match was to be played to a finish: at least, six days were set aside for it, and nobody could imagine a cricket match, in England, going on for longer than that. In fact, with frequent interruptions from rain, the match lasted until nearly the end of the fourth day, and as it pelted down for the next two there might have been the final anti-climax of a drawn series (though no doubt England would have been adjudged the tournament winners on the strength of their extra win over South Africa). As it was, with much the best of the wicket, they had time to beat Australia by 244 runs.

There was one more series of Tests before the First World War, in 1913–14 to South Africa. Once again, most of the leading amateurs were not available, but Douglas, with his Australian success behind him, was an acceptable captain, and had a strong side: certainly the strongest so far to have visited South Africa, arguably indeed the strongest ever to do so, with Hobbs, Rhodes, Woolley and Barnes. Hobbs averaged 76 in all matches, 63 in Tests. Barnes took 125 wickets at 9·64, 46 of them in four Tests, at 10·93. This remains the record for the number of wickets taken in a series, though Laker equalled it in 1956. Barnes would doubtless have taken a number more, but did not play in the fifth Test, having fallen out with the South African Board of Control. None of the South Africans could play him, except H. W. Taylor, whose 508 Test runs, average 50·80, was in the circumstances one of the outstanding batting feats of history. Douglas himself made 266 runs in seven Test innings, and took 10 wickets though he bowled comparatively little. The Tests were limited to four days each, and the fourth was drawn, but England won all the others.

So much for an outline of the story. Now for a look at the captains.

Although the Edwardian period has often been called cricket's golden age, the great names dwindle and fade down the years, except among the zealots. Yet I suppose most cricketers are still stirred by the ring of the name of MacLaren, and a very good one it is for ringing. Nor is this only because Sir Neville Cardus wrote so much about him, though even he can rarely have written better about anybody.

MacLaren was educated at Harrow. He did not go to a university, but was playing for Lancashire when he was 19, in 1890. His career lasted until after the war, but after the early years he could afford to play only intermittently. Nevertheless, he scored 47 hundreds in first-class cricket, five of them for England against Australia. In three tours of Australia he averaged 41 in Tests, and in 1897–8 he scored over a thousand runs, something that had never been done in an Australian season before, though Hill and Ranjitsinhji did it during the same year. His successes on tour suggest how much more impressive his figures would have been had he been able to play regularly and also, no doubt, that his technique was better suited to hard wickets.

But if it is for style that we remember MacLaren, rather than figures, he does still hold one whacking record of his own. In 1895, he scored 424 against Somerset at Taunton. That was then, by 80 runs, the largest score ever made in a first-class cricket match, and it is still, by 60 runs, the largest score ever made in a first-class cricket match in England. Nor does there seem much likelihood, in current conditions, that it will be beaten.

Somerset had entered the Championship only in 1891, but they were a fair side (they won six matches and finished eighth, out of 14). Their bowlers included Sam Woods, still not far from his best, and Tyler, a spinner who took a hundred wickets that season, the first man to do so for Somerset in championship matches. He nearly bowled MacLaren with the first ball of the innings. MacLaren was 288 not out at the end of the first day. Grace's record of 344 was obviously in danger, and next morning an encouraging telegram arrived from the Doctor, who was scoring so many runs himself at the time that he could afford to lose a record with equanimity.

MacLaren batted, in all, for seven hours and 50 minutes. He hit a six and 62 fours, and was seventh out at 792 (Lancashire declared at 801, still the county's highest, and won by an innings and 452). His wicket ultimately fell, to a catch in the deep, off the bowling of H. T. Gamlin, a boy of 17, who was to become one of the most famous of Rugby full-backs. Woods, struggling as so often to make up the numbers, had invited Gamlin to try his off-breaks in a couple of games. He took 2 for 182 in them, and played only one other game for Somerset.

In comparing this innings with other big ones, it should be remembered that it was made off five-ball overs, and that sixes could be scored only if the ball was hit out of the enclosure – over the ropes, but within the ground, was only four. On the other hand, there was no legislation then for a new ball. So far as I can learn from the accounts I have read, Somerset were using the same one throughout. It must have been like a Bath bun at the end.

As for MacLaren the stylist: C. B. Fry wrote of him, 'He lifted his bat for his stroke round his neck like a golfer at the top of his full swing. He stood bolt upright and swept into every stroke, even a defensive backstroke, with deliberate and dominating completeness. He never hedged on his stroke; he never pulled his punches.' Cardus headed his most famous essay about him 'The Noblest Roman'. 'There never was a cricketer', he wrote, 'with more than the grandeur of A. C. MacLaren.' Beldam's action pictures came in time to give us a glimpse of the magnificence of the MacLaren drive.

Fry, of course, had ample opportunity to watch MacLaren at close quarters, and the quotation I have given, written in later years, was a considered judgment. Cardus saw him with the eyes of a Lancashire boy. I do not suggest that they exaggerate, and many similar tributes could be culled from the writings of those who saw him. Yet it was not a universal view.

In 1898, when most of MacLaren's batting triumphs were already behind him, R. H. Lyttelton wrote: 'He is not a tall man, or a player gifted with any one particular hit, but, nevertheless, he is a fast scorer, can pull a straight short ball to leg, and is altogether a thrusting sort of player with no striking grace of style, but a very strong defence.' Imagine it! 'Can pull a straight short ball to leg'. 'No striking grace of style'. Of MacLaren! The tone of Lyttelton's piece (in *Giants of the Game*) is generally favourable; but clearly for him the golden age of style had gone, as it goes for every generation of cricketers, as they grow older.

MacLaren the captain: it can hardly now be *lèse-majesté* to say he was a bad one. He captained Lancashire from 1894 to 1896, jointly in 1899, and from 1900 to 1907. They were a talented side throughout the period, but only once did they win the championship, under his leadership. This was in 1904, and MacLaren himself had a poor season. Still, it was an emphatic enough win: Lancashire played 26 matches, won 16, and drew ten. He was official captain, as we have seen, in four series against Australia (barring the first match of 1899), and won none of them, another unequalled record. No doubt he did not have the best of luck, or the best of selectors, but the excuses begin to run thin, sieved through such a tale of failure.

I am sure that he was, tactically, a good captain. He knew about tempting a batsman to play his favourite stroke too often. He could set a field. Cardus and some others were teasing him, in later years, about Trumper's century before lunch at Old Trafford, which decided the 1902 rubber. 'You can't have known much about setting a field in those days, Archie. Why didn't you exploit the inner and outer ring?' MacLaren explained. He knew all about the danger of the terrible Trumper scoring a fast hundred while the wicket was easy. He placed his field with great care, setting one man to cover another on the off side, Trumper's favourite territory. But in the first few overs, Trumper landed a couple of balls into the car park (it had become the car park by the time of the conversation). 'Now I couldn't place my fielders in the car park, could I?' Once in a Test match in Australia, when he was captain against Joe Darling, an amiable but tough character, he found, opening the innings, that there was a huddle of fieldsmen on the leg side. 'How,' he asked of Joe, 'can I play my famous hook stroke with all these men about?' Darling replied that he could place his field where he liked (it was long before the days of these fiddling modern rules about field-places). MacLaren hit the bowler for four fours into the empty spaces of the outfield. The field was changed. 'Thank you, Joe,' said MacLaren, 'now we can get on with the game like gentlemen.'

I am pinching a great deal from Sir Neville, but I think he would wish that a book about England captains does his hero justice. I will pinch one more story. The boy Cardus got into the train at (I suppose) Warwick Road, after a day of watching cricket at Old Trafford, and found himself in the same compartment as MacLaren and Brearley. Brearley was the Lancashire fast bowler, an amateur, well described by Patrick Morrah, in *The Golden Age of Cricket*, as 'a Lancastrian Sam Woods: a great-hearted player of enormous energy and grand good humour, varied by occasional outbursts of explosive rage'. Lancashire had not had a good day, and the boy waited eagerly to hear what the great men might say about it, and what they said was, and they both meant it to sting,

'Well, Walter, you're a bloody fine fast bowler, aren't you?'

'And you're a bloody fine slip fielder, Archie.'

There was another interesting exchange between these two men, which was recounted to me by Wilfred Rhodes himself, no less. It was in the last Test of 1905, Australia went in against an England score of 430, and Trumper, as usual, opened the innings. Brearley bowled the first over. Trumper hit a boundary and then Brearley bowled one wide of the off stump, a loose one. While Trumper was deciding where to hit it, it came back off the pitch and bowled him. *Trumper, b Brearley, 4.* Brearley always liked to claim that Trumper was his rabbit, though they did not meet often enough for the claim to be substantiated. As the ball came down, MacLaren, at first slip, was saying 'God, what a bloody ball, what a bloody useless ball – oh, well bowled, Walter.'

MacLaren could change his batting order unconventionally and sometimes effectively. This practice has always been a matter of dispute between captains of different schools of thought. Grace, as we have seen, disliked it. Wyatt, as we shall see, took it to excess. At any rate, in the third Test of 1902, with England so far outplayed and needing 339 to win in the fourth innings, MacLaren sent Jessop in to open the innings on the second evening, and Jessop scored 55 in three-quarters of an hour, scaring Australia and giving England a brief chance. Then in the first Test of 1909, England needing only 109 in the last innings, but the pitch gone, he took the risk of sending in Hobbs and Fry (which meant dropping himself in the order), although each had scored 0 in the first innings. Fry claims that he made this suggestion himself, but MacLaren must at least have agreed to it, and I am not quite sure that in this instance Fry's account can be accepted at its face value.

Hobbs (mostly) and Fry got the runs, easily.

There was the occasion (1901–2) when MacLaren took Barnes with him to Australia, on hardly more evidence than a net at Old Trafford, and was triumphantly justified. In the third Test of 1902, that same match (Bramall Lane's only Test) in which Jessop made his mark, he sent a telegram for Barnes with only a few hours to go. Barnes had not been originally chosen. He took 6 for 49 in the Australian first innings, but only 1 for 50 in the second, and England were well beaten. This was poor going by the standards of Barnes. The other selectors (Hawke, Bainbridge, and Gregor MacGregor) were not pleased. Barnes did not play again for England that year.

The trouble with MacLaren was that if he disapproved of the choice of the selectors, he would tell not only them (which was his right as captain, and an *ex officio* member of the committee) but his unfortunate team, even before the game had begun. After the defeat at Sheffield, the selectors left out not only Barnes for the Old Trafford match (the one which Australia won by 3 runs), but also Lockwood and Haigh, both of whom had been chosen in the 12 for Sheffield but neither of whom had played (MacLaren having the last judgment and access to the telegraph office). They picked 11 for Manchester, indicating that they might add a reserve or two. But they did not want their captain to get up to any last-minute pranks again, and the only reserve nominated was Fred Tate, of Sussex. It seems fairly clear, as one looks back over all the different accounts of this affair, that the selectors chose Tate as a reserve because they thought MacLaren could not possibly pick him, and so their original 11 would stand. It seems fairly clear, also, that this infuriated MacLaren so much that he played Tate, even though it meant dropping George Hirst, who certainly had not done well at Sheffield, but was by this time unquestionably England's best all-round cricketer. MacLaren said that the selectors had wanted to see Tate bowl on a wet wicket, and so they should.

Well, as everyone seems to know to this day, Tate was the last man out in the last innings, and dropped a crucial catch in the deep field in Australia's second innings. MacLaren later spent much breath defending himself upon this point, because Tate was never normally fielded in the deep. Darling was the batsman, and a left-hander, but the explanations were never convincing. MacLaren was doubtless eager to bowl Australia out while the wicket was at its most wicked, and Lockwood had them on the run, but the few seconds taken to switch his field properly for the left-hander would not have been wasted. Left-handers were less common then than now (it is of left-handed batsmen I speak: the natural advantages of left-hand bowlers had long been recognized) but MacLaren had had plenty of experience against two of the best, Hill and Darling.

Fred Tate was a good cricketer, though scarcely an England one. He took 2 wickets for 7 runs in the same innings as he dropped Darling. He was not at all a bad batsman – a few weeks later he scored 60 for Sussex against the Australians, and county matches against tourists were still taken very seriously in those days. He is said to have got out to a silly swipe in the crisis, but he had had to wait three-quarters of an hour, after taking guard, because of rain; and putting him in at No. 11 was no encouragement to his confidence. He was the father of Maurice Tate, and lived to see the triumphs of his son, which probably consoled him for everything.

But he cannot, in that last innings of the 1902 Manchester Test, have had any additional encouragement from the behaviour of his captain. England, 37 behind on the first innings, bowled Australia out for 86 (Darling 37, Sydney Gregory 24 – leg-before to Tate – and nobody else in double figures). England therefore needed 124 to win. It was a difficult wicket on the third afternoon, but probably no worse than it had been for Australia the day before. MacLaren went in first (he had batted at No. 4 in the first innings), tried to knock off the runs, and was third out, caught in the deep off Trumble – who had been bowling for just such a contingency – at 72. Now at this point England needed only 52 to win, with 7 wickets in hand, and batting right down the order to Fred Tate, and plenty of time. Whatever the pitch might do, there was no need to panic. Indeed, panic was the one thing that might cost England the match.

MacLaren nevertheless, arriving at the dressing-room – shared by the professionals at the Oval in those days, so long as it was a Test match – flung his bat across the room, and announced that he had 'thrown away the match and the bloody rubber'. The word 'bloody' had a very powerful impact in 1902. The implication was that if *he* could not score runs, nobody else could, and nobody else did. MacLaren, with 35, was top scorer in England's 120.

This does not say much for MacLaren as a captain. Indeed, it has always seemed to me a shocking performance, from the choice of the team to the chuck of the bat. Yet a curious parallel occurred many years later. In 1954–5, England were playing Australia in the fourth Test match, at Adelaide. The England captain then was Len Hutton. It was a slow, dragged-out match, with a miserable over-rate, but in other respects it corresponded quite closely to the fourth Test of 1902. The rubber depended upon it. England needed only 94 to win in the last innings, and the captain went in first, his customary position. It ought to have been all right, without much bother, but there was a spell of bowling by Miller as taxing to the batsmen as Trumble's half a century before. The captain, though he had not scored a great many runs during that series, was rightly regarded as England's sure hope. Hutton did not bash at the bowling, as MacLaren had, but he was third out, at 18. He is supposed to have said, as he entered the dressing-room, something to this effect: 'It's Miller, the blighter, he's done us again.' Denis Compton, next in, said 'Who's done us? Steady on, I haven't been in yet.' Hutton did not throw his bat across the dressing-room. He sat down with his head in his hands and prayed. England won all right, by six wickets.

This is one of the most famous stories of modern cricket, if one dare call an event of 1955 modern. It comes, in print, in at least a dozen different versions. I have spoken to many of the people who were present at the place and the time, and none of *them* agree about it either. But something of this sort must have happened. My own view of the 1955 incident is that Hutton, who is a deep thinker about the game and rarely discloses his mind to anybody, least of all when the crisis of his life is upon him, had a certain deliberation about him when he put his head in his hands. It was just the thing to get the best out of Compton, and it did. The two men had been, at least in terms of press and public, rivals rather than comrades for some years. People tell this story, even Frank Tyson, one of Hutton's most faithful supporters, as if in some way it reflected credit on Compton rather than Hutton. I believe that Hutton was shrewder than that, and knew just what he had to do to get the best performance out of his best remaining batsman at the critical moment.

We shall never know the truth about this, if only because nobody can really remember what they felt, what they intended, what was exactly in their mind, in so critical a situation. Might this also be true of MacLaren in 1902? Might his throwing the bat across the room, in the presence of his succeeding batsmen – 'I've lost the bloody rubber' – have been an attempt to stir up the best from those about to go in?

I doubt it. MacLaren was not a strategic thinker, however good he might have been tactically. He was just in a bad temper, and threw his bat because he was sick of the sight of it, and possibly also had a guilty conscience because he had chosen Tate instead of Hirst. Still, it is a point worth bearing in mind before we condemn him too harshly.

England under MacLaren must have been a good side to watch, save for the passionate partisans, but an uncomfortable side in which to play. It is not really, when you think about it, surprising that he lost so regularly. I once wrote about him, in an article for *The Times* upon the centenary of his birth, that 'England may have had worse captains, but I would be hard put to it to name two or three'. This was an extravagant phrase, which I would not now seek to justify, but I received a congratulatory letter from a gentleman in Perth, Australia, who using one of MacLaren's favourite adjectives, said 'At last an English cricket writer has had the courage to accept that MacLaren was a bloody bad captain'; and also, though you might not believe it, a congratulatory letter from Cardus.

Bad captain or no, with no doubt, no shadow of doubt, no possible probable shadow of doubt, MacLaren was one of the most entrancing, one of the most glamorous – though that word had not come into fashion in his day – characters of his cricketing epoch. If it were possible to recall a side of that period by a vision (it cannot be done by a computer), down would go MacLaren as No. 1; and probably even, for England, as captain, if only for the fun of seeing what would happen.

He paid his last visit to the southern hemisphere in 1922–3, as captain of an M.C.C. side to New Zealand. He made a score of over 200, and one of the younger members of his side said afterwards 'We realized that we hadn't known anything about cricket at all until we saw that innings.' His later years were not free from worry and strain, which perhaps accounted for a rather querulous attitude towards the younger generation of cricketers, which marred his efforts as a cricket reporter. Yet in most respects he was a man of a generous and warm, not to say fiery sprit. Patrick Morrah tells a good story about him. He was hard up, not an unusual state of affairs, but managed to sell a newspaper article for what was then the very large sum – for such notoriously underpaid commodities – of 15 guineas. Immediately he moved out of his cheap lodgings into the best hotel in town, and threw a large dinner party, champagne and all. That was the grand manner. Not strictly Roman, perhaps: but he was surely the noblest Edwardian of them all.

Jackson.

I must declare an interest in Jackson, because once I wrote a book about him. He was a world away – well, the breadth of the Pennines, which is even wider – from MacLaren. Jackson was cool and clinical where MacLaren was heated and impulsive, yet Jackson the batsman was as dashing a stylist as any of them, with the highest average among his contemporaries against Australia, and a formidable change bowler. It is tempting to put him down as the best England captain of them all, but he only had the leadership in that 1905 series. He never toured Australia. The evidence is insufficient for so drastic a judgment. Nevertheless nobody can doubt that he was a very fine player, and a very fine captain.

His whole life, not just his cricketing life, was very different from MacLaren's. He was born at Chapel Allerton, near Leeds, on November 21, 1870 (the same day as Joe Darling was born). He came from a good 'county' family. In due course he went to a preparatory school, Lockers Park in Hertfordshire, where his interest in cricket was encouraged by the headmaster, Mr Draper. The Head, batting in the nets, once promised a bottle of ginger beer to the bowler every time he was bowled out. The small Jackson earned 18 bottles of ginger beer. He went on to Harrow, where MacLaren soon joined him. (Spare a thought or a prayer for the unlucky school bowlers who had to face these two in the same side.) He was in the XI from 1887 to 1889, and captain in his last year. He did not achieve much against Eton in 1887, but in 1888 his father, then a member of Lord Salisbury's government, offered him a sovereign for each wicket he took, and a shilling for each run he made. He scored 21 and 59, and took 11 wickets for 68. His son's comment was that he had been glad to be successful, 'as it would do father so much good'.

Harrow won by 156 runs, after being 26 behind on the first innings. They still sing at Harrow E. E. Bowen's song, commemorating Jackson's performance:

> Ten score to make, or yield her!
>   Shall Eton save the match?
> Bowl, bowler! Go it, fielder!
>   Catch, wicket-keeper, catch!
> Our vain attempts controlling
>   They drive the leather – no!
> *A gentleman's a-bowling*,
>   And down the wickets go.

Jackson went to Cambridge, where he was expected to get his Blue without any difficulty as a freshman. He began nervously and had several failures. Sam Woods, his captain, took him aside and said 'If you are worrying about your Blue, you can have it at once' – with, I dare say, a blue expletive or two added. Jackson's place in the Cambridge side was never thereafter in doubt. He was captain in 1892, and re-elected in 1893, always a rare honour, and even more so in those days. In three of his four years in the side, Cambridge won.

'A Country Vicar' has written:

I remember the game in which I was first impressed by the complete mastery of his batsmanship. It was a college match – between Trinity and Jesus on Jesus Close. The game – a two-day fixture – was regarded as a contest between the two strongest college elevens of 1893.

Trinity were behind on the first innings, needed 253 to win, and lost some early wickets.

Then F. S. Jackson and K. S. Ranjitsinhji made a remarkable stand, adding 136. 'Ranji' was never a slow scorer, but his share of those runs was 47, which shows the nature of Jackson's hitting! It was magnificent. He used every stroke; but the one which dwells most vividly in my memory was an on-drive, out of the ground, which pitched on the creeper-clad wall of the College buildings.

Jackson's successful captaincy of Cambridge makes it even odder that he was not chosen, instead of MacLaren, to succeed Grace as the England captain in 1899. Perhaps it was because of an incident in the match of 1893, which engendered many bitter feelings. Cambridge had scored 182, and Oxford were 95 for 9. The follow-on was then compulsorily imposed if a side was more than 80 runs behind on the first innings. Cambridge did not want to bat last, and Jackson instructed C. M. Wells to bowl wides deliberately, so as to prevent Oxford from following on. As a result of this – and a similar incident in another University match three years later – a bad law was, ultimately, changed; and the follow-on became optional. Why had not one of the last Oxford batsmen thwarted Jackson's plan by knocking down his wicket? Perhaps I may be forgiven for recalling the remark of one long-dead Oxford Blue, who said that only a Cambridge man could ask such a question.

From this distance of time, Jackson's action seems reasonable enough. Nevertheless, it does suggest a toughness of character, a certain ruthlessness behind the genial exterior, like going on and on for the eighteenth bottle of ginger beer. He does not seem to have been a particularly popular man, though he was always a deeply respected one. There was also the fact that in the same year (1893), when he was chosen for all three Tests against Australia, Jackson preferred not to play in the last one, because he wanted to play for Yorkshire at Brighton. Yorkshire needed to win that match to make sure of the championship. They won it, and it was their first championship. But even then there were those who questioned his sense of values.

It should, however, always be remembered of the young Jackson that he gave

Ranjitsinhji his Blue, a much more controversial thing to do than would seem possible to us now. An Indian – even if he was a prince – playing for Cambridge! Jackson had left him out the previous year (Ranji was in his fourth year when at last he got it) and would often comment afterwards, ruefully, about his mistake. I dare say that his experience of India, in one of Hawke's tours in 1892–3, had caused him to revise his views on Indian cricketers and even upon India, a country which he later served as Governor of Bengal.

Jackson would have been invited to tour Australia with Stoddart in 1894–5, but now that his Cambridge days were over he never had the time to tour in the winter. He became preoccupied with business and politics, and I suppose cricketers can count themselves fortunate that he found as much time for the game as he did. He was an automatic choice for any Test match at home, even if he was not playing regularly for Yorkshire. In 1896, in the Lord's Test, a low-scoring match, his first innings of 44 was important, and so was his innings of 45 in another low-scoring match at the Oval. The Lord's innings ended in a way which throws some light on the customs of the time, and also upon the character of Jackson. There was a huge crowd, which encroached on the playing area. Jackson gave a chance to Darling, in the deep, which was dropped because the fieldsman was impeded by the crowd. He promptly put up another in the same place, which Darling held. The gesture did not, however, meet with unanimous approval. Percy Cross Standing, Jackson's biographer, can go no further than to call it 'a pretty piece of quixotism ... perhaps straining a point to be so generous'. Jackson afterwards denied that he had made the second stroke deliberately. He did the proper thing all right, befitting a Harrovian and a Cantab, but the Yorkshireman in him would not let on.

He had a successful series against the Australians in 1899, scoring his second Test match century, and was England's most reliable batsman, by far, in the wild excitements of 1902. Jessop would never have had the chance of playing his innings at the Oval if Jackson had not earlier stood firm. We have noticed the events of 1905, the year everything went right for England and their captain. Incidentally, Jackson tossed for innings against Darling seven times that season. The last time was when he was captaining C. I. Thornton's XI at the Scarborough Festival. When Jackson visited the Australian dressing-room beforehand, he found Darling stripped to the waist, a Union Jack at his belt, saying, 'Now we'll have a proper tossing, and he who gets on top wins the toss!' Jackson called up the stalwart George Hirst, saying, 'Georgie, you come and toss this time.' Darling then sadly agreed to toss in the old-fashioned way, and lost for the seventh time.

At the end of the season a dinner was held at Scarborough to mark the twenty-fifth anniversary of Lord Hawke's association with Yorkshire cricket. Jackson was among the speakers, and referred to his relationship with MacLaren. Despite MacLaren's unsuccessful record, there were still many who viewed his captaincy with feelings only this side of idolatry, and there were plenty among them who felt that Jackson's victory must have depended largely upon having MacLaren at his elbow. One cannot help suspecting that, in later years, MacLaren did not altogether discourage this belief. But Jackson 'expressed his deep and sincere gratitude to Mr MacLaren for his loyal assistance. (Hear, hear.) The crimes and misfortunes of a side were naturally reflected in a great degree upon the captain, and he sometimes thought they were exaggerated both ways; but he knew of no other occasion on which the luck played so unfair a part as it had during the two seasons when Mr MacLaren captained the English side, just as it had been unfairly kind to himself this year'. These were generous words. To Percy Cross Standing, Jackson went even further. 'It was scarcely an enviable position', he said, 'for any man who was at all sensitive to be practically superseded, but MacLaren played as a cricketer and as a true sportsman.' Whenever he went on to bowl for England, he said, he made over the captaincy to MacLaren; he invariably inspected the wicket with him. MacLaren 'in all ways acted as partner rather than lieutenant in the command'. Jackson also declared once in public that he still believed 'there was one man who would have captained England better than himself'.

This is certainly abundant evidence of the tact which was one of Jackson's qualities as a captain. Certainly, too, he must have owed much to MacLaren's experience. But if and when it came to a clash of opinion, one has no doubt that Jackson would quietly pursue his own way. It would be hard to imagine anyone less capable of being a puppet captain. His great advantage was that he had the knack of keeping his side happy and united. Witness his handling of MacLaren himself. Witness how he got the best from such a stormy character as Walter Brearley, who never played better for England than he did this year. Witness that Fry, though he was to be a successful England captain himself, looked back on 1905 as his happiest season in Test cricket, and says that he 'delighted in Jackson's captaincy'.

He was physically strong and well-built, standing nearly six feet high, with (by the standards of those days) a not unduly lavish golden-brown moustache. Fry says he was 'exceptionally good-looking in the Anglo-Saxon Guards officer way'. He was famous for his impeccable turn-out on the field. He had, says Hubert Preston in the 1948 *Wisden*, 'exceptional courage which amounted to belief in his own abilities'. It is this theme to which those who knew him constantly recur. P. F. Warner: 'He never underrated bowlers, nor did he overrate them; he merely played each ball on its merits.' (This recalls the dictum attributed to W.G.: 'There is no crisis in cricket; there is only the next ball'.) E. H. D. Sewell: 'All that Jackson did on the cricket field he did so easily that it seemed to be the only thing to do.' Wilfred Rhodes: 'He . . . possessed the gift of a fine temperament, with plenty of confidence and pluck, and always appeared at his best on great occasions, especially when fighting with his back to the wall.' Canon F. H. Gillingham: 'He always seemed to have that extra reserve of strength to compete with any cricket crisis, however severe.' Sir Home Gordon: 'It was his unexampled coolness that was so astounding; an unruffled calm arising from justified confidence in what he himself could do. His concentration was abnormal . . . I think it must be no exaggeration to say that no one ever saw Jackson hesitate.' C. B. Fry makes the same point, but one passage he wrote on Jackson is worth quoting amply:

Not only has he an extraordinary number of different strokes, of all kinds, but he has a quite notable ability of adapting these strokes without altering them, except in the matter of timing, to all kinds of bowling and to all kinds of wickets. Many batsmen, and good ones, have one game for fast wickets and another for slow, one for good-length bowling and another for bad-length bowling. F. S. Jackson has one game of a most comprehensive and elastic kind which he plays with consummate confidence always, and which he brings into effective relations with all conditions of play. Perhaps, among modern batsmen, there is no one who maintains what may be described as perpetual uniformity of style on every kind of wicket and against every kind of bowling as he does, with the possible exception of Victor Trumper.

This was the kind of thing that had been said about W.G. Fry goes on:

Probably the secret of this uniformity is nothing more nor less than a settled habit of watching the ball from the bowler's hand to the pitch, and from the pitch on to the bat, and of taking every ball as it comes absolutely and entirely on its independent merits; and then – of just playing it quite naturally. Such a method brings the easy and the difficult into the same plane, provided the batsman has versatility and what, for want of a better name, we call genius.

This does not come from Fry's autobiography, written many years later, but from the text he provided for Beldam's action photographs, published in the year of Jackson's triumph. It remains none the less a thoughtful and eloquent tribute from one England captain to another.

Though he was still under 35 years old at the end of the season, 1905 was Jackson's last cricketing year, apart from the occasional game. From time to time it was suggested that he should be recalled, in practice or not (as happened with MacLaren in 1909), but he was too much of a perfectionist for that. He had reached the captaincy of England after undue delay; given the Australians, and a strong Australian side too, a proper licking; and left the scene at the full height of his ability and success, needing no apologists.

His value to his country neither began nor ended with his cricket. In 1915 he entered the House of Commons, the Unionist Member for the Howdenshire division of Yorkshire. He represented it for 11 years. One day in Parliament Winston Churchill, who had been his fag at Harrow (it must have made a striking combination), introduced him to Lloyd George. L.G. immediately said, 'I have been looking all my life for the man who gave Winston Churchill a hiding at school.'

He was not a great parliamentarian, not of the stature in this respect of his father (Lord Allerton, as he became). It is untrue, however, as I once heard alleged, that he was the original of the famous (and no doubt mythical) back-bencher, whose one speech in many years of service was 'Will somebody please shut that damned window?' When he was nerving himself for his maiden speech, the debate took a difficult turn, and the Speaker passed him a note: 'I have dropped you in the batting order; it's a sticky wicket.' And then, later, when the situation was easier: 'Get your pads on. You're next in.' This story is recounted by Hubert Preston in the 1948 *Wisden*, but I confess I have my doubts of it. The House of Commons gives no maiden speaker, least of all so popular and distinguished a maiden, a troublesome passage, unless trouble is deliberately sought, and that was not Jackson's way.

He became Financial Secretary to the War Office in 1922, and in 1923 was chairman of the organization of the Unionist party (as the Conservatives were still technically known). In 1927 he went to India again, as Governor of Bengal, behaving with exactly the calm, courage, and swift reaction one would expect when somebody took a shot at him with the intention of killing him ('The quickest duck I've ever made in all my life'). His long friendship with Ranjitsinhji must have been of help to him in this job. He acquired the 'Colonel' in his title through service in the Boer War (with the Royal Lancasters, an improbable regiment) and also in the Great War, when he raised and commanded a West Yorkshire battalion.

He was President of M.C.C. in 1921, and chairman of the England selectors in 1934 – a very difficult year in which to be a selector. (MacLaren was never made a selector; partly, perhaps, because of his reporting activities – but that was not held to debar Warner.) In 1943 Jackson presided over the important committee set up by M.C.C. to plan for the rebuilding of cricket in the post-war years.

After retiring from cricket, he took up golf. For six months he practised strokes in front of a mirror, with a text-book beside him, not hitting a ball. Within a year he was a scratch player. I have heard this or a similar story told of others, but Sir Home Gordon assures us it is true in this case, and it would be entirely typical of Jackson's self-control and natural ability for any ball game.

When he died, aged 76, in March 1947, he had become Colonel the Honourable Sir Francis Stanley Jackson, P.C., G.C.I.E. I ended my book about his triumphant 1905 season with this paragraph:

One likes to think of that elegant but businesslike figure leading his team out on to the field. He walked briskly, as if eager to set about the enemy, and immediately on reaching the wicket would begin close colloquy and conning of the pitch with his bowlers. But once proceedings had begun, only rarely did he hold up play for consultations. He controlled his field with gestures which were clear, firm, but never exaggerated. He remained unflurried whatever crisis threatened. On the field his mind was locked in the combat, off it he was the most genial of companions and opponents. He was, and looked, every inch a cricketer; every inch a captain of England. I trust that his achievements were duly celebrated at Harrow, and that there was special gusto on the next school song day when they came to the lines

> *A gentleman's a-bowling,*
> *And down the wickets go!*

He was never, incidentally, the regular captain of Yorkshire. Apart from the difficulty he would have had in finding the time for it, Lord Hawke was still in office.

P. F. Warner became captain of Middlesex in 1908, five years after he had first captained England, and held the post until 1920. In his very last match, dramatically, he led them to the championship. His school was Rugby, and he won his Blue at Oxford, where he read law. Cricket, however, was his life: its playing, its reporting, its administration. He was not one of the greatest batsmen of his time, but certainly a very good one. In rating him, we have to bear in mind that despite his long life (he was 89 when he died in 1963) he was not a physically strong man. Indeed, he tells us with pardonable pride that once when he was in the runs against Yorkshire, George Hirst told him that if God had given him 'a proper stummick' he would have had all the bowlers looking both ways for Sunday.

He was a more complex character than at first appears. On the one hand there are many glowing tributes to the parfit gentil knight, and so on. In a memorable sentence H. S. Altham wrote:

Among the figures that challenge oblivion in the long vistas of the game — W.G., with his black beard and M.C.C. cap, Ranji, in his fluttering sleeves of silk — few surely were more familiar, none certainly was better loved, than that of 'Plum' Warner, the 'Happy Warrior', in his Harlequin cap.

And A. A. Thomson, though Warner had often made his dear Yorkshire suffer, wrote that 'no one has in his person more truly symbolized cricket; its pageantry, its dignity and decency, its sense of "civilization under the sun"'. One could fill pages with such tributes, and there is no doubting their sincerity.

Warner himself idealized the game, and was prone to say things such as:

The very word 'cricket' has become a synonym for all that is true and honest. To say 'that is not cricket' implies something underhand, something not in keeping with the best ideals. There is no game which calls forth so many fine attributes, which makes so many demands on its votaries, and, that being so, all who love it as players, as officials or spectators must be careful lest anything they do should do it harm.

On the other hand, there has been the occasional discordant note in the chorus of praise. A recurring one concerned his journalism. Opposition to his choice as England captain in 1903 came not only from those who thought MacLaren could do no wrong, but those who thought it improper that an active journalist should hold such a position. He has told us how his journalism began. Lord Hawke, setting out on a private tour of the West Indies, was asked if a member of the team could send back an occasional article for the press describing progress, and said 'Here, Plummy, you do it, you're latest from school.' Some of his criticisms of his contemporaries in his early writing years were outspoken, though they became much more discreet later on. In practice I doubt if this handicapped him much as a captain, and he was always popular with the sides he led; but it did encourage an unfortunate trend. He continued his journalism in later years even when he was on the selection committee. It was certainly a rather bizarre situation in 1926, when the chairman of selectors was also the cricket correspondent of the *Morning Post*.

Warner was frequently a selector, and even in those years when he was not, no doubt his opinions carried a great deal of weight. Here, too, he came in for some criticism. Without going into individual choices, which can always be argued, he did sometimes lend his support to dubious policies. E. W. Swanton, who writes of him with admiration and affection, nevertheless adds that 'he could never think ill of a fine cricketer, an amiable characteristic but dangerous in a man of such authority who had to make important judgments'. It was Warner who was chiefly responsible, in the 'thirties, for the choice as captain first of Jardine and later of Hammond, neither of which turned out to be particularly happy appointments, at least on tour. And this was odd, because, as Swanton points out, the qualities they lacked were precisely those of tact and graciousness which had made Warner himself so successful a touring captain.

We shall deal with both these captains in due course, but it is necessary here to take a preliminary look at the events of 1932–3, because a consideration of the 'bodyline' tour and Warner's part in it is essential to an estimate of his character.

He was the senior manager of Jardine's team that winter, and it was in an early interview with the Australian press that he spoke the words in praise of cricket which I have quoted.

Briefly, what happened was that the Australians had given England a terrible licking in 1930, against English expectations, chiefly because of Bradman. Statistically, this was the greatest of the Bradman years. In the five Tests in England that year, Bradman scored 974 runs in seven innings, beating numerous records. He scored 131 at Trent Bridge, 254 at Lord's, 334 at Headingley, and 232 at the Oval. Australia made totals, during this series, of 729 (for 6, declared), 566, and 695. England did not bat badly, but they could not cope with scores of this size, especially made so fast as Bradman did. This was the first season of four-day Tests in England: at the end of the first day at Lord's, with England nearing 400 in their first innings, MacLaren was hopping around in fury demanding to know why they had not declared. He would probably argue, and is probably still arguing, somewhere up in the Elysian fields, that they should have done, even in the light of what happened afterwards.

It would not, though, have made much difference. Through the 'thirties, if Australia were in any kind of trouble, and provided that it was a wicket which he felt he could play on, Bradman would score a couple of hundred to put them right. The efficiency of this awesome machine (he became much more than a machine later, but remained awesome) was recognized by the England selectors as they set about planning for the tour of Australia in 1932. *Something had to be done about Bradman.*

The English attack under Jardine was based on a succession of fast, short-pitched balls on the line of the batsman's body, as many as four or five in a six-ball over, supported by seven or even eight fieldsmen on the leg side. They did keep Bradman under some sort of control. He averaged 56, more than any other batsman in the series (except Paynter, who was only out three times) but that was well short of his superhuman level. His highest score was 103. It was the only time in his career he was relatively quelled. Against Larwood, the fastest and most hostile of the bowlers, he averaged only 29. With Bradman reduced to the level of just another good Australian batsman – though of course he was not the only one to whom the tactics were applied – England duly won the rubber, 4–1.

The term 'bodyline' began as a piece of journalist's telegraphese. For some time it was regarded in England as an insult. Jardine himself insisted on the description 'fast leg theory'. But fast leg theory in more modified forms had been known before and has been known since, and it is 'bodyline' which has passed into history. Nothing like a bodyline attack, sustained over a Test series, has happened at any other time: it was soon, of course, made illegal. Lindwall and Miller bowled many a bouncer, Lillee and Thomson hit a great many batsmen, but neither of those dreaded pairs could employ the packed leg side field, accompanied by five bumpers an over.

Now as to Warner's part. First, he was chairman of the selection committee which chose Jardine as captain, and gave him a team which included four fast bowlers. There would not seem anything surprising in that today, but it was very unusual then. The 1928 England side to Australia, and the 1930 Australian side to England, had included one each. There had been occasional try-outs of the tactics beforehand, and one of them, by Bowes at the Oval, had brought severe criticism from the cricket correspondent of the *Morning Post*.

'Bowes', he wrote, 'should alter his tactics. He bowled with five men on the on-side and sent down several very short-pitched balls which frequently bounced head high and more. That is not bowling. Indeed it is not cricket, and if all fast bowlers were to adopt his methods there would be trouble and plenty of it.'

So Warner, as one would have expected, was against bodyline, and he repeated his criticism of it on a number of occasions after Jardine's team had returned.

But it must be pointed out that, according to Warner's own account (in *Cricket Between Two Wars*), Bowes was not an original choice for the tour. Playing for Yorkshire, the champion county, against the Rest of England in the middle of September, he took, on the second day, 7 wickets for 65. *Wisden* says of this match that 'Bowes, without dropping the ball really short, made it lift to such a pronounced extent that no one played him with confidence'. Bowes did not play on the third day of the match. The selectors had decided to send him to Australia, and he was off packing his bags, since there were only five days to go before departure. 'And when it was suggested it was a bit late to ask him', Warner reports, 'I replied, "Lord Roberts got ready for South Africa in three days!"' As it happened, Bowes did not play a large part in that tour, apart from getting Bradman out for a celebrated duck which is argued about to this day; but he made the fourth fast bowler, and had already tried his hand at bodyline. It does seem curious that Warner, if he was not a party to Jardine's intended tactics, should have been so enthusiastic for his choice. Nor does the military analogy strike a happy note, though we ought not to make too much of such details, for Warner liked a military analogy. During the fourth Test of the tour Paynter was taken ill, and Jardine hauled him out of hospital to bat (which he did very well). Warner had told Jardine that he did not think Paynter would be fit, and Jardine had replied 'What about those fellows who marched to Kandahar with the fever on them?' This, says Warner, was 'a remark which delighted me and was typical of our captain's grit and determination'.

In the preceding Test, at Adelaide – it is often recalled as 'the battle of Adelaide' – Warner was snubbed in the Australian dressing-room when he called to pay his condolences to the Australian captain, Woodfull, who was recovering from a severe hit by a ball from Larwood. The story got into the press, something for which Warner blamed Jack Fingleton, who was already a journalist as well as a member of the Australian team. He offered Harold Larwood a pound if he could get Fingleton out for 0 in the second innings, which Larwood did, completing a pair of noughts for Fingleton. Fingleton was not the culprit, as he has since convincingly explained, but naturally felt bitter about the accusation. In his book *Cricket Crisis* (1946) he has a scathing chapter about Warner's part in the bodyline series. Fingleton may have overdone it a bit, and later the two men became friends: but he has a fair point, which we might summarize as 'What did Warner think he was up to?'

I will not go into all the details of the Warner–Woodfull confrontation again. It is worth remembering, though, that they had got on very well before this series, and that Warner had, earlier in the season, visited the school where Woodfull was a master to talk to the boys about cricket (and we might make a fair guess at the kinds of things he said). We might also quote what seem to me the most significant lines in the conversation (it comes to us in various versions, but I follow Warner's own):

> *Woodfull:* I don't want to see you, Mr Warner. There are two teams out there. One is trying to play cricket and the other is not.
> *Warner:* Apart from all that, we most sincerely hope you are not too badly hurt.

Apart from all that. Those are the key words. Warner had been severe on bodyline, or fast leg theory, or whatever you like to call it, before he had gone to Australia, and he was to be even more severe about it afterwards. But here he was as the English manager in Australia, with the thing going on before his eyes day by day, and he uses such a phrase as 'Apart from all that . . .' at such a moment, to a friend still wobbling as a result of 'all that'.

This raises questions of the relationship between a captain and his manager, questions which have occurred before in this narrative and will again, though never in so acute a form. The early managers were players, or partners, or secretaries and treasurers; hardly more. But by 1932 the manager, especially one in such a position as Warner, captain of two successful teams to Australia, a member of the selection committee both at home and on tour, was expected to be more than that. On the previous two tours to Australia, F. C. Toone (who was knighted for his services to cricket, as Warner was) had been an influence both equable and commanding. Toone's captains had been Gilligan and Chapman, two amiable fellows: he was a Yorkshireman, and I expect would have been tougher than either if any serious moral or tactical problem arose. But this is speculation. Nobody can tell how Toone would have dealt with Jardine.

'Warner was sent to keep the peace', wrote Jack Fingleton. It was not so simple as that, certainly not in Warner's mind, and yet over all these years it is a sentence with a ring of truth.

'Don't put so many men on the leg side, Douglas', he is reported to have said to Jardine. This was an accurate tactical judgment – because it was the combination of the bouncer *and* the leg-side field which made bodyline such a menace. That seems to have been the limit of his protests. 'But what can I do? What can I do?' he is reported to have said to his Australian friends. And Clem Hill, his old opponent whom he had failed to reconcile with the Australian Board of Control in 1912, said 'You can come down off the fence for a start, Plum.'

What *could* Warner have done? These were the choices before him:

(1) He could have condemned bodyline, as he had already done and was to do again, and resigned his managership. It is his failure to have done so that gives all his subsequent plaints a feeble sound. Nothing would have done more to awake English opinion to the realities of the situation. Of course, it would have taken a man of exceptionally strong character to do this. He would have been accused of a lack of patriotism, a charge Warner would have found exceptionally wounding. He would have been told that it was no business of his. The consequences for the future of the tour would have been unpredictable. Still, he would have given a salutary shock to the public at home, which had very little idea of what was going on. (The English press coverage of the tour, for reasons which E. W. Swanton explains in *Sort of a Cricket Person*, was unbalanced and inadequate.) As it was, the mere fact that a man such as Warner, with his unequalled reputation for sportsmanship, stayed at his post, seemed an assurance that nothing could be seriously wrong with Jardine's tactics.

(2) He could have defended bodyline, at least in private. His views would soon have become known to the press. For this to carry any conviction, of course, he would have had to have kept quiet about it the previous summer. But he could have done it. I have been writing about bodyline as if it were an unmitigated and acknowledged evil, and so I imagine almost all cricketers would now consider it, but it had its defenders at the time, some of whom knew what they were talking about. Herbert Sutcliffe, who faced it on a number of occasions when playing for Yorkshire against Nottinghamshire, provides a *rationale* for bodyline in moderate terms in *For England and Yorkshire*. It is true that Sutcliffe, with his mastery of the hook, was probably of all batsmen in the world the best equipped to play it, but there were still several fair points which could be made, and the critics often spoilt a good case by overstating it, as the Australian Board of Control did in its cables to M.C.C. This would have been at least a loyal and courageous thing for Warner to have done.

As it was, he continued to sit uneasily on the fence, shared fully in the triumphant homecoming, and only later said how deplorable it had all been.

This was understandable, but it was not heroic.

However, one cannot condemn a man, even an England captain and manager, simply because he was not born to ride the whirlwind and direct the storm, and there is no doubt that Warner must rank as one of England's most successful captains, both as a tactician and on his record. He is the only man, apart from Shrewsbury (and Shrewsbury's second tour as captain included only two Tests), to have led two successful parties to Australia. Few men have given more to the game: and apart from his administrative work, as wartime secretary of M.C.C. and later its President, one must not forget the score or so of books he wrote, which never fall below a workmanlike standard and frequently rise above it.

Although I was introduced to Warner, and was struck, as everyone else was, by his unaffected courtesy and modesty (a quality he found rather lacking in the modern generation, though otherwise he was well enough disposed to his juniors), the first captain of England I ever talked to properly was Charles Fry. Fry was born in 1872 and died in 1956. His school was Repton, his university Oxford. He is an exceptionally easy man to write about, or an exceptionally difficult one, according to how you look at it: easy because there is so much to say about him, difficult because so much has been said and written about him already. He wrote incomparably about himself. I seriously think I have never enjoyed an autobiography more than *Life Worth Living*. Of the attempts by others to put him into print, perhaps Denzil Batchelor's account in the Phoenix *Cricketing Lives* series best catches his flavour. Denzil was Fry's secretary for several years, and one of the few men who could hold his end up in conversation with the master. Cardus has several times written beautifully of Fry, though not so often as he has done of some others. Sir Neville was also equal to the conversational demands. Indeed, on the 1936–7 visit to Australia, when they were both touring as journalists, he scored a technical knock-out. It was Remembrance Day. As the company rose to their feet to observe the two minutes' silence, he breathed the words to his companion, 'This'll irk you, Charles.' At least Fry had plenty of time to think up his repartee, but we never learnt what it was.

Fry could properly be called a polymath, but he was above all a classic. He was a classic academically, with his Open scholarship, head of the list, and his First in Mods. This was to show that he could do it. He did not bother too much about Greats. He had done enough to demonstrate that he was a scholar comparable with, possibly superior to, John Simon and F. E. Smith, his contemporaries at Wadham. Someone will be saying, 'What are these Mods and Greats? Who are Simon and Smith? What is Wadham?' but these short-cuts have to be taken in writing about him, or he would steal the book, and lead me to break his rule that no sentence should exceed 25 words in length. He endeavoured to apply such a rule to contributors to *C. B. Fry's Magazine*, one of several periodicals which he edited (nor was his editorship nominal), but so noticeably failed to observe it in his own writings that the contributors rebelled: whereupon he offered a dispensation to those who had benefited from a classical education, and therefore 'understood how to frame subordinate clauses'. Yet his writing was not, generally, prolix. He was capable of a pithy sentence. Denzil

Batchelor once said that when Fry was in a mordant mood he became the incarnation of the ablative absolute.

Fry was also a classic cricketer. He played a match for Surrey when young, and many for Hampshire in the latter part of his career, but his principal allegiance was to Sussex, which he captained for most of the time from 1904 to 1908, and his most memorable years, which meant more than his Test years, were those in which he and Ranjitsinhji were playing together for Sussex. They made a good cricketing illustration of the difference between the classical and the romantic. At one end, the forward defensive stroke, perfectly balanced and controlled, but with a poise immediately ready to move into attack should the ball offer the opportunity: at the other, Ranji's astonishing back play, with its misleading air of improvised magic, the bumper flicked to long-leg from the lobe of the left ear. They scored thousands of runs together for Sussex. Even the Yorkshire bowlers, in their all-conquering period, dreaded a visit to Hove, while once the two were well set most of the rest of the Sussex side used to go off for a bathe.

In 1896 Ranji had scored 2,780 runs, the highest aggregate yet recorded (W.G.'s 2,739 in 1871 was the record until then). In 1899 Ranji broke his own aggregate record, scoring 3,159 runs. In 1900, he scored 3,065. At this point therefore the three highest aggregates ever made stood in his name. But Fry was not overshadowed. In 1901 he reached the 3,000 mark himself (as J. T. Tyldesley did – Ranji was not so successful that season, with 2,468). In the three seasons 1899–1901, Ranji scored 8,692 runs, and Fry 7,838. No wonder the visiting bowlers began to feel tired before the train reached Haywards Heath. There followed the anticlimax of 1902, when they had their disastrous season in Test cricket, but even in that year Ranji averaged 46 in all matches and Fry 35. In 1903 Fry was top of the averages again, 2,683 runs at 81, with Ranji (I am speaking of those who played a substantial number of innings) second, at 56. In 1904 it was Ranji's turn to lead, with an average of 74 in 34 innings, and Fry's turn to be second, average 70 in 42, though Fry scored the more runs. That was the last of their great seasons together. Ranji became increasingly involved in other matters. Fry continued to be among the leading batsmen, on several occasions at the top of the list, up to the time of his zenith, when he won the Triangular Tournament. I pause, because C.B. would have corrected the use of the word 'Zenith'. His England captaincy came when, in cricketing terms (and only in cricketing terms), the sun was past the meridian.

It was often said that Fry 'learnt all he knew' from Ranji, but this is manifestly untrue. Every picture shows their styles to have been different. Altham, more restrainedly, says 'It is an open secret, which he himself would be the first to admit, that it was his association with the Indian Prince that raised Charles Fry from a good into a great player'. I am not so sure even about this. It was not a proposition I would have liked to put to him myself. The influence of one upon the other must certainly have been great, but it did not all travel the same way. To put it roughly, I expect that it was the romantic genius of Ranji which determined Fry that he, too, would become a genius, but of course a classical one. If the distant east had its magical gods, then so did the isles of Greece. There was a touch of the godlike about them both.

I have put in all the statistics (well, a few of them) because – as with Grace – the modern generation is inclined to say 'Oh, great characters they must have been, those old boys, but how many runs did they score?' Be assured that they both scored a great many, and were regarded as marvels in their own time. Their career figures would look more impressive if they had not kept returning to the game, out of practice and out of form, because they liked playing it so much. This would not have bothered them, any more than it bothered MacLaren. They were Edwardians. Jackson, it occurs to me, and perhaps Warner, had more of a Georgian approach, tidier, less lavish, with an eye to the future, precursors of the coming age. Fry, like MacLaren, never became President of M.C.C. Canniness was not part of their style.

I suspect that it was because Fry was conscious that he was in all respects a classic, that he turned down the suggestion that he might become king of Albania. He would hardly have had a place in an Anthony Hope romance. This was an interesting episode. After the First World War, Ranjitsinhji was elected Chancellor of the Indian Princes, and as such was a member of the Indian delegation to the League of Nations. He appointed Fry as his adviser, and as Ranji did not usually stay in Geneva very long, Fry often became a *de facto* representative of India, and impressed everybody very greatly with his linguistic fluency and majestic manner, even those who had not heard of cricket. Albania, a small, newly-independent state, was looking for a king, preferably an Englishman, and so Fry's name came up for consideration (by no means, it must be said, the only one).

I mentioned this story, which has often enough appeared in print, in an article in *The Times* some years ago, and it led to an interesting correspondence. There was one school of thought which maintained that no such offer had ever been seriously made: that it was all a leg-pull by Ranji. Duleepsinhji, Ranji's nephew (later, you will remember, an England cricketer himself, and later still Indian High Commissioner to Australia), was cited in support of this view. But there was powerful evidence to the contrary, notably from Professor L. F. Rushbrook Williams, who succeeded to Fry's post in Ranji's service some years later. What happened, said Professor Rushbrook Williams, was that during the 1920 session of the League, at Geneva, an Albanian Bishop had called on Ranji and Fry to intimate that if a candidate could be found who was ready to spend £10,000 a year in Albania, the crown would be at his disposal.

Fry was tempted, and believed that if he had pressed Ranji for the money, Ranji would have found it, but Ranji did not want to lose his services. Nevertheless, Rushbrook Williams concludes, 'the provisional offer was undoubtedly given an airing, and it did not emanate from Ranji in the first instance'.

A little later one of C.B.'s daughters, Faith, who had been abroad and missed the correspondence, at the time of its publication, wrote to me and fully confirmed this account of what was known in the family, irreverently, as 'The Albanian Affair'. 'I have never understood', she said, 'why there have been so many variations on this theme, but they much amused my father!!'

This seems conclusive enough, though I could not help thinking that the variations on the theme possibly owed something to the central character himself, who liked to recount the tale, and, like all good raconteurs, would sometimes imaginatively elaborate a detail.

There is no need to doubt that the event is quite possible. Lord Headley, a British peer who had been converted to the Muslim religion, was approached; and ultimately it went to the unfortunate King Zog. I check myself as I am rising from the typewriter to look up more information about Zog. You will have to seek it yourself. I did indicate that one of the dangers of writing about Fry is the lure of the by-paths.

A business partner of Fry's, Christopher Hollis, wrote to me, in connection with the later versions of this story, that C.B. 'had a great capacity for living a fantasy life'. He went on, 'It pleased him to tell the story, and by the end I fancy that he did not know himself whether he believed it or not.' While one does not doubt the truth of this, it would be a mistake to think that Fry was a fantasist, in the sense that Walter Mitty was. His fantasies were no more than embroideries on what was already the finest silk. His achievements were real.

For instance, at Oxford he broke the world record in the long jump, and would have gone over to Athens to win the event at the 1896 Olympics, had he known they were on. I have not mentioned, concerning his cricket, that he scored six centuries in six successive innings, a feat which many years later Bradman equalled, but did not surpass. He won a Blue for soccer, and would have won one for Rugby but for an injury shortly before the Cambridge match. He maintained that he preferred Rugby to soccer, as a game to play, but he appeared for Southampton in the F.A. Cup Final of 1902. He was on the losing side, though the match went to a replay. Tony Pawson, in *100 Years of the F.A. Cup*, says of Fry: 'The one weakness of his game was the usual amateur's weakness of heading with hunched shoulders. Aiming, as always, at perfection he eliminated the fault by constant practice.'

He had no family money behind him, not even the modest private income of Warner. He went up to Oxford, he would say, with his Open scholarship and 30 shillings in his pocket, and kept himself going there by his own labours, partly by vacation tutoring, increasingly by journalism. There is no need to take this literally, but no reason to doubt it is substantially true. He continued to rely upon his own efforts to make a living, never an extravagant one. As a writer, he was much above the class of Warner, still more that of MacLaren. He was a close and articulate analyst of cricket technique, as several books testify. In the 1930s, he increased, dramatically, the circulation of the London *Evening Standard* by writing 'C. B. Fry's Column', which dealt often with cricket, but as often with other things. This was 20 years after he had captained England: not in the first flush of retirement, when any old England captain can make a few brief bob on his name. It was quality, not glamour, that did it.

He failed, however, despite several attempts, to make a real success of a magazine for boys. *C. B. Fry's Magazine* had a fair run, and is now a collector's item, but it did read a little too pompously, a little too worthily, and you can understand why boys turned to *The Boy's Own Paper*, or even *Pluck*, instead. *The Captain*, which Fry also edited, was livelier, and aimed at a more popular market. Much of it still reads very well. The trouble was not the circulation but the advertising. 'I have always thought', Fry wrote, 'that the disbelief of advertisers in the capacity of boys to absorb soap was the snag which eventually tripped up the career of *The Captain*.' Of his books, apart from the auto-biography, I suppose the best was his treatise on *Batsmanship*, which is still constantly quoted by those writing of the cricket of the time, and was studied by any serious young aspiring player. One of those absorbed by it was D. R. Jardine.

My acquaintance with Fry, though treasured, was not extensive. I met him on the training ship *Mercury* which he commanded in the Hamble River. He and his wife gave the best part of 40 years to this work. It was his most time-consuming achievement, less lauded than most, but he was very proud of it. It was because he took charge of *Mercury* that he changed his cricketing allegiance, in 1908, to Hampshire from Sussex. It was because he took charge of *Mercury* that he became, in time, a captain in the Royal Navy. He rather liked this, and would stride about in his uniform looking, as I think it was Robertson-Glasgow who said, every inch like six admirals. F. E. Smith once visited him in his command, was duly impressed, and ended by saying 'This is a fine show, C.B., but, for you, a backwater.' Fry replied, 'That may be, but the question remains whether it is better to be successful or happy.' Not that Fry disdained politics. Apart from his efforts at Geneva, he stood several times for Parliament. His political career was handicapped by his faithfulness to the Liberal party. He polled very well at Brighton, twice, and at Oxford, but was never elected. This may have been as well. He would have found it difficult to settle to the life of an MP, which even in the 1920s was becoming much more a routine one. After his near-run thing at

Oxford, Gilbert Murray (who was a Liberal candidate for the University on several occasions, and also never elected) said to him 'You know, if you're not careful you'll do this once too often.' At least, that is one version of the story. Another is that it was Fry who said it to Gilbert Murray. At the age of 70, Fry told the Oxford University Liberal Club, 'I think I'll try again.' There was loud applause, but he never did. He still had a strength, both mental and physical, beyond that of most members of Parliament, and there was no absurdity in the suggestion, but I think by then the appeal of it had departed. Only one of the six admirals was in whole-hearted support. Another of them had suggested, a year or two earlier, that he might best serve his country during the war as a Bevin Boy, but this I think we may take to be a little *jeu d'esprit* on the part of that particular admiral, though I have not the least doubt that if the challenge had been taken, the other five would have loyally backed up their colleague.

It was at Oxford, which he unaffectedly loved, granted that occasional cursings are a necessary part of true love, that I mostly met Charles Fry. His build was still magnificent, his carriage still majestic. You could see at once why in the 1890s they had written all those articles comparing him to a young Greek god. You would learn in no more than a minute or two those powers of the conversational monologue which had overcome, even overawed, such masters as Cardus and Robertson-Glasgow. I found myself that you could get in a sentence now and then, and a response to it, given three conditions: (a) the sentence must be a question, meriting an answer; (b) he had just used the word 'however', which, contrary to normal practice, he thought more valuable for ending verbal paragraphs than beginning them; (c) he was taking off his naval cap – for in his cap lay his tobacco-pouch, and he was considering a pipe. He also in those years retained the habit, of which many have written, of demonstrating a point of stroke-play with an umbrella. Indeed, once in the buttery of Queen's College, the umbrella momentarily mislaid, he seized an assegai from the wall to illustrate a description of Ranji. It was a slightly alarming moment, for the buttery was not very large, and Fry's arms were long, and the assegai was sharp. In consequence I failed to absorb information of importance, for never to this day have I been *quite* sure how Ranji played the famous leg glide.

All Fry's Test cricket was played in England, except for an early tour to South Africa, on which he was the most successful batsman. There was this belief among his contemporaries that he would have scored hugely on Australian pitches, which seems very likely, but he was not an outstanding success against the Australians over here, even leaving aside the freak disasters of 1902. The Australians believed they could tie him down, by cutting out his favourite strokes to the on-side. In 1905 he gave them an answer by scoring 144 at the Oval, mostly through the off-drive and the cut. His average in the end, 32 to remind you, was acceptable but not outstanding, not for so good a player. In his career, which began in 1892 and ended in 1921, he scored over 30,000 runs in first-class cricket.

In 1921, when he was playing peacefully for Hampshire under Tennyson, and England were in trouble against the Australians, he was asked if he would consider returning to the captaincy of England. He played against the fearful Australian fast bowlers for Hampshire, and made two good scores against them. He declined the captaincy, though, because of an injury, which was no doubt genuine enough. Yet I feel the old Fry, strained or not, would have sprung to the challenge, confident enough in his own ability – if England had not been such a poor side that year. No amount of captaincy could have won them that rubber, and Fry, brought in after the series had begun, could not have had a commanding hand in the choice of the side. He decided, on balance, that things were best left as they were. He certainly did not feel any compulsion to do or die at his country's call. He knew perfectly well that some Test matches are won by one side and some by the other, and that the world, even the cricket world, does not collapse if the others are winning, indeed that it would very soon collapse *unless* the others frequently won (I think I have the gist of a sentence I once heard him use, but I cannot recapture, or match, the precise words).

MacLaren, on the other hand, in that season of 1921, never ceased to proclaim that *he* knew a way to beat the Aussies, given the captaincy and a side of his own choice. And bless us MacLaren did, at Eastbourne, at the end of the season. He chose a side of his own, all amateurs. He chose himself and Walter Brearley. As the ageing Brearley fell over the fence in trying to jump it, and took no further part in the match, MacLaren's XI played with ten men, effectively. As MacLaren himself failed twice with the bat, his contribution did not, statistically, amount to much. As his best player, G. A. Faulkner, who turned the match with a score of 153, was a South African, it could hardly be called an English victory. Nevertheless, MacLaren's XI, after being bowled out for 43 in the first innings, and looking proper Archies, won the match by 28 runs. It was the first time the Australians had lost that season, and no Australian side had gone through an English tour unbeaten, which they would have liked to do. They also lost the next match, at Scarborough, but by then there was no particular point in trying to win.

Cardus was at Eastbourne, having coaxed the expenses out of his editor because he wanted to see whether MacLaren could make good his boast. After the first day's play, Cardus, who was not then famous but had done a remarkable season's work, saw himself displaced from his customary leadership of the *Manchester Guardian*'s cricket page. On the second morning, hope abandoned, he was walking dismally away, unable to watch the funeral, until, with one eye on the exit and another on the railway timetable, he noticed that Faulkner and Ashton were batting fairly well.

This match irritates Australians to this day, and Englishmen too, at least those who were never on MacLaren's side. All a term-end frolic? Peculiar umpiring decisions? The most absurd freak imaginable? I think, trying to struggle to the truth over many years and through many contradictory opinions, that it must count as one up to MacLaren. First, because the luck, which had so often been against him, had turned his way. Second, because he did have the sense to choose some bright young English cricketers. Apart from the three veterans, the remainder of his team was: G. Ashton, H. Ashton, C. T. Ashton, C. H. Gibson, A. P. F. Chapman, M. Falcon, G. E. C. Wood, G. N. Foster.

The first five of these had played for Cambridge that year. Falcon and Wood had previously played.for Cambridge. Foster was an Oxonian. It was like the early days, when the Australian said 'Show us a light blue cap and we'll run!'

Chapman went on to captain England, Wood to play for England. Hubert Ashton was very close to English selection that summer (it was thought he would have many future chances, but in a changing world he never did, though he did many other important things). Gibson was regarded, and we have reliable Australian evidence for it, as one of the best bowlers they met all summer, but his career too was spasmodic. The full-time amateurs were growing smaller by degrees and beautifully less. Michael Falcon was never more than a part-time amateur, though for many years they would summon him to Lord's to play for the Gentlemen. His county cricket was played for Norfolk. I think you will find, though I have long since lost my tattered copy, that in *Ayres' Public Schools Cricket Companion* for 1932, in a biographical index of cricketers which at one time I almost knew by heart, Michael Falcon's was the only name without a first-class county attached to it. So they were a good lot, these MacLaren boys, and certainly the England selectors, who had cast their nets widely and carelessly that summer, may have had pink touches in their cheeks or noses when they read the final score.

At the end of the match, the crowd, says 'Country Vicar' (who was not there), 'swarmed around the pavilion'. I think the numbers may have been a little few for swarming, but they called for speeches, and Armstrong made one, saying (what else does a captain say in such irritating circumstances?) that they had been beaten by a better side. He does not appear to have been unduly upset. MacLaren did not speak. It was said that he was too much overcome by emotion. It was a romantic moment; not at all Fry's style, not the classical style. (I am speaking of them as men, you understand, rather than cricketers. When it came to batting, 'classical' was an apt enough description of MacLaren.)

In the 1905 series, Fry had looked set for another century against the Australians, in the Lord's match, but when he had scored 73 was given out, caught at the wicket, by Jim Phillips, an old adversary, who had many years before no-balled him for throwing, to his intense and lasting irritation. (Most English cricketers agreed that Fry was inclined to throw on the rare occasions he was put on to bowl, though nobody thought it mattered.) At Lord's Fry maintained that he had hit the toe of his boot with the bat, well away from the ball. Phillips explained that he had heard a click. Fry wrote, 'I asked him – of course, after the match – whether he was sure it was not the slamming of a door in the pavilion.' In 1912, after he had won the rubber against Australia, the Oval crowd cheered him and called for him. Earlier in the same match they had booed him, because of his refusal to agree restarting play after rain, at a time when it would clearly have been to Australia's advantage. Fry had not been pleased, and would not go on the Oval balcony to gratify the fickle multitude. 'Now Carlos', urged Ranji – he always called him Carlos – 'be your noble self.' Fry replied, 'This is not one of my noble days.'

Anecdotes such as these suggest in his character not exactly an acidity, but a certain mordancy, a classical disdain. Despite his politics, he would never have made a tribune of the people. On the other hand (for I must work in a classical quotation somehow)

> Omne tulit punctum qui miscuit utile dulci,
> Lectorem delectando pariterque monendo.

This might be roughly translated: mingle profit and pleasure, delight your audience at the same time as you instruct them, and you will win the votes. C. B. Fry did mingle profit with pleasure, did both delight and instruct, and would always be certain of my vote, as an England captain or anything else.

The remaining captains of the pre-1914 period may be dealt with more briefly.

R. E. Foster was one of the famous Worcester fraternity which caused that county to be known as 'Fostershire'. There were seven brothers, though only five played much for the county, and those irregularly. They were the sons of a Malvern schoolmaster, Malvern was a school known not only for its cricket but for its rackets, and it was often observed that the Fosters played cricket with a racket player's strokes, full of flashing cuts and drives to the off. H. K. Foster was the eldest. He never played for England, but he was in several seasons a selector; indeed, he was on the committee which chose his brother as captain in 1907. He scored a hundred in the University match, and was highly rated; the second brother, W. L. Foster, only slightly less so. R.E. was the pick of the bunch, and the only one to play for England. His Test cricket was limited to five matches under Warner in Australia in 1903–4 and the three against South Africa in 1907, but there is no doubt he would have played much more had he been available. He was the kind of player who could step straight into first-class cricket and look as if he had been batting for months. He too scored a hundred for Oxford against Cambridge – indeed his 171 was the highest in the fixture until then.

He was, of course, famous above all for another record, his 287 at Sydney in 1903. His batting average in all Tests was 46, higher than Ranji's and just below Jackson's. Naturally that was to some extent a false figure, but one is reminded of a story told about Eddie Paynter of Lancashire many years later. Paynter's Test average against Australia, in seven Tests, is actually higher than that of any other English batsman, and a kind but candid friend was pointing out that it was really all due to his 216 not out at Trent Bridge in 1938. 'Oh aye,' Paynter cordially agreed, 'oh aye.' And then added, in a ruminative aside, 'Mind, they had to be made.'

As a captain, Foster aroused little comment. He led Worcestershire regularly in only one season, 1901. His eldest brother Harry was usually in charge. For England he had a good side and led it competently. He was helped by winning all three tosses. He had a successful business career, but his health gave way early. He suffered from diabetes, an illness less understood then than now. He made a trip to South Africa, a common specific then for all kinds of disease, but it did no good. He came back home and died in 1914, aged 36. He was widely mourned, not only in cricketing circles, for he had been an international Association footballer, and indeed the only man to captain England at both games.

F. L. Fane has one distinction in this gallery: he probably liked the job less than anyone else who has ever had it. He disliked even captaining Essex, though he did so, from 1904 to 1906. He led them to victory over the Australians, by 19 runs, in 1905. He toured Australia once and South Africa twice. He never played for England at home, though he was a very capable county bat, of a style rather more restrained than was customary for an amateur of that time, and would have been a useful man to fall back on if an emergency had arisen. In his 14 Tests he averaged 26, with a century at Johannesburg in 1906, a notable effort against the googly bowlers after England had lost three quick wickets. Of his five Tests as captain, as deputy first to Jones and then to Leveson-Gower, he won two and lost three. He had the time and means to travel abroad, and played cricket in the West Indies and New Zealand. He had a high reputation as an outfield, which was one of the reasons he disliked captaincy, for third man or long-on are not the best places from which to lead a side. He died in 1960 at the age of 85.

H. D. G. Leveson-Gower was for many years a father-figure at the Oval, and also at Scarborough, where he was responsible for raising the sides for the festival. For a full account of this entertaining little man (I do not use the world 'little' pejoratively: he was known as 'Shrimp' because of his size) I refer you to his own book, *Off and On the Field*, which is full of good stories and interesting information about the cricketers of his time. As a person he was, at least in his youth, full of bounce and gaiety. As a cricketer he was, as Lamb wrote to Wordsworth of a flower bed, neat, not gaudy. He captained England in three Tests, all in South Africa, and these were the only occasions when he was chosen for the England side. His batting average, with the assistance of a couple of not-outs, was 23.

But we cannot leave him at that. He earned a reputation for captaincy. He had led Oxford in the University match of 1896. This is, at least for Oxonians, one of the most memorable matches of the entire series. Oxford went in to make 330 in the last innings, and got them, with three wickets left. Leveson-Gower himself played a staunch innings at a crisis, but the match was effectively won by a century from G. O. Smith. G. O. Smith was an England centre-forward at soccer, and there are still those who say that England can never have had a better, but as a cricketer he was a more dubious quantity. On the first morning, Leveson-Gower was still undecided about his eleventh choice. It lay between Smith and Raikes. Raikes was not so good a batsman as Smith, but could bowl quite well and was a better fielder. Leveson-Gower decided, and it was a principle he often repeated, that you can never have too much batting in a University match. He was justified by the event, though he had to work his four bowlers very hard. Possibly Warner (who was playing under him that year) might have made a different choice.

He captained Surrey in 1908 and 1909, and was joint captain in 1910. Though he led the side over the years on numerous other occasions, that is the extent of his official appointments, which seems surprising, for though he was not one of the very rich, he was able to afford a good deal of time for cricket, one way or another. He was a popular county captain, much liked by his side, and though he did not take them to the championship, they were third, fifth and second in those three seasons. Surrey never won at all from 1899 until 1914, odd when you consider their playing strength over that period.

Leveson-Gower was an England selector in 1909, which you will recall was a bad year for England, and not least its selectors. It seemed, that year, as if he was taking his belief in packing a side with batting too far. At the Oval England played only two bowlers, *qua* bowlers, with no fast bowler at all, but batted a long way down the order: K. L. Hutchings went in at No. 8 (MacLaren doubtless had some scheme in mind). England, one down in the rubber, needed to win in three days. Leveson-Gower was not appointed as a selector again until 1924, when the South Africans were over here. Then, and from 1927 to 1930, he was chairman of the committee.

In 1924 the England team did not face strong opposition, but a side had to be built for Australia the following winter. Leveson-Gower must have credit for choosing Sutcliffe as the opening partner for Hobbs, despite the contending claims of Holmes and Sandham (Sandham went on the tour, but batted lower in the order; Hobbs and Sutcliffe had established themselves as a pair against the South Africans). He also introduced to Test cricket Tate and Gilligan. That England side was beaten in Australia, but not by so very much when you look back at the scores. It was a pretty good side, but it had not enough bowlers. Tate, who took 38 wickets in the Tests, never had sufficient support. Parkin and Macaulay were both left at home. They were naughty boys, no doubt, writing articles for the press which they had never bothered to read, but one of them might have made a lot of difference to that rubber. England scored heaps of runs, but could never take any wickets unless Tate was bowling, and even Tate could not bowl for ever.

Warner took over the chairmanship of selection in 1926, and flew his old M.C.C. flag (the one he had taken to Australia in 1903 and was to take again in 1932) triumphantly from the Oval mast: but Leveson-Gower was back in office in 1927. There were no Test matches in 1927. The New Zealanders were over here, but did not play Tests. Test trials were played. How one stretches out the hands with longing towards the farther shore, a happy domestic season without Test matches! Never again in this lifetime, I fear. In 1928 there were three Tests against the West Indies, who were beaten easily. England played their full strength, apart from Hobbs, in the first one. After that victory the selectors might have felt free to experiment a bit. But no. The entire side which won the Oval Test (England won all three, embarrassingly, by an innings) went to Australia. The side at the Oval contained three bowlers; a fourth, if you counted Hammond, who certainly was a fine bowler – he took 84 wickets that year – but whose chief function was obviously to be the prop and stay of the batting.

When M.C.C. went on tour in those days, they would add their own representatives to the selection committee, and they would have the last word. Warner, for instance, while not an official selector at that time, explains to us just why Woolley was left out (he had scored over 3,000 runs that season) and Mead and Leyland taken instead. All three were left-handers. Mead had also scored 3,000 runs that season. Leyland was young and promising and a good man in the deep. There was as big a rumpus over this selection as there has ever been about any, but it was reasonable enough to prefer Mead to Woolley in the circumstances. Woolley had not been an outstanding success in the time-limitless Tests of Australia, nor was it in his nature to be. Very sensible to leave him at home. If he had gone, he might have found himself unwanted (Mead and Leyland only played in one Test each). This was the England side to Australia that was founded on the principle of batting or bust. Although Leveson-Gower did not have the final word, one cannot help feeling that he had a lot of influence, and was still working on the theory of the University match of 1896.

Test matches on Australian wickets of 1928 did, as Altham has pointed out, go some way to disprove the theory that 'bowling wins matches'. England won 4–1, by making piles of runs. But I tremble as I look back at the English side for that first Test at Brisbane in 1928. England won by 675 runs. They had three bowlers, plus Hammond. There was nobody else in the side who could even be scratched into a bowler. The bowlers were Larwood, some way yet from his peak, and Tate, some way past his peak, and J. C. White, thought of at the time as a good county slow left-hander and not much more. England scored 521 on a plumb wicket, after losing 5 for 217. Chapman went in at No. 7 and scored 50. They caught Australia on a bad wicket, batted again, and caught Australia on another bad wicket. Record victory! And with three-and-a-half bowlers! The Leveson-Gower theory at its highest point.

But it was too big a risk to take. Just imagine what might have happened had Australia won the toss. They had a young man called Bradman in the side, playing in his first Test. After that match, England brought in another bowler, Geary, who did stout work, and finished at the head of the English averages: even though it meant dropping Mead, who had been the highest scorer in England's second innings at Brisbane.

Further examples of Leveson-Gower's inclination to put all his money on batting might be found in the 1930 series, when England often seemed a bowler short. They went into the last, decisive Test at the Oval with three bowlers and three half-bowlers. England scored 405 after winning the toss, and Australia scored 695, winning by an innings.

On balance, therefore, I doubt if Leveson-Gower's policy was right (though I remember that England risked just the same policy at the Oval in 1938, with memorable results). Nevertheless he was a conscientious selector, a liked captain, a genial chap, and one of those who could make a joke against himself. His was a very Edwardian name, but he did not fuss about the pronunciation, and records this verse from an early tour of America. He and Jessop had had a long partnership against the Gentlemen of Philadelphia, and the passage from a Philadelphian newspaper is worth quoting if only because it also includes the best-known brief description of Jessop.

> At one end stocky Jessop frowned,
> > The human catapult
> Who wrecks the roofs of distant towns
> > When set in his assault.
> His mate was that perplexing man
> > We know as 'Looshun-Gore',
> It isn't spelt at all that way,
> > We don't know what it's for.

But as with Cholmondeley and St John
The alphabet is mixed,
And Yankees cannot help but ask –
'Why don't you get it fixed?'

A. O. Jones was probably the best all-round fielder among the England captains. His contemporaries had no doubt that he was the best up to his time. I put in the cautious 'probably' because fielding is a department of the game in which one can say with certainty that the general standard has risen, and it was easier for a good fielder to shine in the 1900s than it is in the 1970s. This struck me very much when I was reading an account by E. H. D. Sewell of the catches he had caught. In 1903, in first-class cricket, he held 19 out of 23. In 1904 he held 30 out of 39. That is 49 out of 62, nearly 5 out of 6, in various positions over two seasons. Sewell was rated an outstanding field, and certainly that is a good record, yet no better than that of many playing today. Incidentally, the position of gully was invented by Jones when he was at Bedford Modern School in the 1880s, and copied by Sewell who was at the neighbouring Bedford School. They have a strong claim to be the first and second men to occupy the position, and nobody could field there as well as Jones, at least until Percy Chapman came along. But Jones was notable anywhere. A catch he made at short leg in the Birmingham Test against Australia in 1909 prompted Warner to write, and the ring of sincerity prevents it from sounding effusive, 'How positively glorious it must be to field like the Notts captain!'

Jones won his Blue in the Cambridge side of 1893 because of his fielding. He was no bowler, and batted at No. 10. But his batting soon developed. He was a fast scorer and a hard hitter, particularly square with the wicket on the off side. He was not one of the more elegant stylists, unfolding from a crouching stance. He became a good enough player to be chosen for England in this country, once in 1899, twice in 1905, and twice more in 1909. He toured Australia under MacLaren, and went as captain six years later. He was not, it must be said, a successful batsman in Tests. In 12 matches he averaged under 14, with a highest score of 34. He did, however, make 15 catches (compare Chapman's 32 catches in 26 games, or Hammond's 110 in 85). He was considered one of the best county captains of his time. He led Nottinghamshire from 1900 to 1912, and jointly in 1913; in 1907 he took them to the championship, and they were usually in the top half of the table. He never had a proper chance as an England captain, through the misfortune of his own illness which kept him off the field for most of the tour; nor did he have so strong a side as he might have hoped. It may be doubted, though, whether even in happier circumstances he would have been one of the more successful touring captains. His manager, Philip Trevor, wrote later of his lack of decision, his agonized three o'clock-in-the-morning hesitations, his constant fretting about details of administration and finance. Also, and I suppose this is what poor Jones's captaincy is chiefly remembered by, he left Hobbs out of the side in the first match, in favour of George Gunn, who had not been chosen for the tour at all. This was not so heinous a crime as it seemed in retrospect. There was an arrangement whereby Gunn, touring Australia on his own account, was available for M.C.C. in an emergency. Hobbs had not played in a Test before, had been unwell himself, and had not many runs on tour behind him. Gunn scored 119 and 74. Jones may not even have been responsible: at the time he was in hospital a long way away, and Fane was the man in charge on the spot. Still, it hurt Hobbs, and it hurt Surrey feelings, and looked an increasingly absurd decision as the years went by. It did not escape Kennington's attention that Gunn came from the same county as his captain, and rivalry between Surrey and Nottinghamshire was very keen in that period.

There remains, of England's pre-1914 captains, John Douglas, but let us leave him till later, when he has completed his mixed but not undistinguished career.

5

SEVEN LEAN YEARS

One woe doth tread upon another's heel,
So fast they follow

Hamlet

His initials were J.W.H.T., and the Australians, because of his exceptionally dour approach to batting, called him 'Johnny-Won't-Hit-Today'. He made himself into a batsman by taking pains, but he was a fine natural fastish swinging bowler, good enough to be chosen for England before he became captain and chosen again after he had been dropped from the job. He was always a tremendous trier, a man to have on your side: as to his merits as a captain, there have been widely differing opinions.

Douglas, as we have seen, took over the captaincy from Warner in all five Tests in Australia in 1911–12, triumphantly winning the rubber after a bad start. In the first Test he did not open the batting with Hobbs and Rhodes, nor did he open the bowling with Barnes and Foster. The second omission was made worse because he opened the bowling himself. He could never resist a swinging new ball. (He was one of the first to make a fetish of polishing it, though in his earlier years at least he did so on his forearm rather than his flannels.) Barnes was not pleased. Frank Woolley, in *The King of Games*, records the following dialogue, after England had lost the toss and were walking out to field:

Douglas: I'm going on first, Sid, as I think I shall be able to make it swing a bit.
Barnes: Oh, that's all right, but what am I out here for?

Douglas explained that he would only have a few overs, as he might get a quick

117

wicket with the new ball. It was then, Woolley reflects, that Barnes might have remained silent, or worded his remark differently.

Barnes: Well, if you're going to bowl with the new one, you can jolly well go on with the old one, too.

One suspects that Barnes did indeed 'word his remark differently'.

However, Douglas was getting on well enough with his side by the end of that series, and he also had that successful tour of South Africa before the war came. He was chosen at home against Australia for the Oval match in 1912. He was an obvious candidate for the leadership when M.C.C. sent a side to Australia in 1920: though not an automatic choice, for it was hoped at one stage that R. H. Spooner might be able to go.

M.C.C. were reluctant to make this tour, feeling that English cricket had not sufficiently recovered from the losses and the long interruption of the war. Yet the feeling among the public was optimistic. Hobbs, Rhodes, Woolley, Hearne and Strudwick were all there from Warner's last side, as well as Douglas himself. The newcomers had all done well in domestic cricket. What happened was that they ran into an exceptionally strong Australian side – many would still say the strongest there has ever been. England did well enough in the lesser matches of the tour, and scored a fair number of runs in the Tests, but they could not take wickets. In the first innings of the first Test, Australia won the toss and were all out for 267, which sounded hopeful to those at home, but the remaining Australian scores were 581, 499, 354, 582, 389, 211 for 2, 392 and 93 for 1. Australia won all five matches, the only time this has ever been done in a rubber between the two countries. They won all of them easily except for the third, at Adelaide, and even there, though England led by 93 on the first innings, the margin against them at the end was 119.

Poor Douglas! What a contrast with a decade before! Yet there was no disposition to blame him unduly. It was obvious that the Australians were very, very good. The two teams travelled to England by boat together, with another rubber to play in the immediately following summer, and Douglas was in charge again for the first Test of 1921 at Trent Bridge. England won the toss, were bowled out for 112, and lost by ten wickets in two days. Five changes were made in the England XI which Douglas led at Lord's. He won the toss, England were out for 187, and lost by eight wickets. Warner said years later that the England batting, bowling and fielding in this match was the poorest he could ever remember, although Woolley played two innings – 95 and 93 – which he was inclined to believe, looking back, were the best of his life.

Seven defeats in seven matches, despite four tosses won, were too much for the selectors, and that was the end of Douglas's England captaincy, apart from one match against South Africa in 1924, when he was brought back as deputy to the injured Gilligan. L. H. Tennyson took over for the rest of the 1921 series, but Douglas kept his place in the side. He was upset at being replaced, but he served readily enough under the new captain. In the very next match he made 75, his highest score against Australia, going in when England had lost three wickets for 30: that was a characteristic effort. He made a third tour of Australia, under Gilligan, in 1924–5, playing in one Test. In all he played in 23 Tests, scoring 962 runs at an average of 29, and taking 45 wickets at an average of 33. He was captain in 18 Tests, winning eight and losing eight. He was 8–4 down against Australia, yet given the strength of the opposition, and difficulties largely not of his own making, that was not so bad a record. Most English captains, even now, at the outset of their charge, would accept the offer of beating Australia four times. MacLaren beat them four times, in rather more favourable circumstances, but lost 11 times; yet there are still those who hail MacLaren as a master-hand and dismiss Douglas as a poor 'prentice.

Douglas was an Essex man – at least, what used to be reckoned an Essex man. He was born at Clapton, in the East End, in 1882. He went to Felsted School, which was known as a notably tough one, with an initiation ceremony for new boys which was recounted in miserable awe by new boys at other public schools a quarter of a century later. (This, and the fact that Douglas went there, are the only things I can ever remember hearing about Felsted.) He learnt to box, very effectively, and won an Olympic gold medal at middle-weight in 1908. On one occasion on tour, summoned to respond to a toast (something he disliked, though he got better at it), he said, 'I can't make speeches, but I'll box any man in the room three rounds.' I have never discovered the provenance of this story. If he had said it shortly after the Hill–McAlister fight, it might have been quite a witty remark. Nobody took him up on the offer.

Charles Bray, who played many times for Essex and later became a writer on cricket, was introduced to the first-class game by Douglas, and has described him in affectionate detail in *Cricket Heroes*, published by Phoenix House in 1959. Bray found him a hard but satisfying captain. He would make his side turn out early for practice before play, and no excuses were accepted. Bray thought he was a good captain and liked playing for him. He had first led the side in 1911 and continued to 1928. He was then 46 years old, a reasonable time at which to retire, but he did not want to go, and fought the committee bitterly. He particularly disliked the choice of his successor, H. M. Morris, considering, truly enough, that Morris was not a good enough cricketer for the job. He did not play for Essex again. 'You either liked and respected John Douglas or you loathed him', is Bray's conclusion, and he suggests his old captain was one of nature's Yorkshiremen. While the Yorkshire character is by no means so straightforward as southerners are inclined to imagine (I once wrote an essay suggesting, at least half-seriously, that Yorkshiremen are more like Latin Americans than anything else) it is true that Douglas displayed many of the best, and some of the worst qualities of Yorkshire cricket.

Bray, whose delightful essay deserves to be read in full, ranges himself firmly on Douglas's side. On the other hand Sir Home Gordon, writing in 1939, said that as an Essex skipper 'he was not only bad but brutal, almost incredible in his ruthlessness'. He instances that G. M. Louden, who could only play occasionally, began to dread playing for Essex because Douglas would bowl him into the ground; and that 'he entirely ruined Hipkin as a player by bullying him'. Hipkin, a slow left-armer, did fall away sadly after a bright beginning, though he did no better when Morris took over. Louden was certainly better in short spells, but apart from the captain himself there was usually nobody else who could be expected to take wickets in the side. Sir Home's remarks, which came in for some criticism at the time of his book's appearance, were possibly influenced by his long friendship with P. A. Perrin. Perrin had been the obvious choice to succeed to the Essex captaincy in 1911, but Douglas's father, who held the mortgage on the Leyton ground, threatened to foreclose if his son was not appointed. So at least goes the story.

Father and son were always fond of each other, and they were together aboard S.S. *Oberoon* when she was sunk in a collision in the Kattegat in 1930. Both were drowned. From the accounts, rather confused, as they are likely to be in such circumstances, it seems that J.W.H.T. might have saved himself had he not been intent on saving his father. It was at about this time that my family had moved to Leyton, living close to the cricket ground. I asked my mother why the flag was only halfway up the pole, and to this day I never see a flag at half-mast without thinking of J. W. H. T. Douglas.

The selectors in 1921 (H. K. Foster, R. H. Spooner and J. Daniell) came in for some heavy criticism, even from the august *Wisden*, which thought they were too inclined to snatch at straws, and the fact that no less than 30 men played for England gives the criticism force. But after all you have to snatch at straws if there is no other way of making bricks, and their change of captaincy at least was not unjustified by events. Australia won the third match, but the last two were drawn. The England performances were much more respectable in these two matches, although there was a feeling that the Australians were not too much bothered about them. It was at the Oval that their captain, Armstrong, retired to the deep field on the last afternoon and passed the time glancing at a newspaper which had blown his way (he explained afterwards that he was reading the sports page, 'to find out who we were playing').

In declining the suggestion that he might return to the captaincy, C. B. Fry had commended to the selectors the Hon. L. H. Tennyson. There were, however, good reasons for their thoughts to be turning in that direction already. Tennyson had played five Tests in South Africa in 1913–14, and had been chosen as a batsman at Lord's, making 5 and 74 not out. Only Woolley on the English side made more runs, and the way Tennyson went for the fast bowlers was heartening. He had become captain of Hampshire in 1919, an office in which he continued until 1933. He was the grandson of the Poet Laureate, becoming the third baron himself, and thus renewed the aristocratic tradition (Douglas, to be sure, had much of the aristocrat in him, but not of the more blue-blooded variety).

Lionel Tennyson had played for Eton, getting into the side as a fast bowler in the first place, but did not get in, or even near, the Cambridge side. However, he developed into a strong, attacking batsman, liking to get on the front foot, in the approved pre-war style (which was now beginning to give way to what its admirers called the 'two-eyed' and its detractors the 'two-shouldered' stance). He was never really a sound enough player to be in the England side, but his warm, sometimes explosive character was good for a demoralized team. He did not have much luck in the Leeds Test, and yet during it he played one of the bravest innings of any England captain. On the first morning, after he had lost the toss, he split his left hand at the base of the thumb and first finger. He had to leave the field for stitching, handing back the captaincy temporarily to Douglas. Nevertheless, after Australia had scored 407, he went in and batted at No. 9, scoring 63 with only one working hand. This was not a defensive innings: it took only 80 minutes. He had exceptionally strong forearms, and was even able to drive the faster bowlers. England were still out for 259, and Hobbs was off to hospital for an appendicitis operation. It must not be forgotten, in recalling England's disasters of that summer, that Hobbs, through injury and illness, was unable to play a single Test innings.

In the second innings, still handicapped, Tennyson scored 36. Although Australia won the rubber without much difficulty, there was a feeling that England had produced a more spirited performance. At Old Trafford, Tennyson won the toss and England scored 362 for 4, but the figures do not mean much because all the first day had been lost to rain, and nothing but a draw was ever likely. Tennyson did not bat in either innings. He made an illegal declaration, at ten to six, anxious to get Australia in before the close. Because the loss of the first day had brought the regulations governing two-day matches into force, the latest time for a declaration had become an hour and 40 minutes before the close. Now one would not expect Tennyson to be familiar with the niceties of the rules, but there is no reason to doubt his claim that he was advised in his action by the entire selection committee, and also by MacLaren, Warner, and Douglas. The Australians did not know either, apart from their wicket-keeper, Carter (the only Yorkshireman in the match), who pointed out the error. Twenty minutes were lost to argument, and England resumed batting. Armstrong then, enjoying the joke, broke another law. He had bowled the last over before the players went off and he bowled the first one after they had come back. Nobody noticed, or at least nobody spoke. I suppose it could be argued that technically all the remaining proceedings were null and void.

The Oval match was also interrupted by rain, and two high-scoring first innings made another draw certain. Tennyson scored 51, again under difficulty, for he had been severely hit on the chest after scoring only a few. That was the end of his Test captaincy, and indeed of his Test cricket, though he went on playing in many parts of the world for many years, taking a side not far short of Test standard to India as late as 1937–8. The adventures of that side have been recalled by one of its members, I. A. R. Peebles. In *Talking of Cricket* he describes the captain's stern injunctions to his men to show no dissent at doubtful umpiring decisions: advice which on one disastrous occasion proved too much for its giver.

So Tennyson did not win a Test match, but he was head of the English batting averages, and played an innings of over 50 in each of the three Tests he batted against Australia. He retired from the post with affection and with honour.

There are endless stories about Tennyson, many of which he would invent or deny as the mood took him. He wrote a couple of entertaining books of reminiscences. In later years he was extravagant and frequently hard up. Slow horses were his principal enemy, but he could never resist a bet about anything. He backed himself for £50 to score 50 in one or the other innings against Australia at Lord's. When he was captain of Hampshire, he liked to keep in touch with his batsmen, and when the umpires objected to the flow of messages he resorted to sending them by telegram. Sometimes the messages dealt with general principle rather than tactical detail. One Hampshire batsman struggling to play himself in again after suffering a nasty blow from a bumper, was surprised when a boy in blue uniform trotted out with a little orange envelope which contained an enquiry as to what he thought his bat was for.

He did not inherit any special literary talent, though his books read well enough. He did, however, once write a poem, at the suggestion of a London editor, in honour of A. P. F. Chapman's victory in Australia. He demanded £100 for it, because it was the only poem ever written by one England captain about another, and because he had a high opinion of poetry in general, as was only proper, befitting his ancestry. But the editor would not go beyond £50, and in the end Tennyson had to publish the poem, which is quite a competent jingle, himself.

On one occasion he was bet that he could not write down the names of ten poems written by his grandfather. He managed seven without difficulty, and then, with a bit of a struggle, two more. Finally, after a long pause, he wrote down 'If'. It was pointed out to him that this had been written by Rudyard Kipling. 'Oh', he said 'What *An Absent Minded Beggar* I am.' He denied this story, and it does sound a little too subtle for him. His humour tended more to the boisterous. He had many friends and few enemies. He died in 1951, still full of beans, still expressing strong and sometimes contradictory opinions.

Douglas and Tennyson, then, both fighters, both in a sense aristocrats, but otherwise such contrasting characters, were England's first captains after the first world war. After 1921, there was no Test cricket at home for three years, which gave English cricket time to build. The next rubber was in 1924, with the South Africans over here, and a tour to follow in Australia during the winter. However, a touring side had visited South Africa in the meantime, in 1922–3, under F. T. Mann.

These were the only Tests Frank Mann played, and when his son George Mann also became captain of England, after more than a quarter of a century, many people had forgotten that his father had had the same honour. It was a successful tour, won 2–1, without much to spare. The captain, who averaged 35 with a top score of 84, was one of the successes, many of his runs coming when most needed. But his side included only seven of England's unfortunate 1921 sides, and as it happened none of the new men did anything special, except Kennedy of Hampshire, whose medium pace did not stir the imagination (he was never to play against Australia, rather unluckily): so not a great deal of attention was paid at home.

Mann had succeeded Warner in the captaincy of Middlesex. He took them to the championship in 1921 and held office until 1928. He was a big hitter and a fine fielder, Warner calling him 'a veritable sand-bank' at mid-off. His university was Cambridge, though he did nothing exceptional in three matches against Oxford, and his school Malvern. He was not, however, a batsman in the Foster tradition: his was the bludgeon, not the rapier. His drives were tremendous. Once, in an innings against Yorkshire, he landed the ball four times on the roof of the Lord's pavilion. *Wisden* said that he was 'among the most forceful batsmen in the history of cricket'. He was popular with his men and of course with the crowds, perhaps a touch Tennysonian in his humours on and off the field. Once at a fancy dress ball at the Folkestone festival he dressed as a 'Nippy' (who now remembers who 'Nippy' was? Think of Lyons' teashops) and caused much amusement by threatening to go to the ladies' lavatory. Larky transvestism was in vogue in the 'twenties (compare Berry Pleydell in the pages of Dornford Yates). At this ball the Mayoress and Sir Home Gordon, who were the judges, gave the booby prize to Tennyson, who had appeared in judicial robes with 'BLOODY JUDGE JEFFREYS' written on his back. Tennyson had earned his award by hitting the Mayoress in the midriff with a pumpkin. There is no record of whether Mann was a prizewinner.

I remember seeing Mann playing in the early 1930s. He looked a huge, square, formidable figure as he pounded the Essex bowling. He was 34 when he captained England (he lived to 76): a little old to make a first expedition to Australia in 1924, and besides he was not quite a good enough cricketer. His Test average was more than ten runs higher than his county one. Was Gilligan a good enough cricketer? That was the question to be settled in 1924, when he took over as captain for South Africa's return visit.

A. E. R. Gilligan had toured under Mann. He had taken nine wickets in his two Tests, opening the bowling, and batting No. 11. He was another fine fieldsman, also usually at mid-off, and his batting improved rapidly, but it was on his bowling that hopes were founded. In 1922 he had become captain of Sussex, and remained so for seven years. In 1924, with Dulwich and Cambridge behind him, he was 29 years old, an attractive, smiling personality.

The rubber against South Africa was won comfortably enough, three easy victories to England and then two rain-spoilt draws. That was not so important, because the South Africans were not a very impressive side. What did raise hopes was the performance of three of the newer England players. In Herbert Sutcliffe was found the opening partner Hobbs needed. In Maurice Tate, Gilligan's partner for Sussex, we found one opening bowler: and there seemed every chance that the captain himself would make the other.

In the first Test at Edgbaston, after England had made 438 (Hobbs and Sutcliffe 136 for the first wicket), Gilligan and Tate bowled South Africa out for 30. Extras, with 11, was the only one in double figures. Gilligan took 6 for 7, Tate 4 for 12. In their second innings South Africa rallied bravely, but still lost by an innings, and Gilligan and Tate took nine of their wickets between them. Here, surely, was a chance of paying something back to the Australians for what we had suffered at the hands of Gregory and McDonald in 1921! Tate was no more than fast-medium, though a very dangerous fast-medium, but Gilligan was at this stage of his career decidedly quick, and it was a fine prospect to think of them in action together. In the second Test Gilligan took five wickets and Tate four; in the third Gilligan, not bowling much, took only one, but Tate had nine.

It is thereafter a melancholy tale. Gilligan, playing for Gentlemen v. Players at the Oval, was heavily hit over the heart. He insisted on batting the next day and scored a brilliant but unnecessary century (the Oval match between these teams no longer ranked so importantly as that at Lord's). The innings perhaps did as much harm as the original knock. Warner says, sombrely, that Gilligan was never the same cricketer again. Modern medical opinion, so far as I have been able to consult it, is a little doubtful of this finding; and Gilligan's long and hale life suggests that the damage was not too serious. But there is no doubt that he was badly shaken up, and whatever the reason, the magic departed. He could not play in the fourth Test, and did not take a wicket in South Africa's only innings in the fifth. Still, he was second to Tate in the Test averages, and since there was no reason to suppose that the setback was more than temporary, public hopes for Australia remained undented.

In Australia, Gilligan took only 10 wickets in the Tests at an average of 52. In all first-class matches, he took only 28 at 38. This was some way from total failure, for it was a high-scoring series; he was handicapped by further injury, and most of his Test wickets were good ones. But he was no longer the partner Tate needed, and the Australians did not rate him fast. He did not play for England again afterwards. In his full Test career of 11 matches, he took 36 wickets at 29, and 26 of them had been taken in his first five, before his injury. His batting average was 16, with a highest score of 39 not out. He lost the rubber in Australia 4–1.

Nevertheless, that is far from all there is to say about Arthur Gilligan as an England captain. His tour was successful in everything but victory, and this was sensed by the English public, who assembled in large numbers to welcome the side home. It was a general opinion among Australians that 3–2 would have better indicated the difference between the teams. Gilligan won the toss only once, in the fourth Test, and England won that match by an innings. He revolutionized the English fielding, a department in which they began to compare with Australia, for the first time since the war and possibly since the early 1900s. This had much effect on the England sides of the next few years. He was, and is, one of the most popular captains England have sent to Australia. Now popularity, as we have seen, is not everything in a captain, and there were those who suggested that Gilligan was too easygoing on the finer points of law. Reading M. A. Noble's detailed account, *Gilligan's Men*, it is hard to find much evidence of this. There was one match lost to Victoria which most captains would have saved by adopting a tighter bowling policy, but Gilligan did not choose to. Noble sometimes criticizes his tactics, and of course Gilligan was not an experienced tactician at that time, though he won a deserved reputation both in Australia and at home, in later years, as a critic and commentator. He was not a lucky captain, Noble agrees, but 'he never failed to maintain that debonair confidence, that fine spirit and that cheery optimism which carries a team through anything'.

On balance, it was again the England bowling that was not good enough, though Tate took 38 wickets, which surpassed Barnes's record for a series against Australia. There were two bowlers at home who might have helped, Parkin of Lancashire (who had struggled manfully four years earlier) and Macaulay of Yorkshire. Both had talked themselves out of the party, Parkin rushing into print to denounce Gilligan. Lord Hawke told the Yorkshire annual general meeting that Macaulay 'only had himself to blame' that he was not in Australia, and Macaulay's break from the off, at various speeds, would certainly have been very useful, but then it had been planned that Gilligan himself should be the principal support. For the rest, there were two slow left-handers, Kilner and Woolley (not much of a bowler now), and three leg-spinners, Freeman, Hearne, and Richard Tyldesley: all moving the same way off the pitch! Howell and Douglas, the other faster bowlers, only played in one Test between them: I say the 'other' faster bowlers, but that is if one does not count Hobbs, who had the pleasure of using the new ball again in the third Test when both Tate and Gilligan were injured.

Australia won the first Test, by 193. England might have won the second, even though Australia began with 600. Hobbs and Sutcliffe scored 283 together, and in the last innings England needed 372. It would have been a record-breaking win, and at 254 for 4 they seemed to have a chance: then the last six wickets went down for 36. In the third Test, England needed 375 in the fourth innings, and failed only by 11. On the last morning they wanted 27 with two wickets left, and Gilligan was one of the batsmen not out overnight. He has said he did not sleep much. I wonder if a harder man – I am not seeking to make a disguised criticism of Gilligan – but I wonder if, say, a Jackson, or an Illingworth, might have slept better and got the runs. Anyway, it was Australia's match and Australia's rubber, and a few minutes after it was over, Gilligan, all disappointment concealed behind smiles, was signing autographs for the young Australians behind the pavilion. Then came England's win in the fourth Test, with Sutcliffe's fourth century of the series. The flavour of success was not altogether removed by two sad collapses in the fifth against the spinners of Grimmett, appearing for Australia for the first time.

So we move on to 1926, with no other Test matches in the meantime – though 1925 had been Hobbs's finest autumnal flowering, comparable to that of W.G. 30 years before – and the Australians in England again. It did not seem unreasonable to hope that this time it would be England's turn. Grimmett on English pitches was an unknown hazard, but otherwise most of the Australian faces were the same. Much would depend on the choice of captain, and at the beginning of the season there was no certain or even probable candidate. Of the 17 county captains, ten were clearly not good enough to win a place on their merits: Jackson of Derbyshire, Robinson of Gloucestershire, Cornwallis of Kent, Green of Lancashire, Fowke of Leicestershire, Fitzroy of Northamptonshire, Daniell of Somerset, Calthorpe of Warwickshire, Jewell of Worcestershire, Lupton of Yorkshire. Gentlemen all, but it is hardly a glittering list, and indicates how the Edwardian age had departed. Counties were finding it more and more difficult to field an amateur captain who was also a cricketer of high quality. Of the remainder, four had already had the task of leading England – Douglas, Tennyson, Mann and Gilligan – and for one reason and another there was no great enthusiasm for choosing them again. There remained three possibilities, or perhaps it would be truer to say two-and-a-bit; Carr of

Nottinghamshire, who had toured South Africa in 1922–3, with moderate success; Fender of Surrey, who had played against Australia both home and away in 1920–1; and J. C. Clay, the captain of Glamorgan. Clay was to play for England a decade later, and prove himself a thoroughly good county captain, but Glamorgan had only been granted first-class status in 1921, and I doubt if anyone on the English side of the border thought of him seriously in 1926.

Yet as we have seen often enough, it was never considered necessary that the captain of England should already be in charge of a county, and there were other possibilities among the amateurs. There was A. P. F. Chapman, who had gone to Australia under Gilligan. He had been a Berkshire player then, but now was qualified for Kent. There was J. C. White of Somerset, a slow left-hander who had played against Australia in 1921, and would probably have been chosen for Gilligan's team had he been available. There was G. T. S. Stevens of Middlesex, a leg-spinner and batsman of brilliance and self-confidence who already, at the age of 25, had been heard to complain that Gentlemen v. Players was not the match it had been in his youth; there was V. W. C. Jupp, recently arrived in Northamptonshire from Sussex, an all-rounder little, if at all, short of the top class. He had been one of the discards of 1921 but had had some success in South Africa.

There was, of course, another possibility: to choose a professional captain, which meant, in practice, Hobbs (though Sutcliffe would probably have done the job better, at least more zestfully). The selection committee that year was Warner, Perrin and Gilligan. They were granted permission by the Board of Control to co-opt two professionals, one from the north and one from the south, and chose Rhodes and Hobbs. The experiment was not a great success and was not repeated. The professionals were reluctant to express themselves too definitely on questions bearing so sharply on the welfare of their fellows. Still, the innovation did bring the possibility of a professional captain a step nearer, and events later in the season were to take it forward another.

Carr and Fender were the likeliest choices, and it was Carr who was appointed, and thereupon joined the selection committee. He led England in the first four Tests, and was replaced by Chapman for the last, the only one finished, which England won.

The England captaincies of both Carr and Chapman extended beyond 1926, and they need to be dealt with when we can survey their careers in perspective. But in the meantime it might be as well to glance at the course of events in 1926, for it was in several ways an important season for English cricket – not just because England won the Ashes back.

The first Test was almost a complete washout. In the second Australia scored 383. England led them with 475 for 3, and made a declaration, but there was never much chance of a finish. In the third, at Leeds, Carr won the toss and put

Australia in. They scored 494, with a century before lunch by Macartney. Well, that was the kind of thing that can happen to any captain, but there was more to it than that. Tate had had Bardsley caught in the slips off the first ball of the match. In the same over Macartney was dropped, at third slip, by Carr himself, not a difficult one as slip catches go. And that could happen to anyone, too, but there was still more. Carr had put Australia in after leaving out Charlie Parker from those assembled on the ground, ready to play. It was a committee decision, but Warner assures us that Carr had the last word.

The reasons why Charlie Parker, of Gloucestershire, played only once for England (in 1921) are clear enough even to anyone writing, as I am, from the west. He was a poor fieldsman and a difficult man. Nevertheless there is no doubt that he was at the time, and for some years before and after this event, the best slow left-hander in the country. If it was thought proper to invite him to the ground, it was an act of lunacy not to play him when you had decided to put the opposition in because it was a wet wicket. Warner makes the best case for it he can (Kilner was also a left-arm bowler, Macaulay could bowl on soft wickets, if only Carr had held that catch . . .) but the passage of the years does not make the decision any more rational.

England saved the match after following on. Carr had what turned out to be his only innings of the series, and made 13. He was captain again at Manchester. It rained part of the time. Australia scored 335, England 305 for 5. Everything therefore depended on the Oval match, which was to be played to a finish. Carr's ill-luck had continued at Manchester, where he went down with tonsillitis after the first day. In these circumstances the captaincy for the rest of the match went to Hobbs, although there was another amateur playing, Stevens. It was Stevens's first match against Australia, but Hobbs's reaction, on being told the news, was 'What about Mr Stevens?' Warner points out that it had first been offered to Strudwick, on the grounds of seniority (though Hobbs had in fact played for England before Strudwick did) but it was not expected that Strudwick would accept, nor did he. So there was a professional leading England again, even if only as a deputy. I doubt if Stevens was inclined to complain, though he doubtless felt that amateur status was not what it had been when he was young.

Then there was the dropping of Carr for the Oval match. We have widely contradictory reports about what went on in the selection committee. Our old, mischievous, but undeniably interesting friend Home Gordon tells us (a) that after Carr had been dropped, he stayed on in the selection committee, which he strictly had no business to do, and gave the decisive vote in favour of Chapman; (b) that 'a certain amateur', not Chapman, had been standing by a telephone to hear news of his election, and to rush round and help to choose the others. He makes no bones about his authorities for at least the first statement: Carr and Gilligan. Warner dismissed Sir Home's account in general terms in *The*

Cricketer, and in more specific, but not quite conclusive terms, in *Cricket Between Two Wars*. But there was no doubt that it was a fraught meeting, nor that the decision regarding the captaincy (and not only that, for there were other controversial changes, including the recall of Rhodes) caused the first big press rumpus/stunt in the modern style, a storm beside which Warner's preference over MacLaren in 1903 had been a ripple. (I am not old enough to remember this, but I can recall the similar row, the big black headlines, four years later, when in comparable circumstances Chapman was replaced by Wyatt.) Public opinion, or at least press opinion, was mostly on Carr's side. This was understandable, for Chapman was unproved as a captain and there were strong candidates even for his place in the side.

But Chapman won all right, and the rumpus was soon forgotten. English cricket had a new hero who looked the part. England had been 22 runs behind on the first innings, but Hobbs and Sutcliffe both scored centuries on a turning wicket in the second. Australia had not quite the bowlers for the conditions, but England had, when Australia batted again, in the person of Rhodes. Every selector was a champion!

Before I end this chapter, approximately halfway through Test history, at the point where England had started winning again over Australia, I would like to say a word or two about Percy Fender. His Test career, apart from one match against South Africa in 1929, was over. He was never to captain England. Presumably he was the 'certain amateur' of whom Gordon speaks (it can hardly have been Stevens, after Hobbs had been preferred to him at Manchester). Fender was widely considered the best of the county captains of his time. He had been joint captain of Surrey for 1920, and was sole captain for the next 11 years. Surrey did not win the championship during this period, but Fender achieved miracles, it seemed to his contemporaries, with a very limited bowling side on the plumb Oval wickets. He was full of tricks and wit. Opposing captains used to make their young 'fancy-cap' players bat bareheaded, rather than give Fender an unnecessary clue. Once, when Surrey were playing at Weston-super-Mare for the festival, he complained to the hotel manager about the size of the rooms, in which he maintained there was not space to swing a cat. 'Very sorry, sir', said the hotel manager demurely, 'Didn't know you had come down here for the cat-swinging.' Fender told this story against himself with gusto, and I repeat it again because I once, in a scatter-brained moment, attributed it in print to R. W. V. Robins.

Fender's batting average, in 13 Tests, was 19; but he could be a dangerous lower-order batsman, and scored the then fastest century in first-class cricket. He took 29 Test wickets at an average of 40. But his five Tests against Australia were all played in 1920–1, when there were plenty of poor figures about, and there were plenty of people who thought that his captaincy, then or later, would have been worth some poor figures. There were two things, looking back, which told against him. First, it was hard for the more solemn judges to take him seriously. The principal reason for this, though not the only one, was his appearance. Ronald Mason, an admirer, describes him as 'tall, angular, beaky, balding, surprisingly reminiscent of Groucho Marx'. He liked to field with his hands in his pockets until the ball was delivered. This took some doing, as his sweater usually came down to his knees. The second was that he had got into some trouble on Douglas's tour of Australia, along with another amateur, E. R. Wilson, for writing press reports. These were cabled back to Australia, sometimes in garbled form, and caused a good deal of ill-feeling. Players were shortly afterwards banned from writing about Tests in which they were taking part, by the Board of Control, although as we have seen the ruling did not necessarily apply to selectors. Thus Fender does not take his place in our ranks, but Herbert Sutcliffe, at the end of a perceptive chapter on captaincy (written in 1935), after paying due tribute to Jardine, and Sellers, and a number of others, declares that Fender was the best captain he had known.

England were on top of the world again by the end of the 1926 season. Australia faced a time of rebuilding. South Africa were in one of their leaner patches. Other opponents were bobbing about on the horizon, but so far no bigger than a man's hand. It was one of our happier moments in the history of Test cricket.

6

THE BRADMAN PROBLEM

It was easier to conquer the East than to know what
to do with it

Horace Walpole, *Letters*

The English victory at the Oval in 1926 marked more than the end of a period of Australian supremacy. Test cricket was now half a century old, and its second half-century was to be very different from its first – most obviously, in its sheer quantity. Nineteen twenty-seven was the last domestic season without Tests (even in the abbreviated season of 1945 there were the 'Victory' Tests). Tests became not only more frequent, but longer. They began to attract much more publicity, as news events as much as sporting encounters. There were many who deplored, and there are some who still deplore, this change of character, not least because of the inevitably diminished stature of the county game. But its full extent only gradually became apparent, and in any case it is hard to see what could have been done to stop it. The spacious Edwardian days were gone. The game had to pay its way, difficult in the straitened post-war economy, and if it could only be done through more and more Test cricket, more and more Test cricket was what we had to have.

Australian visits now settled down on a basis of one every four years, until the Second World War, with return trips in between. But South Africa, and then – in order of seniority – the West Indies, New Zealand and India filled up all the gaps. In 1930 the Australian Tests were lengthened to four days, though the others stayed at three, and the newer countries played only rubbers of three matches. After the Second World War there came a further expansion, with the arrival of Pakistan, until the situation was reached of two sides touring here in the same

131

summer, with a total of six matches lasting five days each. One effect of all this was to cheapen the England cap. It became common enough to find three or four in a county side. It meant even some cheapening of the England captaincy. And since the amateurs-only custom was maintained until 1953, and even those amateurs who played full-time tended to have shorter cricketing careers, the turnover was high, even for matches at home. There are still towering figures among the England captains, but fewer who will demand such extensive treatment as the giants of old.

England v. Australia remains our principal theme, and though other countries in due course achieved parity and sometimes superiority in playing standards, there is still, for Englishmen, nothing quite to match an Australian series. However, before resuming that tale, let us glance at developments on other fronts.

Between 1926 and 1939, England made three tours to South Africa, and South Africa two to England. In 1927–8, over there, the series was drawn, 2–2, after England had won the first two matches. The English captain was R. T. Stanyforth. G. T. S. Stevens took over from him in the last Test. In 1929, at home, England won 2–0, with three drawn. Chapman was still the established England captain, but he played little that summer, staying on for some time in Australia after the winter's tour. J. C. White, his vice-captain in Australia, was captain in the first three Tests against South Africa, and A. W. Carr in the last two. They each won one. In 1930–1, on his last tour, Chapman lost the only Test in South Africa to be finished.

In 1935, South Africa again won the only match finished out of five, the second Test at Lord's. This was the first time England had lost a rubber at home, or even a match, to anyone but Australia. After all these years I can remember what a shock it was, at least to a small boy. England might well have won the series, it seems in retrospect, had the matches been longer. Four times they led on the first innings, but they did not have the bowling to get a strong batting side out twice in three days; nor were their sides very well chosen, even according to Warner, who was one of those responsible. R. E. S. Wyatt was the England captain. He was already established in the post, as was Hammond when he led the side to South Africa in 1938–9. Again, only one match was finished, but this time it was England who won it.

It had been decided, in 1938–9, that the last match should be played to a finish if neither side was more than one up in the rubber. This rule, which had also applied in England for the Australian tour of the previous season, was a bad one. There was certainly a case, and still is, for playing the last match to a finish if the rubber is level, but there was none for the arrangements of these years, which were as likely to produce stalemate as prevent it. England's 1935 experiences against South Africa probably had something to do with this stupid regulation.

The consequence at Durban in 1939, even more than at the Oval in 1938, was a match hovering between the monstrous and the farcical. South Africa won the toss, and scored 530. England then were out for 316. South Africa batted again and scored 481. This left England 696 to win in the last innings. They scored 654 for 5. The match lasted nine playing days, plus one completely lost to rain, and still had to be left drawn at the end, because otherwise the English would have missed their boat home. It was this match that, virtually, put an end to what was called (inappropriately) the 'timeless' Test. On balance this has proved a blessing (though, again, there is a case to be argued): it is possibly not too fanciful to say that the nature of the match, and its pointless result, symbolized the phase, of history more than just cricketing history, which was about to pass. So England's last tour abroad before the Second World War, as before the First, was a victorious one, to South Africa.

Lieutenant-Colonel R. T. Stanyforth, captain in 1927–8, was not one of what I called just now the towering figures. Nevertheless he must not be passed over, for he was unique. He had never played for his county before he captained England. His only matches for Yorkshire (three of them) were played in the season after his return from South Africa. He was the first Yorkshireman to lead England since Jackson, and the last till Yardley, nearly 20 years later. Most of his cricket was played for the Army. He was a wicket-keeper, and quite a good one, though he did not get his flannels at Eton, nor win a Blue at Oxford. He made 73 dismissals in his first-class career, nine of them in Tests. This was his only Test series. Though he went to the West Indies a couple of years later, he was injured early in the tour, and a replacement had to be sent.

He had himself been only a replacement as captain. G. R. Jackson, the Derbyshire captain, had been chosen to lead the side, but when he was taken ill before leaving England, the call went to Stanyforth. He performed very capably. At a reception early in the tour, Field Marshal Smuts said, 'I don't know how good a cricketer Major Stanyforth is, but there can be few better speakers.' His side was a happy one, if it was some way short of England's best, and we have some happy recollections of it from its youngest member, Ian Peebles, who had gone out in the first place as the captain's secretary, but played in four Tests. It was on this tour that Peebles achieved his memorable line on the scorecard, *absent bathing 0*.

Stanyforth was 35 at the time of the tour, and lived until 1964. He had been decorated in the First World War. He was a trustee of M.C.C. at the time of his death. He wrote a useful little book called *Wicket-Keeping*. A gifted and likeable man.

An injury to Stanyforth before the last Test gave Greville Stevens the opportunity to lead England which had been denied him at Old Trafford in 1926. The match was lost, so his record as an England captain was one of 100%

failure, something which would not have perturbed him too much. Before the start of this match the English batsmen were worried about the South African fast bowler Bissett, who had taken eight wickets in the previous Test. Percy Holmes, who was partnering Sutcliffe in the absence of Hobbs, and had some reason for confidence because he had been among the runs, cheered them up by announcing that he 'could play bloody Bissett wi' a broo.n-handle' – with the following result:

> Holmes, c Cameron b Bissett 0
> Holmes, lbw b Bissett 0

Whether the bouncy Stevens would have been one of the more notable England captains had he been able to give more time to the game, it is hard to say. He had not been a successful captain of Oxford, though neither had he been a lucky one. Leg-break bowlers do not often make good captains, at least at the highest levels. There had been, for England, A. G. Steel, and later there were to be R. W. V. Robins and F. R. Brown, but it is fair to say that in all these cases they would not have been chosen for the job primarily for their leg-breaks. (Nowadays, of course, the leg-breaker has practically vanished from the English first-class game, much to its loss.) But there is no doubt that Stevens was one of the finest amateur cricketers of his time, from his days at University College School, where he scored 466 in a house match, to his later occasional appearances for Middlesex in the 'thirties. He was born in 1901 and died in 1970. He played twice against Australia, ten matches in all for England. In first-class cricket he scored more than 10,000 runs at an average of 30, and took nearly 700 wickets at an average of 27. In Test cricket his batting average was only 15, and his bowling average (for 20 wickets) 32. But this is not sufficient evidence to say he would have been a poor Test player, had he been able to give himself more opportunities.

England's other captains against South Africa in this period will recur, even Carr, who, though his Test cricket ended in 1929, was still to be a potent influence on international events some years later.

The West Indies had toured England several times at various levels, and in 1923 they startled a strong side in a match at Scarborough which gave some glimpse of what was to come. In 1928 they were granted three Test matches. The results were disappointing, even embarrassing. England, captained by Chapman, won all three by an innings. There were occasions on the 1928 tour when the West Indies showed something nearer to their proper form, but the stresses of a Test match far from home, against sides which approached England's full strength, were at this time too much for them. They toured England again in 1933, losing two out of three Tests with one drawn; and in 1939, losing one out of three with two drawn. These series were more closely contested. The England captain in 1933 was Jardine (Wyatt taking over for the last because Jardine was injured) and in 1939 Hammond captained the side.

In return, England sent two sides to the West Indies. The first, in 1929–30, was under the Hon. F. S. G. Calthorpe. It contained only three men who had played for England against South Africa in 1929, but it still looks, in retrospect, a useful if venerable side. The average age was 35, and the combined age of Wilfred Rhodes and George Gunn, its senior members, was 102. The West Indies did well to draw the rubber, one-all with two draws.

In 1934–5 Wyatt was the English captain, and the West Indies won by two to one, with one drawn; it was that tour which drew to the attention of the general English public that a formidable new opponent was appearing.

Calthorpe, aged 37 at the time of his captaincy, about the right age given his team, had been a Cambridge Blue, and played for Sussex before moving to Warwickshire, whom he captained from 1920 to 1929. His captaincy of his county had intermissions because of poor health, and he died at the early age of 43. He was a good county player, though below England standard: these were his only Tests. A competent lower-order batsman, he was an inswinging fast-medium bowler, who took a curving run-up to the wicket, which was then considered unusual. He had little success in the Test matches. Wyatt, who was one of his side in the West Indies (and for Warwickshire) did not consider him to be an 'astute' captain, but this was partly because Calthorpe planned Wyatt's future as a bowler rather than a batsman, and Wyatt, justifiably as events proved, had different plans. Wyatt does, however, pay tribute to the encouragement which Calthorpe gave him in his early days, and also comes to his defence over his failure to enforce the follow-on in the last Test, something for which Calthorpe was sharply criticized at the time.

This last Test match of the 1929–30 tour deserves a little attention. It was a forerunner of the enormity at Durban a decade later, and of a good deal more boring cricket. The first three matches had been limited to five days each. The last one was to be played to a finish, since the rubber was level. It lasted for nine days and had to be abandoned as a draw, because otherwise boats would have been missed. England scored 849 in the first innings, Sandham making 325 of them. This would have been the world record individual score in a Test match, had it occurred to anyone outside the West Indies that a Test match was in progress. It has been retrospectively hallowed, and as I write remains the sixth highest, surpassed only by Sobers, Hutton, Hanif, Hammond and Bradman. The West Indies were bowled out for 286, but Calthorpe batted again. He had a precedent for doing this in Chapman's tour of Australia the year before, when Chapman did not enforce the follow-on after England had led by 399 runs on the first innings. But Chapman's match at Brisbane was the first Test of the tour, with no boats hovering on the horizon. Calthorpe declared at 272 for 9 in his second innings, but there was not time to bowl the West Indies out. They scored 408 for 5 when it was ho! for home. Calthorpe's desire to give his ageing bowlers a rest was understandable, but it still seems an odd piece of captaincy, and Wyatt's defence of it, which requires us to believe that the West Indies could have made 700 in their second innings and then caught England on a sticky wicket, is possibly influenced by the fact that he made a few bad guesses himself when captain in the West Indies five years later.

New Zealand played Test matches in England for the first time in 1931, and again in 1937. Only one Test had been arranged in 1931, but New Zealand did so well in it (at the end England needed 94 to win with five wickets left, after leading by 230 on the first innings) that two more were arranged. England won the second by an innings, and the third was nearly a washout. The England captain was Jardine, in his first term of office. The New Zealand side of 1937 was rather a disappointment after the previous one had done so well. They had a poor season against the counties, but did not do badly in the Tests. England won the second, the only one finished, but at one point in the match England were only 152 on, with three second innings wickets left. The England captain in these matches was R. W. V. Robins, and they were the only matches in which he ever *did* captain England, which is a little surprising as we look back, because his was a name often put into contention for the job, and continued to be for more than another decade.

England's arrangements for touring New Zealand have never been very satisfactory, from the days of Ted Pooley onwards. Not that there have been any more disasters of that kind: but the financial resources of New Zealand cricket have not been enough to make a long tour over there a sound proposition, so the Tests have usually been tacked on to the end of tours to Australia, with an inevitable feeling of anti-climax, at least from the English point of view. Lillywhite and Shaw and Shrewsbury had preferred to take the New Zealand matches in the middle of the tour, but they found that that also had its problems, especially from the weather.

In 1929–30, however, M.C.C. sent a side to New Zealand, taking in a state match or two in Australia on the way. They appointed as captain Harold Gilligan – A. H. H. Gilligan – younger brother of Arthur. Four matches were played against New Zealand. Three were drawn, and M.C.C. won one. This was the winter when two 'England' sides were playing simultaneously in different quarters of the world. Still, Harold Gilligan comes into the list of England captains. He had the young Duleepsinhji and the old Woolley to bat for him, and a fine all-rounder in Nichols of Essex, and his side was much too strong for all the opposition but the best. The tour also produced a pleasant book, *The Book of the Two Maurices*. The two Maurices were M. J. Turnbull and M. J. C. Allom. It was an enjoyable tour, and did something to bring along New Zealand cricket, but lost a good deal of money.

England played two Tests in New Zealand at the end of Jardine's Australian tour, in 1933. Both were drawn, with England overwhelmingly the better side. Wyatt captained England in the second Test. Hammond scored 227 in the first match, and 336 not out in the second. Allen's 1936–7 side to Australia also played in New Zealand on the way home, but their match against 'A New Zealand XI' was not given Test rank. In the meantime, another M.C.C. side, led by E. R. T. Holmes, had visited New Zealand, in 1935–6. This tour also lost a lot of money, although of its 14 players, eight were amateurs: an economy measure. It was still a good side, probably as strong as the 1929–30 team, but its four matches against New Zealand – none of which was finished – have not been counted as Tests.

Errol Holmes of Surrey was at the time of this tour very much a candidate for the captaincy of England in Australia the following year. He handled his side well (they played all the Australian states before going on to New Zealand) and had a gift for getting on with his hosts which was much needed in Australia at that time. He had played four Tests in the West Indies under Wyatt, and a fifth at home against South Africa in 1935. He was in fact chosen as a member of the team for Australia in 1936, but withdrew, because of the illness of his father. I suppose it is possible (I do not intend this as an unkind reflection on Holmes, who has described the circumstances in his book, *Flannelled Foolishness*) that if he had been offered the captaincy instead of Allen, he and his father might have agreed that he should take it. He was out of form at the time the decisions were taken, and much depends on these chances. I am not suggesting that Holmes was a major loss to the England captaincy – it would only have been in a weak batting period, as that was, that he could have justified his place in the side – but he undoubtedly would not have disgraced it, and must have come as near to it as any except those who formally turned it down. Besides, it was rough luck that his New Zealand Tests were only 'unofficial' and Gilligan's were 'official'.

But no disrespect, either, to Harold Gilligan, who certainly adds a touch of distinction to the list, though his first-class cricket career and his Test career (batting average 18, did not bowl) hardly do his merits justice. At Dulwich he had been thought the best of the three Gilligan brothers (the third, Frank, the oldest, could give less time to cricket than the other two). Somehow Harold could not regularly reproduce his school form when he entered the first-class game, though two or three times a season he would play an innings which would momentarily convince the watchers that he was one of the best batsmen in the country. He took over the captaincy of Sussex from brother Arthur in 1930, handing over to Duleepsinhji the following season, and although that was his only year of official captaincy he was on many occasions their acting captain. He was a cheerful captain, though he could be firm. He was not, perhaps, a great tactician, but his sides liked playing for him. Turnbull and Allom sum him up in the old story –

'Cap'n, Cap'n, we struck a rock an' we're sinkin' fast!'
'That's all right, me boys, I think I can swim to yonder lightharse and attach a roap on 't.'

'Handsome and bronzed', they add, 'he likes his lettuce and he likes his glass, alas not only one.' But Gilligan still wrote a cheerful foreword to their book. He was an excellent cover-point, very little inferior to Arthur; and a holy terror on the roads of England, which did give terrors rather more unholy scope in the 1920s than they do today. He once travelled from Tunbridge Wells to Horsham in 25 minutes, which must have been nearly a mile a minute along twisty roads; and even faster, Sir Home Gordon (who was a passenger) says, was the last 11 miles to Trent Bridge one morning, which took only 14 minutes. They arrived at 11.25, and Gilligan was changed and leading Sussex into the field at 11.30.

It was a pity Frank Gilligan, the third brother, did not play more. He played for Essex, on the strength of an educational qualification, and became a housemaster at Uppingham. He sounds to have had the right stuff in him as a captain, for when he led Oxford in 1920, he had to cope with the brilliant and glorious young freshman Greville Stevens. As they walked out for the first match, Stevens archly asked 'And shall I field in the place which I've made famous?' (He had made a great reputation in the then relatively unfamiliar position of gully.) 'Yes', said Gilligan, 'long-on at both ends.'

There were some similarities between Stevens and Walter Robins. Both were leg-spinners, both attacking batsmen, both lively characters, both played for Middlesex. Neither made as big an impact on the game as he would have done given more time, though Robins managed to play more than Stevens, and also was able to be more active in cricketing matters after his retirement. Both were outstanding schoolboy cricketers, Robins at Highgate. Robins was in the Cambridge side, as a freshman, in 1926. He played the first of many matches for the Gentlemen in 1928. He captained Middlesex from 1935 to 1938, and again in 1946, 1947 (when they won the championship) and 1950. He played 19 times for England, with a batting average of 26·60 and a bowling average (64 wickets) of 27·46. He was an outstanding fielder in the covers and the deep. In all first-class cricket he made nearly 14,000 runs and took nearly 950 wickets.

Robins played in one Test against South Africa in 1929, and in at least one Test in every home season thereafter (except 1934) until 1937. He was invited to tour Australia in 1932–3, and could not go, but went four years later under Allen. He made a century against South Africa in 1935 (going in at 141 for 5) and took 6 for 32 against the West Indies in 1933. He is better remembered, though, for his efforts in the first two Tests against Australia, in 1930. At Trent Bridge, Australia needed 429 to win in the last innings, which would have been by far the highest score of the match, but Larwood was off the field, injured, and with Bradman going very well it began to seem quite likely that they would get them, until Robins bowled Bradman with a googly which he left alone. Robins had 7 for 132 in the match. At Lord's, in one of the most famous of all Tests, Robins had the spectacular figures of 1 for 172 in the first innings, but a few overs in the second (he took 2 for 34) gave Australia some anxious moments when they went in again needing only 72 to win. At one point they were 3 for 22. Robins took the wickets of Ponsford and Kippax, and had Woodfull dropped at 1. He was criticized in that match for his impetuous running between the wickets. He very nearly ran out Chapman and did comprehensively run out White, these things happening at a crucial stage, when England still had an excellent chance of saving the match. Well, young men do such things. Robins was not chosen again in that series, and there were many who thought it a mistake to drop one who was called, by E. H. D. Sewell, 'by far the best of our young all-rounders'.

His running between the wickets, though speedy, remained an occasional cause of concern to his colleagues. Once in Australia he was batting with Maurice Leyland, who had already been in a long time on a hot day. England were in a hopeless position, needing about 700 to win, 6 down for 195. Robins set about knocking off the rest with great vigour, and suddenly found himself running alongside Leyland, he on his third run and Leyland on his second. The muddle was sorted out without disaster, and Leyland sternly adjured him to go steady. 'We can't get all these runs to-neet'. Leyland did get 111 not out, and Robins 61, but he did not generally have a successful tour. He broke a finger in the first week and could not spin the ball properly for a long time afterwards.

Robins would have played for England more often had there not been several other high-class leg-spinners about during his best years: Freeman (not that the selectors ever gave him much of a chance), Richard Tyldesley, F. R. Brown, Mitchell of Derbyshire, and in the years just before the war, Wright of Kent. His England captaincy was popular and effective. If there does not seem much to say about it, that is because he did not have much to beat. There was more than once a move to recall him to the post after the war, particularly before the last Test of 1948. England had already lost the rubber, and though N. W. D. Yardley had by no means proved a poor captain, it was felt that Robins, still a fine player, might have brought a touch of dash and adventure which would have enabled England to end the series on a brighter note. But it would not have been a policy with much future, and the selectors stuck to Yardley.

Before we take a look at his later activities, we should remember how Robins galvanized Middlesex in those pre-war years. In 1937, Middlesex and Yorkshire were engaged in a competition for the championship which stirred the feelings of

139

north and south as had never happened in cricket since Warner just managed it over Lancashire in 1920. I remember the closing stages of that summer well. I was a Yorkshire boy, you must understand, though I had been living for some years in London, and the thought of Middlesex beating Yorkshire for the championship was therefore especially repellent to me. I would never be able to look my London friends in the face again. We were on holiday at Swanage and heard on the six o'clock news, in our unsatisfactory digs a long way from the beach, that Middlesex had won, and that Yorkshire looked like losing against Glamorgan. Deeply depressed, I walked down into the town with mother, to find father, as usual, on the bowling-green. As soon as he saw me, he waved his evening paper in the air. Could it be? Yes, Yorkshire had won after all, and were still on top of the table.

Next day, we learnt from the newspaper, which I rather fear was the *Daily Telegraph*, that if Yorkshire and Middlesex continued to win all their matches for the rest of the season, Middlesex would be champions: the system worked on percentages at that time, and Middlesex played only 24 matches, the minimum permitted. Only Warwickshire and Northamptonshire played so few. Sussex and Lancashire played as many as 32, Yorkshire 28. Thus if both Yorkshire and Middlesex won their last two matches, Middlesex would overtake Yorkshire.

Dirty work! This was my youthful feeling, though it was absurd, because the conditions of the championship were well known to all participants before they entered, and it was not the fault of Middlesex that they played fewer matches (Lord's was so often in use for other matches, sacred in the calendar, like Tonbridge *v.* Clifton or the Royal Artillery *v.* the Royal Engineers). But still, 'dirty work' was the thought of every irritated northerner, and it may have been this thought which prompted Robins to send a telegram to Sellers, the Yorkshire captain, challenging him to a four-day match on neutral ground, irrespective of the championship result. Sellers at once agreed, adding '£10 a man'. The Yorkshire committee did not approve of gambling, and the bets were off, at least officially, but the match took place, at the Oval, the profits (which were substantial) going to charity. Yorkshire won the toss, caught Middlesex on a turning pitch, and won by an innings. I was, at the time, passionately glad that Yorkshire won so conclusively, but looking back, I admire Robins for making the challenge even more than I admire Sellers for accepting it. Cardus watched this match, and wrote some of his best reports about it, though so far as I know they have never been reprinted.

In 1938, when Yorkshire had again won the championship, more comfortably, with Middlesex second, Robins did not offer another challenge, but sent a telegram of congratulation, beginning 'Your team is too good for us'. It was a generous gesture (I wonder if Sellers, also in his different way an admirable captain, would have done the same had Middlesex won).

So Robins does not, quite, rank among the great captains. When he did manage to take Middlesex to the championship, after the war, it was because he had two astonishingly good batsmen, Compton and Edrich, and a dry summer of hard wickets upon which they could play their strokes almost endlessly. He insisted on fast scoring that summer, because he had not much of a bowling side, but his batsmen (there were Robertson and Brown, too) did score so many runs so quickly that they had enough time to bowl the others out. His position was comparable to that of Fender at the Oval 20 years before. But Fender never managed to lead a championship side, or to captain England, and Robins did both.

Robins was a Test selector from 1946 to 1949, and in 1954, and chairman of the selectors from 1962 to 1964. I doubt if he was good at this. He did not get on very well with the press, which ought not to be a qualification for a selector but has now, like it or not, become one.

Robins tried, in 1954, to replace Hutton by Sheppard as the England captain, and did it in a cloak-and-dagger way which reflected no credit upon him, though we shall come to that disquieting story later. When he became chairman of the selectors in 1962, he issued what *Wisden* described as an ultimatum: 'Play aggressively at all times. Otherwise you will not be chosen for England.' This was not entirely borne out by the events of his chairmanship. Barrington was England's principal batsman in those years. Robins was also manager of the England side which went to the West Indies in 1959–60. The captain was May, who fell ill in the middle of the tour and was replaced by Cowdrey. England won the series by the only match finished, the second one, and in the last one Robins tried hard to persuade Cowdrey to declare to make an entertaining finish. Cowdrey declined. In his autobiography, *M.C.C.*, Cowdrey describes what happened. It is a book in which Cowdrey is never unkind to anyone, but one feels he has to struggle a bit to maintain his kindness to Robins. Other English cricketers on the tour have been, or have allowed their ghosts to have been, more unkind. He was not very popular with the cricketers of the succeeding generation, was Robins. I dare say he deserved it, because he never troubled to understand them, but I remember what Ian Peebles wrote about him – Peebles often played under him for Middlesex and followed him, in 1939, as the county captain: 'The most enthusiastic and joyous cricketer I played with.' That is not a tribute to be dismissed lightly. I worked with him on a number of occasions in radio and television programmes (he was an excellent broadcaster) and found him a stimulating and entertaining companion. He was only 62 when he died, in 1968, at his home near Lord's.

England first played a Test against India at Lord's in 1932. It was the only Test of the tour. The English captain was Jardine. Curiously, three of the side did not go on the tour to Australia the following winter. England won comfortably in the end, by 158 runs, but suffered some early shocks. I shall always remember this match because of the further misadventures of Percy Holmes, he who had failed to play Bissett with a broom-handle. Holmes was unlucky to play for England so rarely. He coincided, of course, with Hobbs, as well as Sutcliffe and Sandham. He had been chosen for the first Test of 1921, made top score in the first innings, and was dropped for the rest of the series. Apart from the South African tour, that had been all his Test cricket, and he was now 45 and nearing retirement. However, a few weeks earlier, at Leyton, he and Sutcliffe had scored 555 for the first wicket, a partnership most of which I saw. That was then the highest stand for any wicket anywhere, and is still, as I write, the highest for any wicket in England. So with Hobbs now retired from Test cricket, the selectors graciously invited Holmes to partner Sutcliffe against India. At Leyton their scores had been:

Holmes, not out 224
Sutcliffe, b Eastman 313

At Lord's, they were:

First innings
Holmes, b Nissar 6
Sutcliffe, b Nissar 3
Second innings
Holmes, b Jahangir Khan 11
Sutcliffe, c Nayudu b Amar Singh 19

In the autumn of 1933 England set off for the return visit. The captain was still Jardine, who had overcome Australia the previous winter and the West Indies, at home, in the summer. Tests were played at Bombay, Calcutta and Madras. England won the first and last, and in the second had much the better of the draw. This was a capital performance by Jardine and his team, which although a good one was below the full England strength. No English team won a rubber in India again until 1976-7, when Greig was captain. Nowadays we do not take Indian cricket lightly, but the 1933 tour raised little interest at home. Well, so we were winning again? Only to be expected, eh? Poor show if we didn't. No 'special correspondents' were sent. Cardus was listening to music. Swanton was touring the West Indies with Sir Julien Cahn (the Knight of the Bicycle-Pump Pads). Robertson-Glasgow was playing snooker's pool, probably. The rest were speculating whether peace would be made with Australia in time for the 1934 tour to take place. As a result, this English side has never received sufficient credit for one of the best achievements of the decade. For if a tour of India is considered physically arduous today, and we all know how much the correspondents suffer, without even the stress of playing, how much more must it have been so then? This was also a strong period in Indian cricket. It is doubtful whether they have ever, until the last few years, been stronger. (It was, of course, before partition, which has deprived India of some of the tall fast bowlers of the north – at least this is one theory.) As late as 1967, as you may see from *Wisden* for that year, D. J. Rutnagur offered a list of the best 11 cricketers ever to have played for India. The article was the result of a conversation he had had with several other knowledgeable and experienced Indian cricketers. No less than six of his 'all-time' Indian XI played in the 1933–4 series. They were V. M. Merchant, Wazir Ali, Amarnath, C. K. Nayudu, Amar Singh, and Nissar, and I suppose that all of them, except possibly Wazir Ali, would walk straight into an Indian side today.

But the Indian tour of England in 1936 was not a successful one. The captain was the Maharaj Kumar of Vizianagram. He was an agreeable companion in the commentary box in later years ('Call me Vizzy') but he had difficulty in holding his talented but mercurial side together. Amarnath was sent home before the first Test. England won the first and third Tests, both by nine wickets, and the second was drawn. This was India's brightest moment, when, after England had led by 368 on the first innings, Merchant and Mushtaq Ali put on over 200 for the first wicket, and the match was saved. The English captain was G. O. Allen, taking over from Wyatt, and it was Allen who took the side to Australia in the following winter.

And now let us return to the Australian saga, which we left at the moment of Chapman's triumph in 1926. There was never any doubt that he would be the leader in Australia in 1928–9. England won the first four matches, and when they scored 519 in the first innings of the fifth, there seemed every likelihood that they would win all five (something they have never done); but Australia won it in the end, by five wickets, chiefly because of the youthful Bradman. Chapman stood down from the last Test. He was reported to be injured, but acted as twelfth man, and there was an impression that he had been dropped, with his own approval, partly because his form was not specially good and partly to let Maurice Leyland have a go. J. C. White therefore captained the side. Despite his absence from cricket for most of 1929, Chapman was also the obvious choice against Australia at home in 1930. When England won the first Test of that series Chapman had been captain in nine Tests, six against Australia and three against the West Indies, and won them all. He was to be captain in eight more, three against Australia and five against South Africa, and did not win one of them.

The second Test of 1930, one of the memorable ones, marked the turning point in Chapman's fortunes. He scored a brilliant hundred, but it was widely felt that England should have saved the game (this was the match in which Walter Robins was so impetuous between the wickets). The scores were: England 425 and 375, Australia 729 for 6 and 72 for 3. Duleepsinhji scored 173, Woodfull

155, Bradman 254, Chapman 121. It has often been said that this match changed the general approach to Test cricket, and that more emphasis began to be placed on saving a match, less on winning it. Chapman went on hitting right to the end of his innings, even though the chance of victory was forlorn. This is perhaps a retrospective judgment, but those four golden days at Lord's do have something of the glamour of departed pageantry about them.

Chapman was also criticized for his field-placing, particularly because his bowlers were sometimes to be found fielding in the deep. Things are different today, but at that time it was accepted doctrine that bowlers should be cherished in positions close to the wicket. G. O. Allen's analysis of 0 for 115 was excused on the grounds that he had too much running about to do. But that did not happen until the Australian batsmen were well on top, and in any case, with Woolley, Hendren and White playing – 123 years between them – it was a difficult England side to place in the field. And what is a captain to do when faced with a scoreboard showing 393 for 1, and 585 for 2?

In the third Test, Australia scored 566, Bradman 334 of them, breaking Foster's record individual score. England, 391 and 95 for 3, saved the match with some help from the rain. It rained again in the fourth Test: Australia 345, England 251 for 8. There was more criticism of Chapman's field-placing, and of the way he handled his bowlers; and, for the first time in the series, he failed with the bat. And so to the Oval, once more in a match without a time limit, with the Ashes depending upon it: and once more with a fresh England captain, for Chapman was dropped, and R. E. S. Wyatt, who had played in none of the preceding matches, was brought in to lead the side.

The rumpus of 1926 was repeated, with embellishments. Press opinion and, it was believed, general public opinion, was this time even more unanimous in hostility to the selectors. In 1926 there had been a feeling that Carr was not proving the ideal captain, even though it was a shock when the inexperienced Chapman replaced him. In 1930, despite the occasional criticisms, Chapman's position did not seem in any danger. He was still the popular, boyish, debonair hero. He had been having his most successful series with the bat, and as a close fieldsman England still did not contain his equal. He could not seriously be blamed because the English bowlers could not get Bradman out (though this was perhaps more apparent in retrospect than at the time). Wyatt, though nothing was known against him, and he had shown himself in the past capable of performing well at the top level, was a figure markedly lacking in glamour.

Matters were made worse when the news of the change in captaincy leaked to the press before the official announcement. Chapman was said (but it was not true) to have learnt of it from a radio bulletin. Wyatt received hundreds of letters and telegrams, many of them abusive. 'If you play at the Oval, pistols await you', said one. Chapman himself gave an interview to the *Daily Mail*, headed 'Why have I been dropped?' which, as Warner said mildly, 'was in a style and manner which did not sound in the least like Chapman'. (All the same, we may think that the appearance of such an interview gave the selectors' decision some retrospective justification.) Even *The Times*, in a leading article, expressed regret at the change, though pointing out that the sporting instincts of the team would probably lead them to support Wyatt in the field. The qualification 'probably' cannot have brought much comfort to Wyatt. *The Times* did, however, point out that the selection committee could hardly be thought less anxious for an England victory than the rest of the public, and also said: 'There are many more important things in life than Test Matches, though at the present moment an intelligent foreigner passing through England must be tempted to doubt whether Englishmen are of that opinion.'

It does seem, after all these years, an odd decision to have taken. Wyatt himself, who has given a balanced account of the episode in his book *Three Straight Sticks*, thought that Chapman had been dropped because his batting style was thought too chancy for a timeless Test, and because he did not sufficiently appreciate the difference between three-day and four-day Test cricket, two reasons which carried some weight even if they were slightly contradictory. The selectors that year were Leveson-Gower, White, and Mann, not the strongest combination. Leveson-Gower was generally held to blame for the choice, though he later denied that he had given the casting vote. Indeed, he added, not once during the season did he have to cast a vote at all, something unique in his experience.

In 1926 England won: in 1930 England lost. That is why the echoes took so long to die down, and why the selectors remained villains. Wyatt came out of the business very well, none the less. He won the toss, not that there is any merit in that, and England lost their first five wickets for 197, a poor score on the plumb Oval wicket. Wyatt then went in to join Sutcliffe, who had as usual opened with Hobbs, and together they put on 170, a record sixth-wicket partnership for England against Australia at that time. England ultimately scored 405, which was an acceptable total even in a match of that sort, but Bradman provided another double century, and England were caught on a turning wicket after rain, Hornibrook, a lanky slow-medium left-hander, taking 7 wickets in the innings for 92. (He only took 17 wickets in the six Test matches in which he played in his career.) Victory to Australia, and the Ashes, by an innings and 39. Nobody suggested that the captaincy had made any difference, though Wyatt's first innings (he failed in the second) had kept England in the match, when an impulsive gesture from Chapman might have lost it there and then. Or so it could be argued.

Wyatt and Chapman, despite of all temptations to belong to other nations, remained friends. Wyatt gave Chapman the freedom of the England dressing-room throughout the match, and toured under him in South Africa the following winter. It was not a successful or particularly happy tour, but that was not Wyatt's fault. Wyatt wrote many years later, 'I always liked Percy Chapman – it would have been difficult to dislike such a cheery, good-natured fellow.' There is no reason to suppose that the words were insincerely written. Wyatt's qualities as an England captain, which were considerable, may be better surveyed later in his career.

Chapman's career as captain, indeed all his Test cricket, was over in 1931. Born in Reading, in Berkshire, in 1900, he was in the Uppingham XI for four years, from 1916 to 1919, captain in the last two. He gained a Blue as a freshman at Cambridge, and was chosen for the Gentlemen in the same year. In 1921 he was one of MacLaren's side which beat the Australians at Eastbourne. In 1922 he scored a century in the University match, followed it with one for the Gentlemen, and in due course one for England against Australia, also at Lord's. This triple feat had never been done before and has never been done since; and will never, I suppose, be done again, unless some unexpected twist of development restores the Gentlemen v. Players fixture. Martin Donnelly, another left-hander though of a very different build and style – and a better batsman than Chapman, I will risk saying, with the prejudice of a contemporary – scored a hundred at Lord's for Oxford, and for the Gentlemen, and in a Test match: but he was playing for New Zealand in the Test.

After his Cambridge and Berkshire days, Chapman played for Kent, spasmodically in the latter years, until 1939. He was Kent's captain from 1931 to 1936. It is ironic, and not the only irony of Chapman's career, that he succeeded to the captaincy of his adopted county only after he had lost the captaincy of England. G. B. Legge was in command of Kent during Chapman's proud years. Legge was a naval officer, of the reserve. He had been preceded for a season by A. J. Evans, who is remembered best for his escaping exploits in the First World War, and the book he wrote about them, even more than his choice as an England player at Lord's in 1921. When the subject of the worst player ever to be chosen for England crops up, as it sometimes does among journalists late at night, one senior member of the company will draw attention to the claims of Evans, with force in his arguments. Before Evans, Kent had been led by Captain Cornwallis, later the second baron. Lord Harris presided, more or less benignly, in the Canterbury scene. It occurs to me that this patrician, military setting may not have been the happiest background for Chapman. He usually gave the impression of being an exceptionally happy man, but that is the way some men disguise their unhappiness.

He scored more than 16,000 runs in first-class cricket, with 27 centuries, at an average of 32. These are good figures however you look at them, and do not begin to take into account his marvellous fielding, but there were many who said he should have scored more, given his talents. No doubt they were right. When Chapman was going well, he looked quite as good as Woolley at the other end, and in the mid-1920s there was no other English left-hander, possibly no other England batsman at all except Hobbs, of whom that could be said. Chapman scored 260 against Lancashire, at Maidstone, when MacDonald, the dreaded Australian, the fastest bowler in the world (Larwood had not then reached his peak of pace and Gregory was in decline), was bowling for Lancashire. Kent lost wickets quickly to MacDonald, Woolley's among them, before Chapman began to smash him all over the place, while Legge scored a decorous century at the other end. Fortunately for historians of cricket, the young Cardus was there, as a *Manchester Guardian* reporter, and has described how Chapman wrecked the bowling.

> He stood on tiptoe to MacDonald and hooked him so that the ball sometimes soared away like a helicopter for six. He lay back and cut him. He put his right foot down the wicket and, laughing as he did so, drove Tyldesley's potential leg-spin into the next field amongst the ruminant cows. In this incredible innings, Chapman hit five sixes and thirty-two fours. MacDonald ... applauded when Chapman pulled him for a huge six, which promised to pass beyond recall. 'It was infectious', said MacDonald, after Kent's and Chapman's innings was over: 'infectious! I felt that I was taking part in Percy's cricket.'

In Test cricket Chapman made 925 runs at an average of 29. He bowled a few overs but did not take a wicket, though in his youth he had been a useful left-armer, first slow and then fast-medium. He made 32 catches, some of them historic. In Larwood's first over of the 1928–9 series Woodfull snicked him between third slip and gully. E. W. Swanton writes: 'The ball flew at terrific speed off the bat, and was next seen in the outstretched left hand of Chapman, whose leap had taken him from the gully almost into Hendren's lap.' The fear of this kind of thing happening again was a constant worry to the Australian batsmen. It was the kind of catch that inspires a fielding side, and it is said that England did not drop a single catch from that moment until the Ashes were won. When Chapman caught Bradman at Lord's in 1930 in the same position, Cardus was watching with Sir James Barrie (I am sorry to keep quoting Sir Neville's stories, but who can resist it?) 'But why is he going away?' asked Barrie, as Bradman departed. 'Surely, Sir James, you saw that marvellous catch?' 'Yes', said Barrie, 'but what evidence have we that the ball which Chapman threw up in the air is the same ball that left Bradman's bat?'

Not everyone liked his carefree style of captaincy. Northcountrymen especially were inclined to be suspicious of it. At the Oval in 1926, in the last innings, he took off Wilfred Rhodes, who had taken four wickets and had every

147

hope of collecting a couple more. Rhodes, a selector you will remember, queried the decision. Chapman explained that he thought it would be pleasant to share the wickets round a bit, and put on Geary and Stevens, each of whom took his only wicket of the innings before the end. Now that was a pleasant gesture, and Australia were hundreds of runs behind, but scarcely one to gladden a Yorkshire heart. Leave nowt to chance.

Chapman's last years were sad. The magnificent physique grew heavy and muscle-bound. He was lonely, and drank too much, as lonely middle-aged men will. He died at the age of 61 after years of illness and depression. But just as a good end can redeem a sad life, so a good life can redeem a sad end, and he had known his hours, his years of glory.

In 1931 there was a new selection committee. Warner returned as chairman, and was joined by P. A. Perrin and T. A. Higson. Since Perrin was to serve in this capacity until 1939, and Higson until 1938, a word about them might not be out of place. Higson was the representative of the north on the committee, He became chairman of Lancashire. He had been a useful cricketer for that county, and for Derbyshire, though he had missed his Blue at Oxford. He was a worrier, and a bit of a fusspot at times, but had a high reputation among his contemporaries as a judge. Perrin was an Essex man, who was perhaps unlucky not to have played for England. He was undoubtedly a fine batsman, but slowness in the field was said to have counted against him, for he was a heavy man. Perrin holds the record for the highest number of boundaries in an innings, 68, at Chesterfield in 1904. Perrin scored 343 not out, and Essex lost an astonishing match by nine wickets. The point about the choice of such men as these was that they had the means and the time to give to a selector's task, not just for an occasional season but for several, thus providing the committee with some continuity, more than ever necessary now that every season was a Test season. Warner was still correspondent of the *Morning Post*, and it had been laid down that no selector could write for publication about Tests and Test trials – though permitted to do so about any other match – but Warner's editor, H. A. Gwynne, accepted this stipulation. This was generous of him, but it was not a compromise particularly satisfactory to anyone except Warner.

They chose as captain neither Chapman nor Wyatt, but D. R. Jardine, and Jardine, as was customary though not invariable, joined the committee. Warner says of the choice, in *Cricket Between Two Wars*, 'he was a keen student of the game and a close and intelligent observer, versed in every avenue and aspect of the game. . . . He had a genius for taking pains, he was always helpful in debate, and I have no hesitation in saying that this Committee was the best on which I have ever served. We worked harmoniously together and everything went like clockwork.' He is writing, remember, of 1931. Three years later he was writing, to a friend Alexander Gore-Ruthven, the Governor of South Australia, that

1 William Clarke (Radio Times Hulton Picture Library)

5 *Opposite above left: P. F. Warner (David Frith)*

6 *Opposite above right: A. C. MacLaren (Radio Times Hulton Picture Library)*

7 *Opposite below left: F. S. Jackson (David Frith)*

8 *Opposite below right: C. B. Fry (David Frith)*

2 *Above: Lord Harris (David Frith)*
3 *Top left: W. G. Grace (David Frith)*
4 *Top right: A. E. Stoddart (David Frith)*

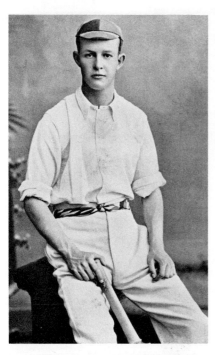

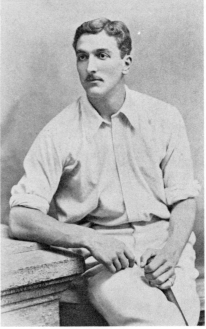

9 *Opposite below right: J. W. H. T.*
Douglas (right) with Warwick
Armstrong (Central Press)

10 *Opposite: Douglas Jardine (Press*
Association)

11 *Opposite below left: Walter*
Hammond (Press Association)

12 *Right: Len Hutton (Colorsport)*

13 *Below: Peter May (Colorsport)*

14 *Above: Colin Cowdrey (Patrick Eagar)*

15 *Left: Ted Dexter (Patrick Eagar)*

16 *Below: M. J. K. Smith (Patrick Eagar)*

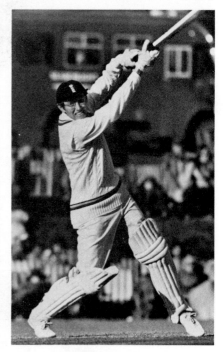

17 Above: Brian Close
(Patrick Eagar)

18 Right: Ray Illingworth
(Patrick Eagar)

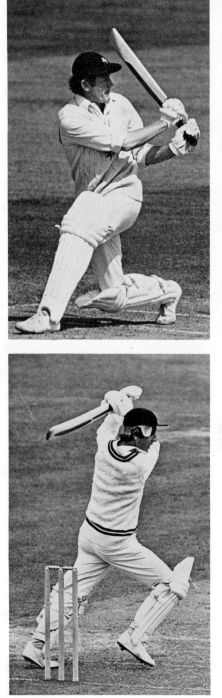

19 Top left: Mike Denness (Patrick Eagar)

20 Top right: Tony Greig (Patrick Eagar)

21 Left: Mike Brearley (Patrick Eager)

Jardine 'is a queer fellow. When he sees a cricket ground with an Australian on it he goes mad! He rose to his present position on my shoulders, and of his attitude to me I do not care to speak.' Swanton prints this letter in his autobiography, *Sort of a Cricket Person*, which among its many other merits contains the best long-distance view of that battle long ago. The appointment of Jardine was fraught with consequences which echo to this day, and will doubtless continue to reverberate so long as cricket remains a sport which people pay to watch. His reign as the captain of England lasted for three years, taking in 15 Tests, five against Australia, two against the West Indies, four against New Zealand, four against India. Of these matches nine were won, and one lost. His batting average was 48 in 33 innings, just below F. S. Jackson's. He took 26 catches in the 22 Tests in which he played, a figure which approximates to Chapman's. He was never a dramatic fielder, as Chapman was, but he did not miss many. He was not a bowler, though he had one Test over which cost 10 runs.

The question, as it occurs to me looking back nearly half a century later, is why the new selection committee chose Jardine in the first place. Chapman had been discarded, very well (his choice as captain for South Africa had been made before he had been dropped in the last Test of 1930). What was wrong with Wyatt? He had done tolerably well in South Africa, bearing the unusual responsibility of opening the innings in the Tests, and taking a wicket now and then, often a valuable one. I suppose the truth, even if it was only subconsciously realized, was that the selectors were only too anxious to put the Chapman–Wyatt controversy behind them, and make a fresh start. White could still have captained England, and so could Fender, but they were getting old. It would be a step backwards rather than forwards to appoint either. M. J. Turnbull of Glamorgan, who had scored a few runs in South Africa and had the captain's touch, might have done it, but it would have been a daring appointment. The other county captains in 1931 were Richardson of Derbyshire, in his first season; Morris of Essex, whom we have noticed in connection with Douglas; Lyon of Gloucestershire (a marvellous captain, but not a good enough player for England); Tennyson, plugging on for Hampshire; Eckersley of Lancashire, an able and agreeable man who later became a Member of Parliament, but was never really worth his place even in the Lancashire side; Dawson of Leicestershire, certainly a good player, Eton and Cambridge and a dasher in the old style, who had toured South Africa under Stanyforth and New Zealand under Harold Gilligan – but there was doubt whether he would be good enough against Australia, or have the time to give to the game (and the real object of the selectors in 1931 – they had been appointed for two seasons – was to build the side for Australia in 1932–3). Haig of Middlesex was too old. Jupp of Northamptonshire might have briefly come into the reckoning again, but he too was 40. There was still Carr of Nottinghamshire. The Sussex captain was

Duleepsinhji. Worcestershire had a new captain, C. F. Walters, who had moved there from Glamorgan, but nobody knew much about him yet. The Yorkshire captain that year was F. E. Greenwood, a man of some quality but not a cricketer who, had he been a professional, would have been near the Yorkshire side.

Given that it was unthinkable that an Indian should captain England, even if he was permitted to play for them, Duleep was out. Even his uncle Ranji had never captained England. Besides – and this was, alas! all too valid a reason – Duleep's health was frail, and although invited to go on the 1932 tour, he had to decline. He had tuberculosis, much less easily dealt with than now, and though he survived and became the High Commissioner for an independent India to Australia, his cricket career was almost done. But then, Carr, that still formidable figure looming in the background? Might he not still do the job, though he was 39 that year? He was fit, fierce, and put his faith in fast bowling. He had become the Nottinghamshire captain in 1919, and held the office until 1934, though he could not play regularly, even in his earlier years. He had been the first choice as England's captain in 1926, and recalled to duty against South Africa in 1929, in which year he took Nottinghamshire to the championship. In his career, Carr played for England 11 times, six of them as captain. He never lost a Test, though to be sure he only won one. His other five Tests had been under Mann in South Africa in 1922–3.

Here we come to the bumpy bit: for all the encomiums loaded upon his batting, and they were many, his Test average was less than 20, and he played only one innings of over 50, though he scored a great many runs for Nottinghamshire. There was one day at Hove in 1925, when Tate was at his best, with the sea-fret which he so much enjoyed, when Carr scored a hundred in 48 minutes, most of them in boundaries. Let us grant that if Carr had been a professional, with the added discipline that status would have imposed, he would have been a sufficiently good player to challenge for a place in the England side.

But more than that, Carr was a man thought from boyhood to be destined for leadership. He was born in 1894, and went to school at Sherborne, in Dorset. Sherborne was then one of the more highly respected public schools, though not one of the poshest (it was not, and never has been, a 'Lord's School', that is to say a school which has, or used to have, an annual match at Lord's). Carr was captain of all games there except, oddly, cricket, the one which he played best. He was chosen to play for Nottinghamshire, in the vacation, when he was only 16 years old. Alec Waugh, a writer more prolific though less gifted than his brother Evelyn, was also at Sherborne in Carr's time, and drew a picture of him as 'Lovelace' in his book, *The Loom of Youth*. I doubt if Alec Waugh, many of whose books I have enjoyed, has done anything better than *The Loom of Youth*, written though it was in the first few months after he had left school, with war broken out and the call to the colours sounding, and he expecting to be killed and therefore risking revelations then considered scandalous, such as that homosexuality was not unknown in public schools. When Waugh went to Sherborne, Carr was captain of his house. Lovelace is described as 'haughty, self-conscious, with sleepy-looking but watchful eyes . . . afraid of nothing'. He 'towered over his contemporaries by the splendour of his athletic achievements, and the strength of an all-mastering personality'.

Carr could be temperamental, though. After a failure he was known, more than once, not just to throw his bat about the dressing-room, but to give it away, and the rest of his gear as well. His players were familiar with this habit and would return it next day: but he did it once too often, and everything had mysteriously vanished. (This story comes in various versions but obviously something of the kind happened.)

Leveson-Gower tells a singular story of Carr. His name was brought up at a selection meeting. Lord Harris was among those present and said: 'Rather old – but Kent – we can't go wrong there.' So Carr was chosen and made a good score. It later transpired that Harris had been thinking of D. W. Carr, a Kentish leg-spinner whose only Test had been in 1909, when he was already 37 years old. I find this story hard to believe, but perhaps they were choosing the teams for Gentlemen *v.* Players or some other match in the nature of a trial.

Sutcliffe thought very highly of Carr – 'as good a captain to play under as any I have met' – and particularly of his handling of the fast bowlers, of whom Nottinghamshire usually had an ample supply. As Larwood and Voce were expected to be among England's principal assets in Australia, there was a case for recalling Carr to the captaincy. Against him was his age, and a doubt whether he would have the patience for a series of timeless Tests (but you might have said that of Chapman). All the same, Carr was a powerful influence on the 1932–3 series. He had made some experiments in the way of fast leg theory himself, and he attended the famous dinner at the Piccadilly Hotel at which – it was said with some exaggeration – the bodyline campaign was plotted. Jardine learnt a lot from him.

We still have not done with Carr. He was to be at the centre of other storms in the next few years. He has been called a stormy petrel, which is not the best of analogies, for the petrel (*procellaria pelagica*) was named for its gift of walking upon the water, as Peter did, even during a storm. But Carr did not walk upon the water. He kept sinking at the critical moments (yes, well, it occurs to me, so did Peter). I feel Carr would have been a mighty captain of England, if his luck had run better. But when you put Australia in, after leaving out Charlie Parker, and drop a catch in the first over, and the man you have dropped makes a hundred before lunch. . . . Nobody ever forgot that. When he scored his century against Australia at Lord's, Chapman gave an easy chance before he had scored. Two

Australian fieldsmen left it to each other, and it fell peacefully to earth about a dozen yards from the bat. It was scarcely remembered in the subsequent sound and fury, though it was a useful recollection when the time came to drop Chapman.

But if we have not yet done with Carr, we have, so far as this book is concerned, almost done with J. C. White, who played the last of his 15 Tests in South Africa in 1931. He might still have gone to Australia, though hardly as captain, in 1932, had it not been for the swift rise of Verity as England's leading slow left-arm bowler. By then White had ceased to be captain of Somerset, an office which he held from 1927 to 1931, officially, and unofficially on a great many other occasions both before and after. He did not much relish captaincy, even of Somerset, but he led England four times, once against Australia and three times against South Africa. He won one match and lost one. Probably he ought not to have lost that last Test against Australia in 1928–9, but he was then only nominally captain, with Chapman bringing out the drinks.

In Test cricket, White took 49 wickets at an average of 32. As most of his Test bowling was done in a high-scoring period, and most of it abroad, these are reputable figures. I would not guess, however, that he was in the highest class of slow left-armers. He did not spin the ball much; less than Parker or the Australian Ironmonger, among his contemporaries, less than Rhodes and Woolley had done when they were young; probably no more than Verity, and Verity was taller and faster and one of the most thoughtful of bowlers.

I do not imply by this that White was a thoughtless bowler. Length and flight were the weapons by which he got batsmen out. Hendren said that no bowler made him more tired than White. Woolley, a left-hander, would sometimes knock him around a bit, but no right-handed batsman, not even Hobbs, treated him lightly. He suffered from Bradman, like everybody else who had to bowl at the blighter, but in the Lord's Test of 1930, that match to which I keep recurring, when Bradman scored 254, it was White who got him in the end, and his figures of 3 for 158 in 51 overs do not look so bad against a total of 729 for 6. The other batsmen he got out in that innings were Ponsford (81) and Kippax (83). He was never a man to give in.

In all first-class cricket, White took 2,356 wickets at an average of 18·57 (there are some variations in the authorities, but I follow, as always when in doubt, Bill Frindall, in *Wisden* of 1976). Of bowlers who have taken more wickets, only Rhodes, Freeman, Hearne, Grace, Tate and Blythe have had a lower average. By taking pains he became a useful batsman, twice scoring a thousand runs in a season, and more than 12,000 in all: but not quite so good as he would, in later years, half-seriously claim. In the field, even in his youth, he was no flier, but he did not miss much, especially in the slips, or off his own bowling.

White's great season in Test cricket was 1928–9, when he was vice-captain in Australia, an amiable and steadying support to the mercurial Chapman. In that series he bowled 406 (six-ball) overs, 134 of them maidens, and took 25 wickets for 760 runs, average 30·40. No other English bowler took 20 wickets, and none but Tate (371 overs) approached the amount of overs bowled. In the first Test, when Australia were caught on a bad pitch, White took 4 for 7 in their second innings. In the fourth Test, on a plumb pitch, which Australia lost by only 12 runs after batting second, his figures were

	O	M	R	W
First innings	60	16	130	5
Second innings	64·5	21	126	8

This was at Adelaide, in hotter weather than a farmer from the Brendon Hills would expect to encounter in a lifetime of harvests. White was bowling when the last Australian batsman, Blackie, came in. Pat Hendren, close up at short-leg, said to Blackie sympathetically and subtly, that he wouldn't be in his shoes for all the money in the world. Blackie played a ball or two, lashed out, and was caught by Larwood at deep square-leg. Oldfield, a capable batsman, was well in at the other end. When they asked Blackie afterwards what he was thinking about as he played the fatal stroke, he replied 'I was thinking how the boys would cheer when they saw me hit him for six.' Many better batsmen than Blackie made similar miscalculations when faced with those innocent-looking slow balls, asking to be hit for six. The only Australian White did not get out in that match at least once was Bradman, who was run out in the second innings when he was winning the match. M. A. Noble, in writing about the tour, says that Blackie was caught off a long-hop, and that Grimmett, out just previously, was also caught off a long-hop. Ho, hum? Twenty years before on the village greens of Somerset they could have told him about those long-hops which somehow did not *quite* turn out to be long-hops. But nobody could be more generous than Noble was to White in his summary of the tour: 'This stalwart farmer–cricketer undoubtedly played the leading part in the downfall of Australia. He was the great rock and standby of his side and one of the most tireless workers with muscle and brain that this or any other English team of cricketers has ever possessed'. That is pitching it up on the high side, unlike the supposed long hops, but it was a tribute to be cherished, and White did cherish it.

'Farmer White', 'Jack White', 'J.C.': I cannot even now bring myself to utter these familiar abbreviations. For me he was always 'Mr White'. He was the first captain of England ever to bowl a ball at me, even if it was only in a net at school. (Though not the last, and I still live in hope that I will demolish the dreaded googly of A. R. Lewis on some suitable carnival occasion.)

Mr White was educated at Taunton School. He was the first Test cricketer which the school produced. In his spare time he used to come and play at the school, and lend a hand at whatever nets happened to be going on. His hair then was grey, his face ruddy, his manner genial, his advice spare. But he did bowl at me. Taunton has produced two Test cricketers since then, J. H. Cameron, who was vice-captain of the West Indies in 1939, and might have become their first black captain if the war had not spoiled his cricketing career; and, in more recent years, John Jameson, who is now back there as a master. White, the farmer and the son of a farmer, was an unmistakably Somerset man. He used to call everybody 'cock', or, if you were a boy, 'young cock'. He was a placid man, though known to murmur, when an important catch was put down off his bowling, 'the trouble with that cock is he's fast asleep'. He accepted decisions given against him, when he was bowling, with equanimity; and as a result possibly got more than his share of favourable decisions when he was batting, or so Robertson-Glasgow suggests. He was fond of all country sports and, like Ranji, lost an eye in a shooting accident. He kept up his interest in cricket, and became President of Somerset in 1960. He died, aged 70, the following year.

There was another cricketer who might have succeeded to the captaincy of England in 1931, if things had happened a little differently a few years before; and a man who for certain – or as certain as an hypothesis can be – would have done it very well. This was Herbert Sutcliffe. It was still accepted doctrine that only an amateur could captain England. It was at the Yorkshire Annual General Meeting in 1925 that Lord Hawke made his celebrated remark about professional captaincy. It ought to be said that it did not form part of his original speech, but was made without forethought in a reply to the vote of thanks. There had been some criticism of the behaviour of Parkin, who – as we have noticed – had attacked Gilligan in the press. (Parkin had played one match for Yorkshire before it was discovered that he had been born 20 yards inside Durham.) Hawke said

> Pray God, no professional shall ever captain England. I love and admire them all but we have always had an amateur skipper and when the day comes when we shall have no more amateurs captaining England it will be a thousand pities.

So it was not so bad as the first sentence, taken on its own, implied, but it was still far from happily put. In 1926 there were two professional selectors, and a professional acting-captain. In 1927 Yorkshire did not win the championship. It was their second consecutive failure, after four consecutive wins. Major Lupton, the Yorkshire captain, was retiring. He had been the only amateur in the side, as was usually the case with Yorkshire sides in the 'twenties, and some of the Yorkshire public were growing a little irritated at having to play a man short, especially as Rhodes and Robinson took most of the decisions.

154

The question therefore arose whether Sutcliffe might be appointed captain of Yorkshire. Hawke was one of the sponsors of the proposition. He doubtless discussed the matter with many people, for though not garrulous he could be indiscreet, but he had special reason to discuss it with Sir Home Gordon, an old friend who had recently published (and ghosted) Hawke's autobiography. According to Sir Home, Hawke deliberately asked him to sound out other counties as to whether it would be acceptable to them if Sutcliffe, after formally becoming an amateur, were to become captain of Yorkshire. It seems an odd request to make. Yorkshire could appoint as captain whom they liked. Transfers between amateur and professional status even then were not unknown, one way round or the other. Amateurism was increasingly becoming a matter of style rather than finance, and no doubt some arrangement could have been made to see that Sutcliffe was not the poorer by the change. Indeed, even if he stayed professional, was there any compelling reason why he should forgo the captaincy? In 1935, Astill, a professional, became the captain of Leicestershire, and there were plenty of nineteenth-century examples.

What happened then is something of a mystery. 'Hawke certainly vacillated', according to Gordon, and it was of course rather a comical predicament for his lordship, who had made the press ring with his views on professional captaincy, and was now recommending a professional captain. The rest of the Yorkshire team had mixed views on the proposal. There was some feeling among them, among the committee, and among the public, that if a professional was to be appointed, it should have been Rhodes, the senior man (this belief that a professional captain must be 'the senior man' produced some poor county captains in the years after the Second World War, which in turn made a strong argument for the abolition of amateur status).

When I say that amateurism was becoming a matter of style, I am referring to life-style, rather than batting-style. There were fewer dashers among the amateurs. Jardine and Wyatt were excellent batsmen, but they did not play as Foster or MacLaren had done, or indeed Carr and Chapman. Sutcliffe, though he could score runs fast enough now and then, and had a fearless hook and an effective cover-drive, batted like a product of Pudsey, which he was – not Malvern. But he was a gentleman all right. His table manners, if I may so put it, were perfection, both on and off the table. Cardus, who was fond of Sutcliffe but enjoyed teasing him, said he spoke in accents of purest Teddington. He was nevertheless a notably smooth and efficient public speaker in his own style. He did not in the least resemble your usual Yorkshire professional (or what has been so often thought of as your usual Yorkshire professional), except in high skill and infinite determination. He was said to use eau-de-Cologne in the dressing-room. He had a touch of hauteur. He wrote his own biography, every word of it, which put him one up on Hawke, who wrote an admiring introduction. If he was not exactly loved by his fellow-professionals, he was immensely respected by them. He combined southern courtesy with northern toughness. His place in an England side from 1924 to 1934 was never in doubt, and it was absurd that he was left out of the side that toured Australia in 1936–7, when Verity had to be used as an opening batsman. In 1930 Sutcliffe was the best batsman in England, better even than Duleepsinhji, and I doubt if the Lord's Test, in which he could not play because of an injury, would have been lost had he been there. He has the highest average of any Englishman against Australia, except Paynter, and while one admires Paynter and relishes his comment about the 216 not out at Nottingham 'having to be made', Paynter played against Australia seven times, Sutcliffe 27.

The point of all this is that if Sutcliffe had been made captain of Yorkshire for the 1928 season, as he should have been, he would have been an established county captain by 1931, as well as one of the first choices for an England side. Would we then have had the bodyline dispute? Well, it is not impossible, for Sutcliffe admired both Carr and Jardine, but I doubt very much if he would have sought to carry so contentious a business off with a high hand. Once established as captain of England, I expect he would have retained the post until 1934, very likely until 1938, and think how different the course of events might have been. However, when controversy sprang up over the Yorkshire suggestion in 1927 Sutcliffe, in South Africa with Stanyforth, tactfully withdrew, and that was the end of the matter.

Jardine was in the XI at Winchester, and won his Blue at Oxford in 1920 as a freshman. His county was Surrey, whom he captained in 1932 and 1933, after Fender had retired. He was thus another of those who captained England before his county. In four seasons at Oxford, he was not made captain. It was not that he was unpopular there, but even then he presented an austere, reserved front to the world. In his second year there occurred an incident which J. H. Fingleton thinks may have had something to do with his subsequent hostility to Australians. Armstrong's Australians had required, not unreasonably, a day's rest before each Test, and so it came about that their match against Oxford was reduced to two days. At the end of the second day Jardine was 94 not out. No English batsman had scored a century against the conquering Australians at that point. As Oxford had forfeited a day of their fixture, the Australians might have bowled an extra over or two. Sam Woods, for instance, would certainly have done so. As it was, Jardine was deprived of a century to crown an innings played in the distinguished, assured, upright style which was to become so familiar.

Both as a player and a personality he was a great contrast to Chapman, though the received picture of a grim, unyielding man is over-simplified. Certainly he was a tough opponent; but off the field, relaxing with friends of his own background, he could be a genial and witty companion. He was from

156

Oxford days a warm friend of R. C. Robertson-Glasgow, who has written about him with affection and understanding. They were both men of moods, though with Robertson-Glasgow it was the sunshine which usually showed, and with Jardine the shadow.

'As for bodyline', Warner wrote in *Cricket Between Two Wars*, 'he thought that this type of bowling was legitimate and within the rules. I think, however, he would agree that it was stern action.' Jardine might have replied that Test matches were occasions for stern action. In the fourth Test, when Paynter was stricken by tonsillitis and it seemed improbable that he would be able to bat, Warner was delighted by Jardine's reference to the fellows that marched to Kandahar.

The march to Kandahar was a feat of arms in the Afghan Wars, which made the reputation of the future Lord Roberts. The march, 313 miles in 22 days with a column of 10,000 specially chosen men, was an heroic success, despite the fever and the hostile country. The war was a pointless failure. Ramsay Muir wrote of it 'Evidently adventures amongst the fierce clansmen of the mountains were costly and dangerous', and soon there was a change of government in Britain, and Gladstone returned to power, and the troops were withdrawn. I wonder if Jardine had noticed this parallel when he made his remark to Warner. He was intelligent enough, and knowledgeable enough, to have done so.

I have touched on bodyline before, when writing of Warner, and will not dwell upon it too long now. But it was a blot upon the game, the worst in the history of Test cricket, and Englishmen should not tire of repeating this, though it would probably be better if Australians did. Remember it was the *combination* of bouncers aimed at the body, and seven or eight men on the leg-side, which made the mischief. Warner says that in the first Test Larwood bowled 39 balls out of 42 'on the line of the batsman, or just clear of him', and gives this merely as an example. Other estimates were much the same, though there has always been difficulty in defining just what is a bouncer, or bumper, and just what is 'on the line of the batsman'. Jardine maintained that he instructed his bowlers to attack the leg stump, and the Australian batsman Kippax said that he would accept that if the leg stump was two feet wide and six feet tall. But opinions grew so heated (or so icy, I suppose would be the better word, at least in Jardine's case) that you can never quite believe what anyone involved in the bodyline series says about it.

These tactics would no doubt have been less successful, by far, had England not possessed Larwood. Comparisons of the speed of bowlers of different periods, even more than comparisons of the merits of batsmen, are bound to end inconclusively, but to this day I doubt if anyone making a list of the half-dozen or so fastest bowlers the game has known, would omit the name of Larwood – not at the pace he was bowling in 1932. Jardine perceived, or possibly Carr had perceived it first, that in Larwood he had the weapon which could beat Australia.

That meant, in effect, getting Bradman out, because England were at this period clearly the better side if only they could put a devil into that terrible little machine.

There was not much evidence to encourage this faith in Larwood, on the face of it. He was certainly fast, and willing, and a beautiful sight when he was bowling (I saw him myself in 1932, and can capture the memory now) but his Test record really was not very good up to that point. He had taken 31 wickets in three series against Australia, at an average of 41. On the other hand he had not been very fit in 1930, and in both following seasons he headed the first-class bowling averages, with these figures:

	O	M	R	W	Av'ge
1931	651·3	142	1,553	129	12·03
1932	866·4	203	2,084	162	12·86

It has sometimes been suggested – by Warner himself, among others – that Larwood would have been as successful on the 1932–3 tour had he kept to orthodox methods. As evidence for this it is pointed out that Allen, who refused to bowl bodyline, took 21 wickets in the Tests at 28 (Larwood 33 at 19), and although Allen was a fast bowler, he was some way short of Larwood's speed. But would Allen have been so successful without the demoralization spread by Larwood (and, to a lesser extent, Voce) among the Australian batsmen? It seems very doubtful. Jardine did not think so.

E. H. D. Sewell thinks that the improvement in Larwood's health and performance was due in part to a series of visits to the dentist, and it is true that before the touring party set sail Jardine insisted that every member of it should have a clean bill of health from the dentist; a point typical of his attention to detail.

England won the first Test by ten wickets after losing the toss, but Bradman had not been fit to play for Australia. For the second Test England dropped Verity, their only spinner, and Bowes came in as a fourth fast bowler. Bradman was back. He was cheered all the way to the wicket, and Bowes bowled him first ball. He pulled the ball on to his stumps. It was just outside the leg stump, but not a bouncer, which Bradman was clearly expecting. This was one of the rare occasions when Jardine showed emotion on the field. He was briefly to be seen hopping up and down with delight. It was Bowes's only wicket of the series, of which he has nevertheless given us one of the best accounts. In the second innings, Bradman scored 103, not out, and Australia won.

But that was his only century of the series. It was the only rubber England won while he was playing, apart from that of 1928–9 when he was hardly more than a boy. Bodyline therefore achieved its purpose. It also ended the Test career of Larwood. He limped off the field during the Australian second innings in the last Test, with a broken bone in his foot. Jardine would not let him go until Bradman was out. He returned to play for Nottinghamshire with success, but was never the same man again.

England won the third Test, 'the battle of Adelaide', by 338 runs. This was the match in which both Woodfull and Oldfield were struck by Larwood, and there was a substantial force of riot police on the ground, and Warner had words with Woodfull in the Australian dressing-room. England won the fourth Test by six wickets and the last by eight. There was an angry exchange of cables between the Australian Board of Control, and M.C.C. M.C.C. were much better at drafting cables, and also had a strong card in threatening to cancel the rest of the tour, though they put it much more delicately than that. But the verbal victory proved a hollow one, once it was realized at home just what had been going on. That took some time. The English mood at the end of the tour was aptly described by Swanton as 'foggily resentful'. Jardine was received home with much public acclaim. When Surrey played Yorkshire at Bramall Lane he was given a standing ovation all the way to the wicket. Larwood went home early, nursing his injury and his grievances. He had, after all, only done his duty and bowled to orders as a professional should, and had been abominably treated by some members of the Australian public. Arthur Carr came halfway to meet him. But as far as Larwood was concerned, no grudges were borne, and indeed he settled in Australia after the war. Very few Australians, however, ever brought themselves to forgive Jardine. This, we may be certain, did not disturb him.

In 1933 the West Indies were here, with two fast bowlers, or rather one-and-a-bit. Martindale was fast, probably as fast as anyone in the world except Larwood. Constantine was not as fast as he had been a few years earlier, but could still bowl a very fast ball from time to time: but he was under contract to the Lancashire League club Nelson, and could only play in a few matches for the tourists. One of these was the second Test at Old Trafford, and they decided to bowl bodyline. Constantine did not want to bowl it, not there. 'No', he told Grant, his captain, 'not at Old Trafford – it's too slow. Bowl it at Lord's.' But he could not play in the Lord's Test. He did play at Lord's in the M.C.C. match, but Grant did not want to waste his surprise on a lesser match. So Old Trafford it was, with Martindale and Constantine flinging the ball down short of a length with a packed leg-side field. Hammond was hit on the chin, though he was able to resume batting. Four wickets fell for 134, but Jardine scored 127 and England 374. Jardine never flinched. He played right back to the bouncers, standing on tiptoe, meeting them with a dead bat (he was not a hooker). It was, in its way, magnificent: but Martindale and Constantine at Old Trafford were not the same proposition as Larwood on an Australian pitch. Martindale took 5 for 73, Constantine 1 for 55. Clark of Northamptonshire bowled bodyline in the second West Indies innings. It was a valuable match, in that it gave many Englishmen a clearer knowledge of what had been going on. Farnes, who was very fast for an undergraduate, also bowled bodyline in the University match, and several Oxford batsmen were hit. It was to be seen from time to time in county matches, usually when Nottinghamshire were involved. But opinion was rapidly swinging against it, and its outlawry was not distant.

Jardine's position as England's captain was still unchallenged, but during the tour of India in the winter he announced that he would not play against the Australians in 1934. He accepted a contract to write about the series. He wrote his own account of the Australian tour, and a very interesting book it is, though Bradman had a point when he observed that you could read it from one end to the other without ever discovering just what bodyline was. Larwood also wrote a book, or put his name to it, and some explosive newspaper articles. The situation had reached the point when it was clear that if the 1934 tour was to go on, Australia would require an assurance that bodyline would not be bowled, and it was also clear that Jardine would not give such an assurance. (That does not mean to say he would have bowled it, but he would certainly have reserved the right to.) His resignation therefore resolved the problem, though it caused disappointment among the more warlike Englishmen. I have never felt he has had sufficient credit for it. If he had stayed on to be sacked there would have been such an outcry, such bitterness, that cricketing relations between the two countries might well have been endangered even more than in 1932–3.

'But apart from all that, Mrs Lincoln. . . ?' How good a captain was Jardine in other respects? He commanded great loyalty from his team, even though there were others, besides Allen, who disapproved of his tactics. While stern in his discipline he was zealous in looking after their welfare. One hot, fierce day Larwood lunched off sips of champagne, personally administered by the captain. He was not very good at communication. He upset Bowes early in the tour by giving him orders which he made no attempt to explain, though a word or two would have been sufficient. But he struck up an excellent relationship with Sutcliffe, the senior professional, though on the 1928–9 tour of Australia Sutcliffe had thought him 'a queer devil'. He offered to drop himself from the side because he was not getting many runs, and insisted on leaving the rest of the selection committee while they discussed it. They talked about the weather. Ray Robinson, the Australian cricket writer, thought he was inclined to panic when wickets were not falling, fussing his fieldsmen around unnecessarily, but this is not a widely held view: most critics praise him for his meticulous field-placing. He had immense courage and immense pride. Once he was severely hit, and the crowd cheered, but he would not rub himself. At the end of his innings he entered the England dressing-room, apparently unmoved, said 'Close the door', and collapsed. There was blood on his flannels. He batted in a Harlequin cap, which infuriated the Australians. Of course it was not really the cap which infuriated them, but its wearer. Warner had often worn a Harlequin cap. Chapman had worn all sorts of odd caps and they loved him for it. Jardine was so insistent on the cap because he knew it infuriated them, and they knew he knew, which infuriated them still more. He would not have been a popular captain with the public even without bodyline, but he would have been, in his own style, a pretty good one.

He was a man of irony rather than humour, but Robertson-Glasgow records that, for all his taciturnity, 'his cursing, at its best, was Elizabethan in scope and variety'. He was a stern judge of himself as well as others. Once after batting a long time in Australia, and scoring very slowly, he apologized to an Australian for playing 'like an old spinster defending her honour'. Test matches, for all his success in them, did not bring out the best of his batting style.

The last match in which he captained an English side was at Bombay, a special match added to the tour for the benefit of the Indian Earthquake Fund. According to *Wisden*, he 'packed the leg-side with fieldsmen': which may have been a last gesture of defiance, but then again, since his only fast bowler on that occasion was Morris Nichols, a worthy performer but no hurricane, may not.

With Jardine absent, and the 1934 series going ahead after some hiccoughs, the obvious choice as England's captain was Wyatt, who had been vice-captain in Australia, and had taken over when Jardine was injured for the third Test against the West Indies in 1933. Wyatt was not one of the more successful England captains. He led in 16 matches, of which three were won, five lost and eight drawn. He never won a rubber. Nevertheless his tactful handling of the situation in 1934 was of great service to cricket. Fortunately, too, the Australian captain was again that true sportsman, Woodfull. Bodyline was still in the air, especially when Bradman began getting among the runs again. When he was piling them on at Leeds a spectator called up to the press box 'We want you out there, Jardine', and tactical questions apart, Jardine was missed as a batsman in a series when the English batting too frequently crumbled after a fair start. Voce bowled bodyline for Nottinghamshire against the Australians. Carr was not playing in the match but was still the county captain, and nobody doubted who was responsible. The Australians finished the match, but protested. Voce did not appear on the last day, suffering, it was announced, from sore shins. Nottinghamshire were required to apologize and did. There was a full-scale row in the Nottinghamshire club that winter, as one of the results of which Carr departed from the captaincy. Before the following season M.C.C. instructed the umpires that 'the persistent and systematic bowling of fast short-pitched balls' was forbidden, and any bowler who offended could be barred until the end of the innings. The bumper is with us to this day, sometimes to excess, but that instruction, and the later legislation about limiting the leg-side field, made it impossible for anyone to bowl bodyline as Larwood and Voce had bowled it in Australia.

The match at Nottingham was as unpleasant as could be, and there was a good deal of wild English talk about Australian 'squealers', but thanks to Wyatt and Woodfull the Tests passed off in relative harmony. Australia won the first Test by 238 runs and the last by 562 runs. England won the second by an innings and 38 runs. The third and fourth were drawn. This suggests a fairly close series, but in fact Australia were much the stronger side. Wyatt points out that if England had saved the first Test, which they failed to do by only ten minutes, they might have won the rubber, since the last Test would not then have been played to a finish, but such a result would have been unjust. There were far more 'ifs' on the other side – if, for instance, Australia had saved the follow-on at Lord's, where Verity bowled them out on a damp pitch; and if it had not rained at Leeds when England were in a hopeless position.

In the first Test Wyatt, with a damaged thumb, was unable to play – he was prone to broken bones, and Ray Robinson once called him 'Brittle Bob' – and Walters was made captain, as the only other amateur in the side, except for Pataudi and Farnes. He seems to have done the job well enough, and Wyatt was on the spot to advise him, but it was his first match against Australia. Sutcliffe was playing, yet even if the amateurs-only rule had not been followed, the captaincy – bearing in mind the custom of going by seniority among professionals – would presumably have gone to Hendren, who had been recalled to the England side. Hendren was thought not to want the job very much. What would have happened if Walters had not been chosen for the team (he was not by any means a certainty)? Would the job have gone to young Farnes, just down from Cambridge and the fast bowler? Would we have had an Indian captain? Or would somebody have been called in specially to lead the side, Allen perhaps? It did not arise, but it could have been an awkward situation, and once again stirred thoughts of professional captaincy.

A word about Walters. He had played three times against the West Indies in 1933, and three times under Jardine in India. With the five matches against Australia this year, that was all his Test cricket. He was a handsome, attacking batsman, who opened the innings in the old-fashioned style. Six times in the series he passed 40, with a highest score of 82. His average in all Tests was 52. He gave up cricket early. He was born in 1905, a Welshman, and played for Glamorgan for several seasons, but in 1928 left them to become secretary of Worcestershire, for whom he qualified by residence. He was captain of Worcestershire from 1931 to 1935. There were many who thought him too rash for Test cricket, but many more who relished him. His Test career was too brief for a conclusive judgment.

Wyatt continued as captain in the West Indies in the winter, and at home against South Africa. Although he did not captain England again, he went to Australia again, under Allen, and was not far from the England side in 1938. He continued playing cricket after the war, moving from Warwickshire to Worcestershire. He was the Warwickshire captain from 1930 to 1937, the Worcestershire captain in 1950 and 1951. He enjoyed his cricket, despite all the knocks he took, and was reluctant to give it up. He played in 40 Tests altogether, with an average of 32. In his earlier days he was a useful medium-paced bowler, and took 18 wickets in Tests at an average of 35. He was a Surrey man by birth, born at Milford in 1901. He was always ready for a tour abroad in the winter, and was the first man to visit all five of the then Test-playing countries, as well as several others. Altogether he scored nearly 40,000 runs at an average of 40, and took nearly 900 wickets. He scored 85 centuries. These figures show what a thoroughly sound cricketer he was. His style, however, was marked more by stubbornness than gracefulness, and though he could hit the ball hard he never quite became a public favourite. He did not *look* the kind of person it is easy to warm to, though he was both liked and respected by his teams. He fell out with Warwickshire in somewhat perplexing circumstances, upon which his own book throws no very revealing light, but he played on for them until the war under the new captain, Peter Cranmer, with whom he soon established an amicable relationship. If Wyatt is not a name to give the eyes a reminiscent sparkle, it is very rarely you hear anyone speak unkindly of him. His deep love of animals, an attribute shared by many reserved men, seems very much in character.

As a Test captain he had a reputation of being unlucky, and in the sense of injuries he certainly was. The criticism frequently made of him is that he was too much of a theorist, and it does seem to have some force. He was always ready to change the batting order to suit the circumstances of the game. In the first and second Tests in the West Indies he almost reversed it, winning the first but losing the second. It was absurd, however you like to look at it, that the last three batsmen in the England order, when England were trying to save the match in Trinidad, were Leyland, Iddon, and E. R. T. Holmes. Leyland was then potentially England's best batsman, since Sutcliffe had not been chosen for the trip, and Hammond was not making many runs. Iddon had scored 73 and Holmes 85 not out in the first innings. England lost the match with only two or three minutes to go. Wyatt's explanation of this at the time, repeated many years later, was that he was afraid of what the new ball might do on the matting wicket. It was not a convincing explanation then, and it is not a convincing explanation now. That Leyland was given out to a bad decision – Constantine, the bowler, agreed afterwards that he had only appealed in the heat of the moment for a ball which hit the batsman high on the thigh – does not affect the unwisdom of the tactics. There were possibly some hidden animosities lying behind England's failure on this tour; I doubt if Wyatt was responsible for them, except in the sense that he failed to control them. But he was not to blame for the depressing collapse with which England ended the series. He had suffered a badly fractured jaw early in the first innings, and Holmes, the vice-captain, took over.

Warner has told us how Wyatt's stubbornness could extend to selection. Particularly he describes Wyatt's insistence on having Mitchell of Derbyshire in the side for the second Test in 1935. The wickets at Lord's were poor ones that year because of a plague of leather-jackets, and Wyatt was sure that Mitchell's leg-breaks would win the match. The other selectors would have preferred Robins, but Wyatt had his way. He then over-used Mitchell in an attempt to demonstrate his point. Then in the last Test of that series he put South Africa in to bat on a plumb Oval wicket. The reasoning was that England, one down in the rubber, were going to find it difficult to bowl South Africa out twice in three days. By putting them in first they might hope to avoid too long a stint in the field, and take advantage of any early life in the pitch, as was sometimes to be found at the Oval at that time. As against that, Australia had scored 475 for 2 on the first day there the previous year, and the South African morale cannot have been too high after two consecutive defeats in county matches. The gamble looked as if it might be coming off when South Africa were 333 for 8, but there was a long partnership between Dalton and Langton, and they reached 476. Although England led, the game was comfortably saved. Wyatt had taken the risk with his eyes open and had to bear the criticism, as Carr had to do nine years earlier.

He was asked to take the M.C.C. side to New Zealand that winter, but reluctantly declined in order to take a rest, bearing in mind the tour of Australia in the following winter. He might have been wiser to go, because for a long time in 1936 he could find no form, and was only chosen for Australia at all when Holmes withdrew.

Allen was to become one of the father-figures of M.C.C., though his England captaincy was limited to the three matches against India, the five in Australia, and four in the West Indies after the war. In Australia he was faced with the same kind of problem as had confronted Wyatt in England: restoring good relations. In this the tour was outstandingly successful, though the rubber was lost, after England had won the first two Tests. In 1937, with Allen unable to give much time to cricket, Robins took over against New Zealand, but Allen was obviously a strong candidate for the captaincy against Australia again in 1938. However, in the autumn of 1937 Hammond had announced his intention of playing in future as an amateur. From that moment, according to Warner's later account – he was still the chairman of selectors – there was never any real doubt that Hammond would be England's next captain, and so it was. He drew the rubber in 1938. After two drawn matches and one wash-out, Australia won a low-scoring match at Leeds, and England the famous match at the Oval, when they scored over 900 and Hutton broke Bradman's individual record.

Hammond continued for two more series before the war and two more after it. His reputation as a captain, like Allen's to a lesser extent, would stand higher had he not returned in the post-war years. An assessment of the careers of these two men, so different yet so often interwoven, may be more properly made when we reach that period.

7

THE LORD DESERTS HAWKE

It is beginning to be hinted that we are a nation of amateurs
Lord Rosebery (in 1900)

In time all haggard hawks will stoop to lure
Thomas Kyd (in 1592)

There have been so many Test matches played by England in the last quarter of a century or so, with not only every summer but nearly every winter occupied, that it seems best to set them out in chronological order, before we begin to look at the captains in more detail. Here is the pattern from the time when Hammond resumed command, in 1946, to the retirement (as it proved) of Hutton, the first modern professional captain, at the end of the Australian tour of 1954-5.

Year	Opponents	Result			Captain
		W.	L.	D.	
1946	India	1	0	2	W. R. Hammond
1946–7	Australia	0	3	2	W. R. Hammond (4)
					N. W. D. Yardley (1)
1946–7	New Zealand	0	0	1	W. R. Hammond
1947	South Africa	3	0	2	N. W. D. Yardley
1947–8	West Indies	0	2	2	G. O. Allen (3)
					K. Cranston (1)
1948	Australia	0	4	1	N. W. D. Yardley
1948–9	South Africa	2	0	3	F. G. Mann
1949	New Zealand	0	0	4	F. G. Mann (2)
					F. R. Brown (2)
1950	West Indies	1	3	0	N. W. D. Yardley (3)
					F. R. Brown (1)
1950–1	Australia	1	4	0	F. R. Brown

166

Year	Opponents	Result			Captain
		W.	L.	D.	
1950–1	New Zealand	1	0	1	F. R. Brown
1951	South Africa	3	1	1	F. R. Brown
1951–2	India	1	1	3	N. D. Howard (4)
					D. B. Carr (1)
1952	India	3	0	1	L. Hutton
1953	Australia	1	0	4	L. Hutton
1953–4	West Indies	2	2	1	L. Hutton
1954	Pakistan	1	1	2	L. Hutton (2)
					D. S. Sheppard (2)
1954–5	Australia	3	1	1	L. Hutton
1954–5	New Zealand	2	0	0	L. Hutton

The most immediately striking things about that list are the resemblance of the Australian matches to those following the First World War (a heavy defeat in Australia, a heavy defeat at home, a 4–1 defeat in Australia which yet contained signs of hope, and then the recovery of the Ashes at the Oval by the only match settled in the series); the first victory of the West Indies in England, in 1950; and the appointment, in 1952, of a professional captain.

One or two of these England captains need not detain us too long. Kenneth Cranston deputized for Allen in the first Test of the West Indies tour, in 1947–8. He was a relative newcomer to first-class cricket, who captained Lancashire in 1947 and 1948, in his early thirties. He played in all four Tests of Allen's tour, and at home three times against South Africa in 1947, and once against Australia in 1948. He was a bowler of brisk medium pace, and a useful batsman in the lower middle of the order: about the nearest thing England had in those days to an all-rounder. He took 18 Test wickets, average 26, and scored just over 200 runs, average 15. In the Test at Leeds in 1947, he brought the South African second innings to an end by taking their last four wickets in an over, which gave him an analysis of 4 for 12. This is another example of how hard it is to judge a man's potential merits on a brief career. A few more years in the game, and he might have become a regular England captain. Jim Swanton, who had come across him during the war in the Liverpool and District Competition, had recognized Cranston as 'a spirited and gifted cricketer'.

Nigel Howard, the son of a former Lancashire secretary, Rupert Howard, succeeded Cranston as captain of Lancashire in 1949, and held the post until 1954, when, professional captaincy having been accepted even at the England level, Washbrook succeeded him. He was a good player, Howard, not of England standard, but good enough to be chosen to play for the Gentlemen. He averaged nearly 40 for Lancashire in 1950, in which year he led them to a joint championship with Surrey. He only played for England when taking the side to India in 1951–2. His Test match average was 17, with a highest score of 23, and he did not bowl. He was a good fieldsman, particularly a good catcher: a young man to be captain, born in 1925. He once scored a century before lunch, and though we must not make too much of this, because it was for Lancashire Second XI against Nottinghamshire Second XI, it is not a feat to be despised. He was a proper Lancastrian, born at Preston and educated at Rossall. His teams liked him. I once heard it said, on a Lancashire ground, that he would have made a better captain than MacLaren, 'given the talent'. Ah, 'given the talent'! Many of us would consider ourselves to be better England captains than MacLaren, if it was not for that little matter of the talent.

In the last Test of that Indian series, D. B. Carr took over the team. I am now moving into the period where some of these England captains have been acquaintances, and even friends, of mine, which makes judgement more difficult. It is easier to judge a captain on what he has done, or what he has written – provided you can be reasonably sure he wrote it himself – than on what he says, especially in moments of stress, such as a radio interview or just after a bad lbw decision. Still, I have always liked and admired Carr, who has done much for the game since his retirement as a player. He is the only England captain ever to be born in Germany: at Wiesbaden in 1926. He went to Repton, where he was captain in 1944, and the following year, when the 'Victory Tests' were played against Australian sides, was chosen for the England XI. He was already marked as a possible future England captain. He played for Derbyshire in 1946, went to Oxford in 1948, captained them in 1950. He became assistant secretary of Derbyshire in 1953, and their captain in 1955. He never quite fulfilled his youthful promise as a batsman, although he could look very good at times, and his Test cricket was limited to two matches on the Indian tour (average 34). He was a fine football player, a member of the Pegasus sides which won the Amateur Cup at Wembley in 1951 and 1953, in that dying Corinthian flourish.

D. S. Sheppard, now the Bishop of Liverpool, who captained England in two matches against Pakistan in 1954 (when Hutton was unfit), has a much more important part to play in the story of the England captaincy than that suggests. Twice it seemed quite likely, even probable, that he would take an England team to Australia, but those episodes can be dealt with in their place. He certainly had the character, and the technical ability, to make a success of it. He was born in Reigate, Surrey, a town which has produced many excellent cricketers (as well as W. G. Bunter), but Sussex was his playing county. He was their captain in 1953, and the year before he had captained Cambridge. He had been at school at Sherborne, but except for his skill at cricket did not resemble A. W. Carr. He played in 22 Test matches, and had a batting average of 38. Had it not been for his call to the church, he would have played in many more. He wrote, when still quite young, a book called *Parson's Pitch*, less a cricket book than the tale of his spiritual pilgrimage. It is deeply interesting to read how a man of Christian convictions argued out with himself such questions as whether he ought to accept the England captaincy, whether he should play against South Africa, and even such tactical questions such as whether he should ask his players to bowl defensively down the leg side. This last may sound trivial, but for Sheppard his faith is his life, and there is no part of his life where his faith does not enter. A great many cricketers were grateful to him for his leadership when the question of the proposed 1970 South African tour was dominating our minds. Not even those who disagreed with him doubted his integrity, and he proved to be better informed (though scrupulously refusing to use private information) than most of his critics. For myself, in general terms, I find his theology a little on the evangelical side (which may sound an odd thing to say, coming from a Baptist local preacher to an Anglican bishop) but I have no doubt he will be reckoned one of the Christian leaders of Britain in his time, and he was a pretty good cricketer too.

G. O. B. Allen, known from his initials as 'Gubby', was another of those England captains born abroad. He was born, of all places, at Sydney, in 1902. He learnt his cricket, however, at Eton and Cambridge. Here was yet another who was unable to give so much time to the game as he would have liked, but he managed to make 25 Test appearances, 11 of them as captain (won four, lost five). He was a fast bowler, not quite of the highest class – he gained in accuracy as he grew older, but naturally lost something in speed – with the additional advantage of being a hard-hitting batsman in the middle of the order. He took 81 wickets in Tests at an average of 30, good figures when you consider how much he had to bowl against Bradman – he played his first Test in 1930 and his last in 1948, which nearly covers the Bradman years. He once got Bradman out for 0, but that was on a bad pitch, and on only one other occasion did he get him out in a Test. His Test batting average was 24, for 750 runs.

We think of Allen in latter days as a patriarchal, though not aloof, figure at Lord's, but his playing days could be tempestuous. Of his earlier career, Robertson-Glasgow wrote, 'he was perhaps too easily depressed by failure'. When he became captain, he was well liked by his teams, though there were occasional storms in the West Indies in 1947–8. He did not have much practice at captaincy, since he could never give the time to be the regular captain of Middlesex. He was not a lucky England captain, though he was within distance of winning the rubber in Australia, and with the weaker side. That was not a well-chosen England side. It was not that any duds were picked, but better men were left at home. Sutcliffe, for instance, was discarded, and Paynter. Wyatt, at least in retrospect, felt that a risk might have been taken with Hutton and Compton, rather than, say, Fagg and Fishlock. In one Test, Allen made the experiment of opening the innings with Verity, since none of the supposed openers were scoring runs, except Barnett. Barnett and Verity made 53 together, the best England opening partnership of the series, and 45 in the second (the second-best) but the experiment was not tried again. Allen's tactics on the whole were orthodox – no doubt he was reacting to the assorted unorthodoxies of his predecessors, Jardine and Wyatt. In the earlier part of the tour he acted as a University captain, choosing the sides himself, but later a selection committee was set up. It was the last time, I think, that a captain assumed such powers, though there have been tours where you might not have noticed the difference. Allen's services to cricket on that Australian tour were, it must be stressed, immense, even though the rubber was lost. That he was Australian-born undoubtedly helped. In 1938, he was asked to captain the Rest in the Test trial, but had to withdraw because of injury. It would have made no difference. The selectors were set on Hammond.

It was probably a mistake for Allen to go to the West Indies in 1947, though it seemed a good idea that he should impart his wisdom to the young men of the side. It was not much better than an England Second XI, and suffered from injuries even more than most touring sides do. The captain himself, at the age of 45, had difficulty keeping fit. England lost the rubber, indeed did not win a first-class match on the tour, but the public atmosphere was happy, at least compared with some visits to the West Indies since.

He was chairman of selectors from 1955 to 1961, and has been one of the most influential men in English cricket over the last 25 years. Probably his most successful committee was that of 1956, when to strengthen the batting first Washbrook, then Sheppard, then Compton were recalled to the side, and in every case with success. Not that it was an entirely satisfying rubber for England, though it was comfortably won. It was the year that the Australians felt, with some justification, that the pitches offered to them unduly favoured the bowling of Laker and Lock.

And now Hammond. He played in 85 Tests, scoring 7,249 runs, average 58·45, and taking 83 wickets, average 37·83. He made 110 catches, nearly all of them in the slips. He scored 22 centuries, with a highest score of 336 not out against New Zealand, in its time a Test record. In all first-class cricket he made 50,493 runs, average 56·10, took 732 wickets, average 30·58, and 819 catches. There it is in massive figures, but even they cannot tell of his mastery, the brilliance of his youth, the poise of his maturity. Fortunately we have many witnesses to them.

He captained England in 20 Tests, from 1938 to 1947. He was born in 1903, so he was 35 when he became captain, after turning amateur. Of these matches, four were won (one against Australia), and three lost (all against Australia). He won some praise for his captaincy before the war (not just conventional praise; Fingleton, for instance, thought he was a good captain). After the war, he had some blame. Jim Swanton, in his later books, has been severe about him. I think it is fair to say that Hammond was not temperamentally well suited to the job. After his death, I introduced a radio programme about him, in which many of his contemporaries recorded their recollections of him. A word that kept cropping up was 'moody'. Even Tom Goddard, an old pal with whom he had shared rooms for years, used the word: with an affectionate shake of the head, to be sure, but he used it.

Hammond died in 1965, and not long afterwards, talking to a Gloucestershire friend who had seen many of the great innings, I was moved to quote Hardy's words – at the end of *Tess* – 'The President of the Immortals had ended his sport'. My friend was familiar enough with Hardy's bitter Aeschylean reference, but would not have it. 'Why', he said, 'Wally was just about the President of the Immortals himself!'

Yet Hammond's career, for all its grandeur, was pursued by an ironic fate, from its beginning to its end. His father was killed in action in the First World War, something that should not be forgotten in any judgment of the man. In 1918 the family moved to Cirencester, and it was at Cirencester Grammar School that he drew the attention of Gloucestershire, for whom he first played in 1920. He had no sooner begun than Lord Harris, you can bet, pointed out that he was not qualified for Gloucestershire, since he had been born in Kent, at Dover. Lord Harris was correct, but this was not one of his more gracious acts. If somebody in Gloucestershire had been a little more careful, the trouble could probably have been avoided. That meant there was little first-class cricket for Hammond, for two years. However, when he did start, qualified by residence, he did not waste time. In 1923, he scored 1,400 runs, average 28; in 1924 1,300, average 30; in 1925 1,800, average 35. In 1925–6 he went to the West Indies with Calthorpe's first team, which did not play recognized Test matches, and there was infected with a bug by a mosquito or some other creature. Early tours abroad for young and lusty cricketers are often hazardous. His illness was serious, and kept him out of cricket for all the 1926 season at home. Warner visited him in hospital, and cheered him up. Hammond nearly died, because British doctors did not then know much about Caribbean infections. In 1926, it has often been said, he would have been England's No. 3 or 4 against Australia. I dare say so, but when you look back at the sides of that time, who would have been dropped for him? Not the sacred Woolley, nor the hero of Lord's, Hendren? Chapman, perhaps, and then who would have succeeded Carr as captain, and taken the next side to Australia? But I will not go into that again.

In 1928, Hammond set off to Australia under Chapman, and seemed to have put his disappointments behind him. In 1927, he had played an innings of 187, in three hours, against Lancashire at Old Trafford. He batted against MacDonald, then at his peak, and anxious to polish off the match on the third morning to get to the races. Cardus always regarded this innings as one of the best he had ever seen, and so did another young Lancastrian, Arthur Wrigley. The match was saved, and MacDonald had no racing that day.

Now that Hobbs was approaching his end, nobody doubted that Hammond would succeed him as England's most dominating batsman, and this he was, for a decade. Herbert Sutcliffe, it must not be forgotten, had a higher average, and Herbert was the man to score a hundred runs for your life when the going was grim, but his batting never gave quite the sense of majesty and excitement that Hammond's did. (But I revert to the thought that Sutcliffe would have made a better England captain.)

In 1928–9, in Australia, Hammond scored a record number of runs for a series: two double centuries, and then two centuries in the same match. He would, of course, be the greatest batsman, not only in England but in the world, for as long as he cared to play. But in this same series, a youngster called Bradman appeared in the Australian side, and after an uncertain start – he was dropped for the second Test – played an innings which won Australia the last one. Maurice Tate, meaning it kindly, told Bradman that he would have to keep his bat a bit straighter when he came to England. What Bradman did to Tate in 1930 an Englishman can hardly bear to recollect.

For in 1930 Bradman, in a display of flawless batting which has never been equalled, not even by himself, not even by Grace in 1876 or 1895, not even by Hobbs in 1925 nor Trumper in 1902, broke Hammond's 1928–9 records for a Test series, in both aggregate and average. Hammond himself had, in comparison, a poor series. He was troubled by Grimmett, who got him out five times in his first six innings; though according to some accounts he was England's best bowler. So there it was. For the rest of his career, Hammond was destined to be only the *second-best* batsman in the world (possibly not even that, but we had not learned to take the West Indies and George Headley seriously then): and he was not, so far as his cricket went, a man content to be second-best.

His cricketing life, thenceforth, was overshadowed by Bradman. In 1932–3, in Australia, Bradman was 'tamed', as it was genteelly put, by Larwood and Jardine, but still averaged slightly more than Hammond. In 1934, Hammond had an unhappy series, never scoring 50, and Bradman won the rubber with a triple and a double century. Next time in Australia, Hammond scored two hundred at Sydney, to give Allen his 2–0 lead. But Bradman scored prodigiously again, and the rubber was lost. On the last morning of the fourth Test, England still had a chance. They had led by 42 on the first innings, batting second (this was the Test in which Verity opened), and although Bradman had scored 212, they still had a chance. At the end of the fifth day, Hammond and Leyland were together, our two best batsmen. The score was 148 for 3, a total of 392 needed to win. It was not impossible, because the pitch was still playing well.

Hammond was bowled, with the day's third ball, by Fleetwood-Smith. There was a particular irony to this. Fleetwood-Smith was a left-arm googly bowler, a rarity in those days. The England side of 1932–3 had heard all about him, and feared him. In an early match against Victoria, Hammond was adjured to set about him. He scored 203, and Fleetwood-Smith, whose figures were 25–3–124–2, did not play in any of the Tests. After the match Hammond, who was capable of a generous gesture, went out of his way to seek out Fleetwood-Smith, who was 22 at the time, and spent some time giving him words of encouragement and advice (I doubt if Jardine would have approved). Fleetwood-Smith never forgot this act of kindness.

Anyway, that morning at Adelaide four years later, Fleetwood-Smith had his revenge, and Australia won by 148 runs. It turned out to be the decisive moment of the rubber. George Duckworth said sombrely, 'You wouldn't get Don out in first over with Ashes at stake.' This was Hammond's problem. It was not enough for him to do well. He had to do better than Bradman.

So we come to 1938, when the men were rival captains. Two Tests were drawn and one washed out. In the fourth, at Headingley, Hammond scored 76 in the first innings, Bradman 102. This was just about the difference between the totals of the two sides. In the second innings, Hammond was out for 0, and from then on Australia were winning. In England's massive win at the Oval, the fact that Bradman had had to leave the field, injured and could not bat, took a little off the edge of the delight. It is said that Hammond demanded medical assurances that Bradman would be unfit to bat, before he declared England's innings at 903 for 7. Thus the rubber was square, but Australia kept the Ashes, and there was a feeling that England were the stronger side, and ought to have done better.

And then there was the post-war tour to Australia. Was Hammond right to go? Did he believe that one last tilt could square the balance with his ancient enemy? He had scored runs in the 'Victory Tests', when again he had been England's captain. He had scored runs, though his season was limited, in England in 1946, when he was captain against India. In Australia he scored runs, in the lesser matches, but failed in the Tests. Bradman went remorselessly on. It was thought (though I doubt it) that Bradman, who had been unwell, might retire if he suffered a couple of early failures. In the first Test, Bradman had scored 28 when he seemed so obviously caught, by Ikin at second slip, that the English side did not bother to appeal. Hammond, at first slip, sat down with a sigh of relief. But Bradman stayed at the crease, and when an appeal was ultimately made, it was turned down. At the end of the over, Hammond said to Bradman, 'That's a bloody fine way to start a series', and the captains were scarcely on speaking terms for the rest of the tour. Bradman scored 187 in that innings, and in the following Tests scored 234, 79, 49, 0, 56 not out, 12, and 63. Hammond scored 32, 23, 1, 37, 9, 26, 18, 22, and did not play in the last match. He returned home heavily defeated, and that, apart from an odd match here or there, was the end of his first-class cricket.

Do not think that in looking at Hammond's career in this light I am unaware of his merits. I saw enough of him to remember the splendour of his off-side play. He was, for a year or three, the best all-rounder English cricket had had since Grace – and I do not forget Wilfred Rhodes and George Hirst. He was the best batsman England has had since 1918 (counting Hobbs as pre-1914) except possibly Hutton. These are things impossible to prove, but they are my own judgments, for what they are worth. Hammond gave to cricket, and cricket gave to Hammond, everything – except the things he wanted most.

I saw his last county match, in 1951. Gloucestershire were in trouble with injuries, and he was persuaded to come back for the Whitsuntide game against Somerset. I shall never forget his reception, from one of the biggest crowds I have seen on the Bristol ground. They were kept waiting a long time, while Emmett and Milton scored 200 for the first wicket. It might have been better if that partnership had ended sooner. The crowd were no more than mildly appreciative of the graceful Emmett and the steadfast Milton: it was Hammond they had come to see. When he came, he batted for half an hour or so, scoring 7, all in singles. There was not one attempt at a forcing stroke. In the evening we watched him fielding at slip. He stood there immobile, scarcely bending. We discovered afterwards that he had strained a muscle, and he took no further part in the match. We hoped that we might see him play again, but we never did.

His life after that had its measure of disappointments and difficulties. Cardus wrote, in his memorial tribute in *Wisden*, 'His cricket was, I think, his only way of self-realization.' He emigrated to South Africa, but returned to England for a while, shortly before his death, to help Gloucestershire with a financial appeal. It fell to me to be one of his interviewers, and this was the only occasion I talked to him for any length of time. The impression he gave was of a quiet stoicism, of a man who had not found life easy but had come to terms with it. He was 62 when he died.

You can see, I hope, why I spoke to my friend of the President of the Immortals ending his sport.

And now we come to Norman Yardley, who, whatever his shortcomings, which are not numerous, is a much more cheerful person to write about. N. W. D. Yardley takes us back to the older tradition of captaincy, not so much in his own style – his batting was more sound than showy, and his best strokes made to the on-side – but in background. He followed a famous public school, St Peter's (York), with Cambridge. He was the first Yorkshireman to lead England against Australia since Jackson (it must be remembered that Yorkshire amateurs were rare, though A. B. Sellers might have been a possibility in 1938, had not Hammond changed his status). Yardley was destined to the succession before the war. He had been twelfth man against Australia in 1938, then aged 23, and vice-captain to Hammond in South Africa the following winter, though he only played in one Test. His quality as a cricketer and a man was not doubted, and he was again chosen as Hammond's vice-captain in 1946–7, though he had not been showing much form at home. That was a hard assignment for Yardley. He had much of the handling of the side off the field, since Hammond usually travelled apart from the rest, by car. He took over the captaincy on the field for the last Test, when Hammond was injured, or feeling injured. He had a most successful tour as a player, which few others did. Repeatedly he propped up the England batting from No. 7 or thereabouts, and he also turned out to be, unexpectedly, a valuable bowler. He had hardly ever bowled for Yorkshire, but then the Yorkshire attack in the last few years before the war was stronger than the England attack in the first few years after it. Yardley took 10 wickets in the series, including, unbelievably, that of Bradman, three times running. His team-mates christened him 'Spof'. He never *looked* like a bowler. He came perilously near, with his gentle medium-paced seamers, to bowling 'off the wrong foot'.

Yardley played altogether in 20 Test matches, in which he scored 812 runs, average 25, and took 21 wickets, average 34. He was captain in 14, of which four were won and seven were lost. After the Australian tour, he was the obvious captain against South Africa in 1947. This was a rubber comfortably won, thanks chiefly to the astonishing batting of Compton and Edrich in their golden season. In 1948 he was captain again, against Australia, and although there were some complaints when England kept losing matches, and suggestions towards the end, as we have noticed, that Robins might replace him, it was improbable that anyone could have done much better against that Australian team. He could not go to South Africa on the 1948–9 tour. F. G. Mann went instead, and did so well that he was first choice against New Zealand in 1949. But in 1950, with the West Indies in England, Yardley was England's captain again, and there could hardly have been any dispute that he would be the best man to take the side to Australia in 1950, except (or including) Mann. Neither could go, and there have been mild arguments ever since as to who got his refusal in first. Yardley was a man who worked hard at his business, and would I am sure much have liked to lead England in Australia. Nor is there any doubt that he would have done it well, though there is always something to be said, if you are in a losing run, for a change of captains.

In 1953, before the drastic decision to appoint a professional was made, Yardley's was still the name most mentioned as the likeliest England captain. Early that season I was sitting next at dinner to Jim Swanton (I hope he will not mind my recalling the conversation) and he said that if there was to be an amateur captain, Yardley had no serious competitor.

Norman Yardley was, and is, immensely liked and respected. I have hardly ever heard an unkind word said of him. I shall not forget how he guided and helped me in my first Test match radio commentary, at Edgbaston in 1962. He could easily have scored points off a raw and relatively young commentator, who had no first-class cricket behind him; but always was generous, to an extent, among Test match summarizers, which I have known only Trevor Bailey to reach. Norman was also generous, sometimes more than Trevor was, to the players. He could suffer fools gladly, and in one way and another, at one time or another, he has had to.

It has to be faced, though, that his record as a captain is a little disappointing. When he led Cambridge in 1938, they did not win a match. When he was captain of Yorkshire, from 1948 to 1955, they never won the championship outright, though they shared it with Middlesex in 1949. They were fourth in 1948, third in 1950, second in 1951 and 1952, a grim joint twelfth in 1953, second again in 1954 and 1955. This was an admirable record for any captain except a Yorkshire one. They had good enough players to do it, or so it seems looking back, though they had to face one of the strongest county sides ever known, as Surrey approached their peak.

Tactically, Yardley was considered the best county captain among his contemporaries. He never gave anything stupidly away, but was always ready to run a reasonable risk. This was, I remember, the general view among the professionals of the time. He knew more about the detail of a game – how to cut off a batsman's favourite strokes, where his bowlers ought to pitch the ball, and so on – than Stuart Surridge, who led Surrey to six of their seven consecutive championships, from 1952 to 1957 (May took over in 1958). He was worth his place in a Yorkshire side, and usually in an England side, just on his merits as a player. The same could not strictly be said of Surridge, given the Surrey bowling at that time (two Bedsers, Loader, Laker and Lock). Yet Surridge seemed to get a little more out of his sides than Yardley did. Yorkshire were certainly not an easy side to lead, and rarely have been; but Surrey also, in those years, had an awkward cuss or two.

Why was this? Was it because Yardley did not bully his sides, did not lose his temper with them, as Sellers, for instance, sometimes did? I expect Yardley would say that things have come to a pretty pass if a captain, to get results, has to be a bully. Was it because he did not mix with them sufficiently, off the field? This suggestion has been made, but it is sharply contradicted by a number of those who played under him, and I find it difficult to believe. No doubt his tours as vice-captain to Hammond had not given him, in this respect, a fortunate example, but Yardley, though a quiet man, is no introvert.

176

Was it because a Cambridge Blue and, say, a miner's son, found it difficult to strike a sympathetic note in the post-war era? This also has been suggested, but is nonsense. Neither Yardley's accent nor his demeanour suggested any superiority over the professional player. In fact if you heard him in conversation with Herbert Sutcliffe in the committee tent at Scarborough, your immediate thought would have been that Sutcliffe was the former England captain, and Yardley the former lad from the ground staff.

Yet Yardley was aloof in one respect: in the words of Peter Thomas, 'The intrigue and politics sometimes evident under the surface of cricket was repugnant to him'. J. M. Kilburn wrote that 'fighting for its own sake made no particular appeal to him'. The fierce, rude, gamesmanlike Test cricket of today would not have attracted him, and in his own time he could see cricket moving in that direction. It has been said that he was 'too nice a man' to be a successful captain. That will not quite do, because many successful captains have been nice men. Yet 'nice' is a word with various meanings, and if in Yardley's case we interpret it as 'fastidious', we are perhaps getting somewhere near him.

There was a problem about the captaincy to South Africa in the winter of 1948–9. Not only was Yardley unable to go, but so was Edrich, who had brought himself, theoretically, into the reckoning by turning amateur in 1947. Edrich, deservedly or not, had not been thought a good tourist in 1946–7, and in fact was never to captain England, though he still had much Test cricket before him, and several years as captain of Middlesex. The name of Dollery was mentioned as a possibility, although he was a professional. He had been joint captain of Warwickshire in 1948, and made a very good impression, subsequently confirmed. But the professional barrier still held, and certainly it would not have made much sense to ask a professional captain to begin his duties with an overseas tour.

George Mann had also made a good impression in his first year's captaincy of Middlesex, and it was not forgotten that his father's England captaincy, though brief, had been admired – also in South Africa. I am not suggesting any nepotism: heredity is a legitimate thing for selectors to take into account. The difficulty with Mann was that he was not, on the form he had shown so far, a good enough batsman. His batting average was low. He had scored only three centuries in first-class cricket. He was a natural leader, full of enthusiasm, a fine fieldsman: but suppose he failed with the bat, who then would lead the side? In the event S. C. Griffith went as vice-captain. It is true that earlier in the year Griffith had scored a century, opening the innings in his first Test, under Allen in the West Indies, when called into the side as very nearly the last of the walking wounded available: but that had been something of a miracle. If you played him as an opener in South Africa, you would have to drop either Hutton or Washbrook. If you played him as a wicket-keeper, he would certainly do the job well, but then you would have to drop Evans, which at the time seemed unthinkable.

The selectors were therefore taking a big risk with Mann's batting. It was justified. On the first day of first-class cricket, at the Cape against Western Province – not at the time a particularly strong side – M.C.C. bowled and fielded feebly, and faced a score of 386 for 4. On the second day, Mann went in with three wickets down and scored a century, which he completed with a six, and from that moment his side began to grow and flourish together like the green bay tree.

England's 2–0 win in the rubber was narrower than it sounds, since they won the first Test by only two wickets (the occasion when Gladwin and Bedser ran a leg-bye from the last ball) and the last by three, when they had been set to score 174 in 95 minutes. With no really fast bowler, they had difficulty in getting South Africa out. But they were the more enterprising side, scoring their runs at much the faster rate, with Mann prepared to take risks and judging them skilfully, as well as making a useful contribution himself, including a century in the last Test. In fact the series was something of a triumph for him. 'As a captain', wrote *Wisden* in its survey of the tour, 'he was ideal, zealous to a degree, and considerate in all things at all times.'

He was captain against New Zealand in 1949 for only two matches, since business was making its demands upon him. He gave up his captaincy of Middlesex at the end of that season. He was a real loss to the game, for he was only in his early thirties, having been born, at Byfleet, in 1917. He had been captain of the XI at Eton, and won his Blue at Cambridge in 1938, the year Yardley was captain. He was therefore captain of England seven times, winning two and losing none, and never played except as captain. His batting average was 37·60, a couple of points higher than his father's had been. He had gone to his father for advice, before setting out for South Africa, and had been told two things: never to accept a private invitation to dinner, and have as little to do with the press as possible. He carried out the first injunction, but not the second (his relations with the press were happy). The point about staying in for dinner is explained by Swanton:

> He thought his place was in the hotel dining-room with his team, irrespective of how many or how few happened to be there. They may not be many, but they were perhaps inclined to be the same ones who had either not been asked anywhere or had preferred to relax among their companions. It was one time and place where the captain could always be found.

As a wise, though different, piece of captaincy, this ranks with Jardine's insistence on visits to the dentist.

I must add a word or two about S. C. Griffith, known (cricketers rarely have gifts for nicknames) as Billy. He became secretary of M.C.C., a post which he held with dignity and restraint in tricky times. He played in only three Tests, that in the West Indies in which he scored his unexpected hundred, and two more on this tour of Mann's, when, since Evans had struck a bad patch, he was chosen as wicket-keeper. At their best, there was not much between them as wicket-keepers. Griffith was quieter, less demonstrative, less erratic. Evans was the extrovert, capable of extraordinary brilliance, and of pulling a fielding side around him by his sheer vigour and sense of attack. He did this more than once in a Test match. He has been known to miss catches by throwing them up before he caught them, a defect of his qualities, and I doubt if Griffith ever did that.

Griffith was born in Surrey, in 1914, went to school at Dulwich, and then to Cambridge, where he won his Blue in 1935. He toured New Zealand under Holmes, returning to Cambridge after his Antipodean winter (they did not find life too bad, the gentlemanly young athletes of those days, especially if they were at Cambridge). His name was often mooted as an England captain, especially for Australia in 1950, but there was always Evans. Griffith would not have shamed England either as captain or wicket-keeper. It was his misfortune that he had so outstanding a contemporary. In some other periods, he might have become one of the noblest names in this book.

That captaincy for Australia in 1950 was a problem. Let us look at the county captains that year, taking them in descending order down the championship.

Lancashire and Surrey were joint champions. Lancashire were led by Nigel Howard, whom we have discussed. Nowhere near the normal Test side. Surrey were led by M. R. Barton, making a brief return to first-class cricket. He had been an Oxford Blue in 1937, a good player, but again, inconceivable for Australia. Yorkshire, who came third, were led steadily by Yardley. Warwickshire came fourth, led by Dollery, who was, you remember, a professional. Derbyshire were fifth led by Vaulkhard, who did not play cricket very well but was, I remember from a fleeting acquaintance, a pleasant man. Worcestershire were sixth, led by Wyatt, but it was a little late to send Wyatt to Australia again, though I dare say he would not have minded. Gloucestershire were seventh. This was the last season of Basil Allen's captaincy. He had both preceded and succeeded Hammond, and was a sound county cricketer, 39 years old. Somerset were joint seventh, led by Stuart Rogers, a fair-haired and engaging hitter, not at all an England cricketer. Kent were ninth, under D. G. Clark, who later became an England manager but was never in the least likely to become an England player. Northamptonshire were tenth. Pause here. Their captain was F. R. Brown, who had joined them the previous season. He had spent many spasmodic years with Surrey, and made scattered appearances for England. He had been called in to replace Mann in 1949, but he had been born in 1910 and was not getting any slimmer. Glamorgan were eleventh, led by Wilfred

Wooller, who was to continue to lead them until 1956. I would give a good deal to have seen Wooller captaining an English side, but he was then also approaching 40, and had never come near making an England side in his prime (he was, of course, one of the best Rugby footballers who ever played for Wales, and his years of service to Welsh cricket are, like the man, formidable). Hampshire, who came twelfth, were led by Desmond Eagar, an excellent captain and a better cricketer than many think, but no, not Test match standard. Sussex, thirteenth, were captained by James Langridge, a professional, who had played for England before the war, and toured Australia under Hammond, without playing in a Test match. Langridge was 44. Middlesex were captained by Robins, returning for a season after Mann's lamented retirement. Robins had been born a month before Langridge. Nottinghamshire were captained by W. A. Sime, who has since become a distinguished (or at least controversial) judge. Leicestershire were captained by C. H. Palmer, in his first year with the county, a likely-looking player, but you could say no more, a personality genial rather than commanding. Essex, who came at the bottom of the table, though winning more matches than two of those above them, were theoretically captained by T. N. Pearce and D. J. Insole. As Pearce resigned at the end of May. Insole was practically their captain, and he was undoubtedly going to be an admirable cricketer; but he was only 24.

Of that list, the only serious possibilities were Dollery, Brown, and Insole. The prospect of a professional captain was again discussed, but there was still the argument that such an experiment would be better begun at home, and also that our batting depended so much on Hutton and Compton that neither of them should be given the extra responsibility – and if you were going to appoint a professional, they were the strongest candidates, despite the claims of Dollery. Tom Dollery, a prolific county scorer, in four Tests for England from 1948 to 1950, had only achieved a batting average of 10. Hutton had every qualification for captaincy, except experience of it. If he had decided to 'turn amateur' in the autumn of 1949, as Hammond had done in the autumn of 1937, he must have been England's next captain, come Yardley, come Mann. He did no such thing. It would have been foreign to his character.

There were, in 1950, several promising young amateurs about, but none of them had been on a major tour. In the meantime, Yardley was captain of England, against the West Indies. He did well for a time. He beat them, captaining M.C.C., at Lord's, and then won the first Test, at Old Trafford. This was an interesting match from the point of view of the future captaincy. Dollery was chosen. He scored 8 and 0, and never played for England again. Hubert Doggart was chosen. Doggart's background was Winchester, Cambridge, and Sussex. He had been appointed joint captain of Sussex, in 1950, by the committee, but the annual general meeting refused to confirm it, and James

Langridge was made the sole captain. This incident, trivial though it seems in retrospect, because Langridge was so near retirement, and Doggart was to spend so little of his time in first-class cricket, shows something of the feeling at the time between advocates of amateur and professional captaincy.

Doggart did rather better than Dollery at Old Trafford, scoring 29 and 22, and was chosen again for the second Test at Lord's, where he scored 0 and 25. That was his last appearance for England. Edrich played in the first two Tests, scoring 7, 71, 8 and 8. For the third Test, at Nottingham, Insole was chosen, still with an eye to the succession. He scored 21 and 0. Dewes, another Cantab, was brought in for the third and fourth, scoring 0, 67, 17 and 3, but Dewes was thought of as a possible batsman (he did indeed go to Australia) rather than a possible captain.

Had Dollery, or Doggart, or Insole, happened to score a hundred, England might have had a different captain in Australia the following winter. With hindsight, it is possible to say that each of them might have made a fair job of it, especially Insole. Insole, a gracious man who later became chairman of the selectors, was mostly a leg-side batsman. He was also a grammar school boy, from an ancient foundation which I attended briefly myself, Sir George Monoux, Walthamstow. If he had managed to play a large innings at Nottingham, he might have continued as England's captain for many Tests, and if he was worth considering for the Australian job at all, he should not have been discarded because of a failure. He ultimately played for England with much success, but not again until 1955.

But the selectors, and for that matter the press, and in consequence most of the public, were not thinking rationally about the captaincy by this time. They were looking, as uncertain and vaguely religious men do in times of stress, for a Sign.

And in the Gentlemen v. Players match that year (so much a better testing-ground than most official Test trials) they were vouchsafed one.

F. R. Brown made a hundred in that match, coming in to bat at 194 for 6. Indeed, he scored 122 out of 131 in 100 minutes. He also took some wickets, and moved about the field with a nimbleness that denied his size and years. After his regular play with Northamptonshire (assisted by a staff appointment, as most amateurs now were) he was clearly as good a cricketer, taking him all round, as he had ever been. Some of the nip had gone from the leg-spinner which first drew him to public notice, but he had developed seam bowling as an alternative attack, and the whacking drives were as powerful as ever. He was made captain for Australia before the match was over.

What seemed almost as important, at the time, was that Denis Compton was made vice-captain. Dollery, who had captained the Players at Lord's, and also scored a hundred, was not chosen for the tour at all, but Compton's appointment was another step forward by the professionals. It meant that if Brown, through a failure of fitness or form, had to fall out of the Test side, Compton, in his own right, would become England's first professional captain of the twentieth century. In fact, Brown was one of the few men on his side who hardly ever became injured, or sick, or lost form. Compton was troubled by injuries, and scored no runs to speak of in the Tests in which he could play. It was by far his poorest series. One conclusion drawn from this was that there was nothing like an amateur captain. Another was that the wrong professional had been made vice-captain. This was a view held with particular vigour in Warwickshire and Yorkshire.

Compton did not make a convincing impression in the matches in which he led M.C.C., and Brown was noticed to consult more frequently, on the field of play, with Hutton. The relationship between Hutton and Compton was never of the easiest. They had entered Test cricket in the same season, 1937, and from the start had symbolized the intense rivalry between Middlesex and Yorkshire, between south and north. They had few big partnerships, surprisingly few considering the vast number of runs they scored in Tests. When Compton was captain in a state match, and M.C.C. were in trouble, he consulted Hutton, and received the advice 'Send home for another bowler.' I am sure Keith Miller is right when he says that this was no more than an example of Hutton's dry sense of humour, but it was a style of humour which Compton did not share. It is no disparagement of either man to say that they could never have become kindred spirits.

On this tour of Australia, so far as the private competition went, the north was the more pleased, because alongside Compton's failures Hutton could set his most successful Australian season. He averaged 88 in the Tests (only Hammond in 1928–9, when runs were much more plentiful, had averaged more). The next in the English list was Simpson, 38. Yet no Englishman, of north or south, could take much satisfaction from the series, for Australia won 4–1, England's only win coming in the last match.

It was very much like Gilligan's tour, except that the scores were lower. Australian pitches were less impregnable, in good weather, than we in England had grown accustomed to think. In the first Test, England (principally Bedser and Bailey) bowled Australia out for 228, and then the weather broke. The second was close, all the way through, but Australia won again, by 28 runs. The next two they won fairly easily. Although England's concluding win was heartening, the series was a decisive defeat.

Apart from Hutton, and Bedser, and to a lesser extent Bailey, the only man to come out of the tour with an increased reputation was the captain. Brown scored 210 runs, average 26 (which made him third in the batting averages), and took 18 wickets, at 21 (which made him third in the bowling). He made his contributions, both with bat and ball, when they were most needed. In the third Test, when England were reduced to three bowlers, because of injuries to Bailey and

Wright, he bowled 44 (eight-ball) overs in Australia's only innings, taking 4 for 153. He also made 79, England's highest score. This was an heroic effort for a man of his age.

He did not have a very good side. Too many of the younger men did not develop as had been hoped; not all of them, it seemed even at the time, were wisely chosen (Edrich was left at home). But Brown led them with a vigorous spirit as well as example, and became very popular with the Australian public, who had greeted his appointment with some incredulity. Tactically, he was sometimes criticized. In the first two Tests, he dropped Hutton down the order. He had a case for this. There were two other capable opening batsmen present, Washbrook and Simpson, and his middle order was wobbly. So why not strengthen it by putting Hutton there? It was not an absurd strategy, but it ignored too much of psychology and history. Nobody, as Cardus pointed out, would have thought of dropping Hobbs down the order, and was not Hutton his successor, the only current batsman who could be compared with him? The plan did not work out, but it did not fail by all that much.

Brown was born in Peru, at Lima, in 1910, attended the Leys School, and won his Blue at Cambridge in 1930 and 1931. He toured Australia under Jardine, without playing in a Test, but played six times for England at home before the war. He was a big man, inclined to burliness even in his youth: a man of warmth rather than subtlety, not perhaps the sort of man you would expect to take to leg-spin. When he turned to medium-pace seamers, he looked more in character. He was a tremendous driver of the ball. He might have been one of the best of all-rounders if – again the point recurs – he had been able to play regularly throughout his career. How would he have fared, I wonder, had his prime years been between 1895 and 1914? He would have been an ornament to that gallant scene, and though he might have found it difficult to hold a place in the England side, especially when Barnes was about, he might still have won a Test match or two. He was the last of the Edwardians.

He continued to captain England in 1951, against South Africa, a rubber comfortably won in the end, though South Africa were a good side that year. He then retired from the captaincy, though he was to play Test cricket again. In 1953, when chairman of selectors, he was chosen to play under Hutton in the Lord's match. This unusual step caused Hutton some perturbation, but all passed off smoothly. Indeed he resumed his captaincy for a short time during that match, when Hutton had to leave the field with an injury. In all he had led England in 15 Tests, of which five were won, six lost and four drawn. His one spectacular failing was in tossing. He won only three times (and on one of those put the other side in).

As a captain, he had served England well at an awkward time, and has continued to do so since his retirement (he gave up the Northamptonshire captaincy at the end of 1953). He was not altogether happy in his capacity as a touring manager, in Australia in 1958–9. Some of his senior players found him brusque and bossy. His trouble was, I suspect, that he was only really content when he was in the middle of the action, on the field of play, and did not take kindly to the frustrations of the pavilion; and also that he had, as he grew older, an increasingly Edwardian distrust of pressmen. I never felt he was quite at ease in a commentary box: subconsciously I dare say he felt he was consorting with the enemy.

Who was to follow Brown when India were the visitors in 1952? The field was much the same. Insole had taken over Essex, Simpson Nottinghamshire. Simpson, who had scored a century in the last Test of Brown's tour, had his supporters, but the general feeling was that this excellent cricketer lacked the personality to lead an England side. Bailey and Sheppard both lacked experience, and Sheppard had the additional disadvantage that it was known he would not be in first-class cricket for long. Edrich and Compton were joint captains of Middlesex. The selectors – Yardley, Wyatt, Brown and Ames – took the plunge and went for Hutton. I have often thought Brown must have been as responsible as anyone for the choice. He often expressed his admiration for Hutton, and well he might, considering how well Hutton had served him. The only other serious possibilities were Yardley and Compton. So at last the barrier was down, and for the first time in the twentieth century England had a professional captain.

Hutton did not have much difficulty in winning the series against the Indians in 1952 (when Trueman made his first appearance) and scored plenty of runs himself. Inevitably, he was chosen again, against Australia, in 1953. He won the Ashes in the last Test, at the Oval, so that strange repetition of the post-1918 pattern continued. His batting was not so dominating as it had been in the previous series against Australia, but he made one of his best hundreds at Lord's, the highest score of the match at the Oval, after his cap (the same one he had worn in 1938 when he broke the record) had nearly dropped on the wicket, and averaged over 50. His captaincy was generally approved, with certain reservations to which I will come later.

That winter there was to be a tour of the West Indies. There were still those who thought that while a professional captain at home might be feasible, a professional captain on tour was a horse of another colour. After Hutton's recapture of the Ashes, his appointment was certain, but critical voices were heard again when he came home.

The tour was not unsuccessful in results. The rubber was drawn, 2–2, after England had been two down. The recovery was principally due to the batting of the captain, who averaged 150 in the last three Tests, though he could not have done it without Bailey's best (ever) spell of bowling, in the last one. But there had been a good deal of trouble off the field, and some on it. England players showed dissent at umpire's decisions. At Georgetown, there was what then passed for a riot, with bottles thrown on the field. Elegant ladies complained that English cricketers had molested them. There was a misunderstanding, to put it no higher, between Hutton and the Chief Minister of Jamaica, Mr Bustamante.

You can find good accounts of this tour if you turn to *West Indian Adventure*, by Swanton (for the cricket), and *Cricket Cauldron*, by Alex Bannister (for the other stuff). As John Arlott observed in *Wisden*, both need to be read. Many of the participants subsequently contributed their views, often contradictorily.

With the passage of a quarter of a century, it is possible to see that deep social causes were at work, of which the appointment of a professional captain for England was a superficial symptom: the decline of Empire, the awakening of the coloured races, the eroding of Victorian ideals of 'sportsmanship'. I record these developments, though I do not necessarily deplore them. The dissent by fieldsmen – even the placid Tom Graveney threw down the ball in disgust when he was denied a catch at slip – would be commonplace today. The bottle-throwing, which Hutton outfaced, keeping his side on the field (he needed another wicket that evening), has been dwarfed by similar events in various parts of the world. It was not so difficult for him to keep his side on, as to keep the umpires on, but he managed to do both.

But in 1954, bottle-throwing was thought to be a habit confined to Australians when Lord Harris was the target, and there was a sense of shock at home that a Test match should be interrupted in this way; and also about the concomitant arguments, which the press (on both sides) did not minimize. There was a disposition among the Old Guard who dimly resented a professional captain, to blame the troubles on Hutton. Hutton had no doubt found it a severe task, and he had his weaknesses in tact (though the youthful and ebullient Trueman would have been a problem for any touring captain, except Jardine, who would have had him tamed or sent home in a month). Yet I am inclined to think, looking back, that this tour of Hutton's was about the bravest effort of his career.

A point not to be forgotten, as Jim Swanton has told us in *Sort of a Cricket Person*, is that Hutton was not fortunate in the choice of the manager. He had wanted S. C. Griffith, who would have been just the man for the job. Instead, C. H. Palmer was made manager, with the additional understanding that he might play (he did in fact play in one Test). This was a ridiculous arrangement, placing the manager above the captain one moment, and below him another. Nobody was in charge. Palmer has always been a much-liked man, but he had not the experience, nor what I suppose might be called the toughness, for what proved to be so arduous a position, and the ambiguity of his appointment did nothing to encourage him to be any tougher. Of Palmer it could be said, as it was of Yardley, that 'the intrigue and politics sometimes evident under the surface of cricket was repugnant to him'.

Nor were Hutton's senior professionals so co-operative as they might have been, at least in the earlier part of the tour. There was an unpleasant disagreement with Evans, who has frankly and, I would judge, fairly described it in his book, *Action in Cricket*. Hutton never found personal relationships easy, though he got better as the mantle of captaincy dwelt upon him. At this time he was conscious that he had grown up among such men as these, his fellow-professionals, and was reluctant to order them about. He did not have the hail-fellow-well-met touch which might have made the ordering easier, and he did not have a manager who could do it for him.

Precisely, said those still suspicious of professional captaincy. Told you so. Disaster. Lost a dominion, near enough. And in 1954, when Pakistan were here to play four Tests, Hutton was unwell, and could play only in the first and last. He had never been a robust man physically, not for an international sportsman, and his nerves, beneath that determinedly calm exterior, were – I am sure – acutely sensitive. The strain of the winter had told upon him. For the second and third, the selectors (H. S. Altham, Robins, Wyatt and Ames -- it did not escape notice that there was no northerner on this committee) called in Sheppard. This was a sensible short-term choice. Sheppard had captained Sussex the previous year, though he had now given place to Doggart, and had shown obvious gifts for the job. He could hardly be thought of as a prospect for the future, since his life lay with the church, but as a deputy he was ideal.

He did what was required of him, cheerfully and unobtrusively. He had no particular personal success (he batted twice, scoring 37 and 13), but on more general evidence it was known that he had matured into a batsman always fit to be considered for an England side. It soon began to be suggested that Sheppard was the man to take England to Australia at the end of the season ('so that Hutton could concentrate on his batting', it was tactfully added, as though the poor man had not scored a run in the West Indies). And Sheppard, without for a moment considering abandoning his call to the ministry, reasonably felt that to set back his studies for six months or so, in order to captain England in Australia, might be within God's purposes. I say this entirely seriously. There has never been any trace of the hypocrite about Sheppard.

What followed he has described, fairly and sometimes hilariously, in *Parson's Pitch*. Robins, it seems, was his chief backer. Sheppard was anxious that the rivalry should not affect his friendly relationship with Hutton. He consulted Professor Norman Sykes, one of his tutors at Cambridge. Norman Sykes (who had also been, as it happens, one of my tutors at Oxford a few years earlier) was a splendid man, a Yorkshireman and a cricketer, as well as being just about the best ecclesiastical historian in the country. (He died, much too soon, as Dean of Winchester.) He enjoyed the corridors of power, and must specially have enjoyed his function as secret emissary between Sheppard and Hutton. Nor was his mission unsuccessful. Relations between Hutton and Sheppard remained happy. Both conducted themselves with dignity. This is of course what one would hope for in England captains, but these two, for a few weeks, had much to endure. The press had a jamboree. A word out of place by either could have done much harm. The *News Chronicle*, I think it was (and I expect others did the same), invited their readers to cast their votes for the captaincy. The poll went, unsurprisingly, heavily in favour of Hutton. All the old stories about the antagonism of the Establishment to professionals were run to death. The north–south rivalry was invoked, with its customary complications. Robins seems to have acted, not for the first or last time, with an indiscretion that was almost light-headed. Altham, as a Winchester master, was a natural target.

It all seems, now, faintly ridiculous. Hutton was duly appointed. Sheppard did not go to Australia. So long as Hutton was in health, the outcome could not be doubted, though there was, I suppose, just a possibility that the ferocity of the press campaign in Hutton's favour might have produced a counter-effect in the committee. *Wisden* said that his captaincy was only confirmed by a single vote, but withdrew the statement the following year.

The rubber against Pakistan was drawn, one–all. After being outplayed for most of the series, they won the last Test. Hutton, already chosen as captain for Australia, had returned to lead the side, but did nothing of consequence (his scores in this rubber were 0, 14 and 5). Fazal Mahmood, a kind of Pakistani Bedser, took 12 wickets for 99 on a damp pitch.

So the entrails could have been more encouraging when Hutton set out for Australia. This expedition – though I doubt if he put it quite this way to himself – was to crown his life or mar it. He won 3–1, after losing the first Test by an innings, and after putting Australia in. He did not bat as well as before (England had six who averaged higher) but he made the highest score of the match, 80, in the fourth Test at Adelaide, when England retained the Ashes.

He went on and won a couple of Tests in New Zealand. In the second, which England won by an innings, he was the highest England scorer, the position to which he had long been accustomed. When he came home with the team, he was greeted by Billy Griffith with a life membership of M.C.C., and the red and yellow tie. In due course he was made a knight. It was hoped that he might be able to lead England again in another Australian series, but he only played a few matches in 1955, and although he was not old as captains go (39) he left the game, gracefully and without rancour.

Hutton was born in Pudsey, the same place as two other Yorkshire opening batsmen, Tunnicliffe and Sutcliffe, and of another notable England captain (who also actually opened the innings for England), Illingworth. When Hutton was hardly more than a boy, Sutcliffe wrote about him in such extravagant terms, in his book *For England and Yorkshire*, that both Hawke, who wrote the introduction, and Home Gordon, who provided the statistics, thought Sutcliffe was overdoing it. Sutcliffe, to the end of his long life, was proud of this little bit of prophecy. When Hutton broke Bradman's record for the highest score in 1938, Warner, who had also been among the sceptics, said that he had 'justified everything his mentor said of him'. Not that Hutton was the same kind of batsman as Sutcliffe, except in concentration. He was no hooker, though he would sometimes do it to show he could. His off-drive was the glory of his game. It was less of a thump than Hammond's – sometimes you could hardly hear the bat hit the ball – but there it was, speeding through between cover and extra, the batsman still following through the long stroke as he took an unnecessary step or two down the pitch.

Hutton first played for Yorkshire in 1934. His best season was certainly 1939, when he not only scored nearly 3,000 runs (in a shortened season) but scored most of them at a great pace. Sellers used to say to him, that season, 'All very well, lad, scoring your seventies and eighties before lunch, but remember tha's opening for Yorkshire, and don't be bloody silly.' (I record this remark as I remember Sellers saying it.) 'Ay', he would add, 'but blighter went on doing it just the same.'

During the war, Hutton had an unlucky accident, in a gymnasium, while serving in the Army. This ultimately, after several variously successful operations, shortened his left arm, the guiding arm, by an inch. You would have thought it almost impossible for a man whose play was founded on the classical off-drive to be so good again after so crucial a misfortune. You would have thought it almost impossible for a batsman so dependent upon his dancing leg-work as Denis Compton to be so good again after his knee had gone. Often have I wished that it had been Compton's arm and Hutton's knee to suffer, instead of the other way round. Both, while unquestionably the best English batsmen of their time, might have been even better, and won more matches against Australia, with a twinge of luck.

Hutton played in 79 Tests, with a batting average of 57, for nearly seven thousand runs. Like Sutcliffe and Leyland, he was at his best against Australia. He would not like me to omit his bowling record, which was 3 wickets for an average of 77. The last one he took in his last game against Australia, with the last ball of the (drawn) match. But he was a good leg-spinner in his earlier days (he took 45 wickets in a season) and it is painful to recall the time when he was put on, unexpectedly and without any practice, at Headingley in 1948, when the extraordinary Australians were romping away with an extraordinary match.

This, I suppose, was one of Norman Yardley's mistakes; yet if Yardley himself had held a very hard, low catch at square leg, off Hutton's bowling, we might be acclaiming him for the genius of his gamble to this day. In all first-class cricket, Hutton scored more than 40,000 runs, with an average of 55, which, we Yorkshiremen meanly note, was a couple of thousand more than Compton, who also averaged four less. He captained England in 23 Tests, winning eight and losing four. As a tosser, he was for a long time worse than Brown, but he had managed to win seven by the end.

I cannot, even now, bring myself to write quite dispassionately of Hutton. He succeeded Herbert Sutcliffe as my boyhood hero, and affections of such a time are not easily effaced. I was a Yorkshire boy, mad about cricket, living – as it seemed to me – in exile among enemies in the south, and consequently intensely partisan. Hutton's 364 is not nowadays rated as one of the greater innings – indeed, as Edmund Blunden noted in *Cricket Country*, Englishmen began to be slightly shamefaced about it, within a few months. But to me, and most other boys of my age, even if they were southerners, boys who had suffered from years and years of Bradman, it was a transcendent moment when Hutton broke Bradman's record. Even ten years later, when I should have been old enough to know better, I was deeply upset when Hutton was dropped from the England side, and wrote indignant letters about it to Sir Pelham Warner and E. W. Swanton, the two people I felt instinctively (and entirely incorrectly) to blame. I never much enjoyed watching Hutton bat. I was always scared that he might get out, like a housewife who is so proud of the best china that she never takes it out of the cabinet.

That third test of 1948 was the only time Hutton was ever left out of an England XI, when he was available. The reasoning of the England selectors was that they had a weak batting side, were up against two very good and very fast bowlers, and that if their No. 1 backed away, as he had done at Lord's (I think this has to be accepted, but I was not there), the effect on the rest would be disastrous. He was a better batsman when he came back. Many years later Jim Swanton wrote to me, 'I never saw Len flinch again for the rest of his career', and he had plenty to put up with from Lindwall and Miller, with some supporting characters. The man who replaced Hutton in the England side was my old friend George Emmett, who made his first appearance, and as it proved his only appearance for England, in the unluckiest circumstances possible. If he had scored 50, they could hardly have picked him again, unless they took the drastic step of dropping Washbrook. Emmett scored 10 and 0, Lindwall getting him both times. Washbrook scored 11 and 85 not out, though he was dropped three times in his second innings, tolerable catches, early on. Emmett, pitched in, was pitched out. This was sad, because he was good enough to have batted for

189

England many times more, an incorrigible stroke-player who would, I dare say, have made as many runs as Washbrook did on the 1950–1 tour, and might well have been a better complement to Hutton as an opening partner.

The conflict with Lindwall and Miller provides the key to Hutton's captaincy of England. What was needed to win Test matches, he decided, was two fast bowlers, a judgment which history, before and since, has generally confirmed. He thought at first that his fast bowlers were to be Trueman and Statham. After Trueman's disappointing season in the West Indies, they turned out, in Australia, to be Tyson and Statham. Hutton's difficulty was that Bedser, who had taken 30 wickets against Australia in 1950–1, and 39 in 1953, had a prescriptive claim to the new ball. In the first Test of 1954–5, England played their four faster bowlers. Bedser, who was not thoroughly fit – he had had a nasty attack of shingles – took 1 for 131 (with some ill-luck in dropped catches). Statham took 2 for 123. Tyson took 1 for 160. Bailey took 3 for 140. Hutton then took what Jack Fingleton called the 'terrific decision' to omit Bedser, and stuck to Tyson and Statham as his opening pair of bowlers for the rest of the series. He was abundantly justified, but came in for some criticism for the manner in which Bedser learnt of the decision to leave him out, from the team-sheet in the dressing-room. Here, again, was a success in tactics, but a failure in communication.

Hutton was a cautious captain. This was in his nature, and even had it not been, the circumstances of his appointment would have pressed him in the same direction. His caution had its dismal aspects, particularly in the slowing of the over-rate. For this he had some reason because so much depended on keeping Tyson and Statham as fresh as possible. It nevertheless set an unhappy precedent, which other captains, not only of England, were only too ready to follow.

These are the major criticisms to be made of Hutton, as a captain, and they are not without force. Nevertheless, he won two consecutive rubbers against Australia. Only one other captain had done this in the twentieth century, Chapman – and Chapman had been captain only for the last match in 1926. Warner won twice in Australia, but not in consecutive series, and in his second tour was unable to play in a Test match.

People have asked me often, in the last few years, people who knew I was writing this book, whom I thought to be the best of England captains. The 'best'? It is a question-begging word. Grace, because he was Grace? Jackson, who did all that was required of him, superbly, in his one season? Fry, because of his Latin and Greek? Chapman, because of his warmth and long run of success? Jardine, because of his ruthlessness? I do not know. But if I *had* to offer, under threat, my own opinion, I would say – remembering all the special problems the man had to face, and remembering my own Yorkshire susceptibilities: yes, I would plump for Sir Leonard.

8

THE AMATEUR REVIVED...
AND ABSORBED

The trenchant blade, Toledo trusty,
For want of fighting was grown rusty,
And eat into itself, for lack
Of somebody to hew and hack
                    Samuel Butler, *Hudibras*

From Hutton's retirement to the present day, Test matches have continued to proliferate, all over the world. There hardly seems to be a day when one is not going on somewhere. Modern transport has made a visit to the other side of the world much more like a Mothers' Union outing than Lillywhite and his company. England had such a crowded programme already, that they could not cram many extra Tests into it, but they did their best, by agreeing to extend tours in Australia to six Tests, and by introducing, at home, the 'double-tour' summer, with two rubbers of three, to accommodate the number of countries (no doubt to increase more yet) anxious, and qualified, to play Test cricket. This is an inevitable development, though not entirely desirable. With every additional Test match played in a calendar year (I notice that statisticians are already taking account of 'calendar years' rather than seasons) the special atmosphere, attraction, perhaps glamour would be the word, of a Test match, diminishes.

Here is a list of the England captains from the time of Hutton's retirement to the Centenary Test at Melbourne in 1977.

Season	Captain	Opponents	Matches	Won	Drawn	Lost
1955	P. B. H. May	South Africa	5	3	0	2
1956	P. B. H. May	Australia	5	2	2	1
1956–7	P. B. H. May	South Africa	5	2	1	2
1957	P. B. H. May	West Indies	5	3	2	0

Season	Captain	Opponents	Matches	Won	Drawn	Lost
1958	P. B. H. May	New Zealand	5	4	1	0
1958–9	P. B. H. May	Australia	5	0	1	4
1959	P. B. H. May	New Zealand	2	1	1	0
1959⎱	P. B. H. May	India	3	3	0	0
1959⎰	M. C. Cowdrey	India	2	2	0	0
1959–60⎱	P. B. H. May	West Indies	3	1	2	0
1959–60⎰	M. C. Cowdrey	West Indies	2	0	2	0
1960	M. C. Cowdrey	South Africa	5	3	2	0
1961⎱	P. B. H. May	Australia	3	1	1	1
1961⎰	M. C. Cowdrey	Australia	2	0	1	1
1961–2	E. R. Dexter	India	5	0	3	2
1961–2	E. R. Dexter	Pakistan	3	1	2	0
1962⎱	E. R. Dexter	Pakistan	4	3	1	0
1962⎰	M. C. Cowdrey	Pakistan	1	1	0	0
1962–3	E. R. Dexter	Australia	5	1	3	1
1962–3	E. R. Dexter	New Zealand	3	3	0	0
1963	E. R. Dexter	West Indies	5	1	1	3
1963–4	M. J. K. Smith	India	5	0	5	0
1964	E. R. Dexter	Australia	5	0	4	1
1964–5	M. J. K. Smith	South Africa	5	1	4	0
1965	M. J. K. Smith	New Zealand	3	3	0	0
1965	M. J. K. Smith	South Africa	3	0	2	1
1965–6	M. J. K. Smith	Australia	5	1	3	1
1965–6	M. J. K. Smith	New Zealand	3	0	3	0
1966⎱	M. J. K. Smith	West Indies	1	0	0	1
1966⎰	M. C. Cowdrey	West Indies	3	0	1	2
1966⎰	D. B. Close	West Indies	1	1	0	0
1967	D. B. Close	India	3	3	0	0
1967	D. B. Close	Pakistan	3	2	1	0
1967–8	M. C. Cowdrey	West Indies	5	1	4	0
1968⎱	M. C. Cowdrey	Australia	4	1	2	1
1968⎰	T. W. Graveney	Australia	1	0	1	0
1968–9	M. C. Cowdrey	Pakistan	3	0	3	0
1969	R. Illingworth	West Indies	3	2	1	0
1969	R. Illingworth	New Zealand	3	2	1	0
1970	R. Illingworth	Rest of the World	5	1	0	4
1970–1	R. Illingworth	Australia	6	2	4	0
1970–1	R. Illingworth	New Zealand	2	1	1	0
1971	R. Illingworth	Pakistan	3	1	2	0
1971	R. Illingworth	India	3	0	2	1
1972	R. Illingworth	Australia	5	2	1	2
1972–3	A. R. Lewis	India	5	1	2	2
1972–3	A. R. Lewis	Pakistan	3	0	3	0
1973	R. Illingworth	New Zealand	3	2	1	0
1973	R. Illingworth	West Indies	3	0	1	2
1973–4	M. H. Denness	West Indies	5	1	3	1
1974	M. H. Denness	India	3	3	0	0

Season	Captain	Opponents	Matches	Won	Drawn	Lost
1974	M. H. Denness	Pakistan	3	0	3	0
1974–5⎰	M. H. Denness	Australia	5	1	1	3
1974–5⎰	J. H. Edrich	Australia	1	0	0	1
1974–5	M. H. Denness	New Zealand	2	1	1	0
1975⎱	M. H. Denness	Australia	1	0	0	1
1975⎰	A. W. Greig	Australia	3	0	3	0
1976	A. W. Greig	West Indies	5	0	2	3
1976–7	A. W. Greig	India	5	3	1	1
1976–7	A. W. Greig	Australia	1	0	0	1

One thing that immediately occurs to you about that list is that, despite the number of matches, the England captaincy was shared around less. No doubt it was a symptom of the 'professional approach'. Once a captain was appointed, he could, barring accidents, expect a good run; and probably he did not have much time to do anything else. The days when someone such as A. O. Jones, or even Warner, or Tennyson, or Gilligan, or Allen, could become captain without having a prescriptive right to the job – happy enough to go after a season or two – were long gone. It had become a long-term rather than a short-term proposition. The fortunes of Sheppard illustrate this point.

The next thing that strikes you is that after the experiment with professional captaincy, successful though it had been, the amateurs took over again. Amateur status was formally abolished in 1962, when there were only a few genuine amateurs left: but both before and after that, the majority of England captains have come from Oxford or (more often) Cambridge, and would have been amateurs, at least theoretically, under the old dispensation.

From 1955 to 1966 the captaincy was in the hands of four men: May and Dexter (both from Cambridge), and Cowdrey and Smith (both from Oxford). Here were four Elizabethans to compare with the four Edwardians whom we noticed earlier. The Englishmen of the second Elizabethan age have been of a different stamp – obviously I speak in general terms – from those of the first. Caution, what in the north is called meanness (southerners must understand that the word is not intended altogether pejoratively) has been a principal note, and this has been true of cricket as much as most other activities. In the time of Elizabeth I, what was to become the British Empire was a healthy fledgling spreading its wings ('Methinks I see her as an eagle mewing her mighty youth, and kindling her undazzled eyes at the full noonday beam'). Good old John Davis, trying to teach the Eskimo to dance and tackle. In the time of Edward VII, it was still, or thought itself to be, an eagle in full flight, and 'the eagle suffers little birds to sing'. In the time of Elizabeth II, it has become more of an ageing robin fiercely defending its own patch.

The north wind will blow
And we shall have snow,
And what will poor robin do then, poor thing?
He'll sit in a barn
To keep himself warm,
And hide his head under a wing, poor thing!

So we would not have expected the England captains of this period to lead their sides with *panache*. Nor, usually, did they, though there were moments in their batting – especially that of Dexter and May – which remembered the buccaneering touch.

May led England in 41 Tests, more than anybody else has done so far, piled into six years. Cowdrey led them in 27, although he never achieved his ambition of taking a side to Australia – he was vice-captain there four times for four different captains: May, Dexter, Smith, and finally Illingworth. Dexter led England in 30 Tests, Smith in 25. As the long dominion of these four began to draw to a close, the 'professional' began to get a look in again: briefly with Close (seven Tests and a self-inflicted wound) and then, more substantially, with Illingworth. Illingworth won the Ashes in Australia, the first to do so since Hutton, and retained them at home. He was captain in 36 Tests. Perhaps he stayed in the job a year too long, but that made a refreshing change from those captains who had given it up several years too soon. After Illingworth came Denness, another Cambridge man, and after Denness came Greig, a South African of an amateur manner and a professional inclination. After Greig came chaos – I mean to the cricket world, though not to his successor Brearley, who seems to be doing the job, as I write, notably well in circumstances of unprecedented difficulty.

The decision to appoint May as Hutton's successor had been foreshadowed by his choice as vice-captain for the 1954–5 tour of Australia. I am not sure whether his appointment was wise. There was a case for Bailey, as Hutton's natural successor. May came to the job young, and in consequence retired from it young. As a further consequence, the same thing happened to Dexter. England would surely have had a few more years of both of them, if we had a season or two of Bailey, after Hutton.

Bailey never captained England, not even in a stray match, and therefore, to my regret, has no proper place in this book. It is astonishing that so good a cricketer, so thoughtful a judge, and so friendly a man, should have been passed over, though he was at a time when there were other strong candidates about. He had been vice-captain to Hutton in the West Indies. He is, or was in his earlier days, a man of contradictions, who sometimes enjoyed being irritating, to his captain, to his colleagues, to the public, but most of all to his opponents. There is a marvellous chapter about Bailey in his friend Insole's book *Cricket From the Middle* – though it ought not to be taken entirely seriously, I can believe it when Insole says of Bailey

> He has been known to assist in the gentle breaking up of social gatherings which have lasted rather too long by changing into his pyjamas and making an obtrusive re-appearance. This is, for him, the subtlest of hints.

I suppose the theory in 1954 was (a) that Bailey was not enough of a dasher on the field, and/or (b) that he was too irresponsible off it. With Hutton as a cautious captain, England could not afford another cautious one as his second-in-command. The first view was rubbish. It has never followed that because a man was a stodgy batsman, he was a stodgy captain (Douglas and Jardine are names that come to mind at once, or Woodfull, if you cast your eye beyond England). The second view was misconceived. I do not doubt that Trevor was a bit of a monkey in those days, but nor do I doubt that he would have responded swiftly, if possibly a shade ponderously, to the challenge of captaincy. But this is, I must confess, a minority view. The Essex committee preferred Insole, and the England committee May. And once May was installed, and had begun with victories against Australia and South Africa, there could be no turning back.

We must note, in passing, the brief captaincies of Edrich (John Edrich, Bill's cousin) and Graveney, both as deputies, but both against Australia. Graveney came in when Cowdrey, though present on the ground, decided he was unfit at Headingley in 1968. The match was drawn. Edrich came in when Denness, who was having trouble scoring runs against the Australian fast bowlers, stood down at Sydney in 1975. The match was lost, and with it the Ashes, though there were only a few overs to spare at the end, and Edrich scored 83 runs for once out.

Graveney and Edrich have been two of the best batsmen of their time, something sufficiently indicated by Graveney's 122 centuries in first-class cricket, and Edrich's 103 (as I write, in play). Graveney was the most elegant of the English post-war professional batsmen, if you count Hutton and Compton as pre-war. He has always been a favourite of mine, both as a player and a man, perhaps because, living as I do in the west, I saw so much of him. His Test match career, though the figures came out acceptably enough at the end (4,882 runs in 79 Tests, average 44), had its bad patches. The selectors did not always have sufficient faith in him, though there were occasions when he tested their patience. His batting was sometimes thought too rash for modern Test cricket. This rashness did not often extend to his captaincy. He led Gloucestershire, and later, more happily, Worcestershire. He did not have any special gift for leadership, though he was a sound enough tactician. Much the same judgment could be made of Edrich, who has captained Surrey faithfully but without *élan*. Edrich scored

5,138 runs in Tests, 77 of them, average 43. He had plenty of strokes, but they were not the more dramatic strokes, and he had the advantage (it usually proves to be an advantage, if you are looking for style) of being a left-hander. I saw his innings of 310, not out, against New Zealand at Leeds in 1965. It was not a slow innings, but I cannot remember much about it, although I was one of the radio commentators, and paying reasonably close attention. There were times when both of these men were mentioned as possible regular England captains, but for one reason and another their chances never came.

Peter May was born at Reading, on the last day of 1929. He was an exceptionally good schoolboy batsman. In 1947, when he was captain of Charterhouse, he scored centuries against both Eton and Harrow. He made his first-class debut for Combined Services while he was in the Navy. In 1950, at Cambridge, he was an automatic Blue, and in the same year won his county cap for Surrey, and played in a Test trial. His first Test was against South Africa, at Leeds in 1951. He scored 138, and his triumphal progress thereafter was rarely interrupted.

Colin Cowdrey's early career had many similarities. He was born at Bangalore, almost three years later than May. He went to Tonbridge, where he was in the XI for five seasons (in those days he was thought of almost as much as a leg-spinner as a batsman). He played for Kent in 1950 while still at school, and won his county cap the following year. He won his Blue in his first summer at Oxford, in 1952. He would very likely have gone to the West Indies in 1953 but for the requirements of Oxford. He was, however, chosen for his first Australian tour, as May was, in 1954.

The slight difference between them in age, and therefore experience, was obviously crucial to their careers as England captains, but it would not be fair to attribute May's greater success to that alone. He bore himself, without being haughty, as one born to command (so did Dexter, but he put in the haughtiness for good measure). Cowdrey, a modest and in many ways diffident man, though with a deep inner pride, was an unobtrusive captain. You could watch one of Cowdrey's England sides in the field for quite a long time without realizing — assuming you did not know already — who was captain. If Dexter was captain you would know in a couple of minutes. Both these approaches had their merits, but the stance of May, somewhere between them, was the best.

May played in 66 Tests, scoring 4,537 runs, average nearly 47. In all first-class cricket, from 1948 to 1963, he scored 27,592 runs, with 85 centuries, at an average of 51. He captained Surrey from 1957 to 1962. He won them two championships in his first two years, taking over towards the end of their invincible run, but no more. The mighty side was beginning to show cracks as it grew older, and he had some troubles with the senior professionals, especially Laker, who was not then (I go by his own account, in *Over to Me*) so mellow a man as he has subsequently become. I dare say (though Jim Laker regrets the book, for which he was not entirely responsible) that May did not handle him so well. Laker was, after all, one of the best bowlers in the world, and suffered more pain from his hard-worked, constantly swollen spinning finger than a batsman who hardly ever bowled might fully appreciate. But as May increased in authority, an authority generated as much by his character as his mastery with the bat, he nearly always had his teams on his side.

Of his 41 Tests as captain, May won 20, and lost 10. All the losses were against Australia and South Africa. From 1955 to the middle of 1959, he was England's only captain, and remained, barring any health bothers, the accepted first choice until he retired from Test cricket, as it proved permanently (though there were occasionally hopes that he might be persuaded to return), at the end of 1961. In his last couple of years as captain, Cowdrey sometimes deputized for him.

Against Australia, May won one rubber and lost two. There was bound to be a swing after England had won, for the first time in this century, three in a row, from 1953 to 1956. Neither the 1956 nor the 1958–9 rubbers were entirely satisfactory. In 1956, Australians felt, England won because they had rigged the pitches to suit their spinners, and in 1958–9, Englishmen felt, Australia won because their bowlers were chuckers. I am not suggesting it was so simple as that in either case, but both series were played to a rising cacophony from the press. May, though not a man easily flustered, must have been tried very hard at times (while keeping his own form well) and I imagine these troubles contributed to his early retirement. The 1961 series was happier, and I suppose we ought not to say that May 'lost' it, since of the three Tests in which he was captain England won one and lost one.

Cowdrey had captained in the first two. He has described the circumstances in his book, *M.C.C.* (his father had deliberately given him the magic initials). May had asked not to be considered for the first Test – which England drew, after being in trouble, thanks chiefly to 180 from Dexter in the second innings, with another century from Subba Row. For the second Test, May returned to the side, but Cowdrey continued as captain. The match was lost. It was not a distinguished performance by England. The batting failed twice. Cowdrey scored a total of 23 runs, and May 39. May then resumed the captaincy. This was a deep disappointment to Cowdrey, he tells us in his autobiography written many years later, though he concealed his feelings well enough at the time. He says that he felt unprepared for the job when it was unexpectedly thrust upon him. Earlier in the season, he writes, he was so absorbed in his captaincy of Kent (he captained them from 1956 to 1971, and achieved a dear ambition when at last he took them to the championship in 1970) – so absorbed in his captaincy of Kent that 'apart from anticipating that I would hardly be dropped from the

England side as a specialist batsman, I gave no thought at all to the Test series that lay ahead'.

This will not, with respect to an old friend, quite do. Cowdrey had deputized for May twice against India in 1959, twice against the West Indies in 1959–60, and had been captain for the whole series against South Africa in 1960. May was unwell at this time, and his sickness – although such a splendid, upstanding figure at the crease, he was never quite one of the strong boys – was another cause of his retirement. While it was expected that May would be fit enough in 1961, and assumed that he would be first choice as captain, there was an obvious possibility that Cowdrey would have to step in at some point. He had no business to be unprepared. This was taking diffidence too far.

Against South Africa, May won 3–2 at home in 1955, and drew 2–2, with one drawn, there in 1956–7. The 1955 series was one of the best, and the last, deciding match at the Oval was open until the last day. May, with two centuries and three more scores of over 80, did as much as anyone for the victory. The 1956–7 series was one of the worst, with appallingly slow scoring rates on both sides. May was criticized for his tactics on this tour. He was on his first tour as captain, the South African tour even then was a delicate one, and he did not score many runs himself in the Tests, though plenty at other times. His vice-captain was Insole, who had a successful tour, heading the Test batting averages, and was another of those a little unlucky never to have been an England captain.

Perhaps this is the time for a passing word on Insole, who is nowadays a great man, chairman of selection committees, manager of touring sides, no doubt destined to be President of M.C.C., if he hasn't been already. He is a shrewd man (he managed to sit on the selection committee which appointed him vice-captain for South Africa, and he had to get the vice-captaincy or his firm would not have released him – well, that's what he says). He is a witty man, and *Cricket From the Middle* is, at least in those parts which Insole may be presumed to have written himself, one of the best books ever written by an England cricketer. It has some stodgy patches, for which someone else must have been responsible. Insole was mostly an on-side batsman, and used to make jokes against himself about his limited number of strokes – exaggerated jokes, for I have seen him drive handsomely to the off. Only once or twice, to be sure, but I did not see him bat very often. He would have made an interesting captain, but could never be sure enough of his place in the side. He played in nine Tests, five on this tour, and four scattered around at home from 1950 to 1957. He scored more than 400 runs at an average of 27, in Test cricket, and would have done better had he ever had more than one match in a home series. He served Essex well, and scored over 25,000 runs at an average of nearly 40 in a career lasting from 1947 to 1963. He was another of the Cambridge men, not so serene and majestic in his younger days as he is, or strives to be, now. As Sydney Smith said of Jeffrey, 'I have heard him speak disrespectfully of the Equator', though Sydney Smith had never heard of Trevor Bailey. Insole established himself as a Test match batsman only on the 1956–7 tour to South Africa – his chance had slipped by years before – and as he was three years older than May, only some oddity would have given him the captaincy then.

Against the West Indies, May was captain in eight Tests, five at home in 1957 and three over there (until his health went) in 1959–60. He won four of these matches and lost none. The 1957 series was a happy one for England and her captain. The West Indies side was reckoned to be a very strong one, with Worrell, Weekes and Walcott to bat, and Ramadhin and Valentine to bowl. Among others present were young men called Sobers, O. G. Smith, Gilchrist and Kanhai. The West Indies seemed to be winning the first Test easily, when they had bowled England out for 186 (Ramadhin 7 for 49 in 31 overs) and scored 474. England had lost 3 for 113 in the second innings, when May and Cowdrey came together. The next wicket, Cowdrey's, fell at 524. He had made 154. May went on to 285 not out, until he declared at 583 for 4. He might perhaps have been blamed for not declaring earlier, since the West Indies had lost 7 for 72 before the close, and were struggling, but slice that how you like, it had been a marvellous recovery.

It had also been a marvellous partnership. E. W. Swanton has written of it:

> The concentration, the restraint, the technical excellence of these two innings could not be over-praised. Never have two young cricketers built such a monument to patience and determination. On a flawless wicket they owed scarcely anything to luck, and gave no clear chance. They simply established a mastery and with unwearying care upheld it.

Although England did not win the match, they had, as it proved, effectively won the rubber, for the West Indies were never the same side again. Although they had to bat on a miserable wicket at the Oval, which once more raised questions about rigged pitches for the Surrey spinners, England had by then already won the series. This was probably May's best moment as a captain.

He took the side to the West Indies in the autumn of 1959, a little chastened by the defeat in Australia the previous winter. He was still unwell after an operation at the end of the previous summer, and after the third Test was ordered home, Cowdrey once more taking over. But he had been there to lead England to a win in the second Test, the one match in the series which had a positive result. It was a high-scoring series. May himself, naturally enough in retrospect, did not make many runs, but Cowdrey did, opening the innings, something he did not much like, and bravely keeping himself to it even after becoming captain. There was another riot in the second Test, the one England won, and this time England did have to leave the field early, though Walter Robins, the manager, agreed with the West Indian authorities that extra time should be played on the following days to make up for that lost. There was a troublesome incident in the third Test, when May declined to grant Kanhai a runner. He was not within his rights. He thought that Kanhai had come into the match injured, as opposed to being injured during the game, and that the West Indies were trying to steal an advantage. In fact, apart from the obvious point that a runner is always more likely to be a handicap than an advantage, to ask the fielding captain for permission to use one is a matter of courtesy, not law. Kanhai was suffering from cramp. The umpires were not sure of the law, and disagreed about what to do. Kanhai batted on in difficulty, and was out soon afterwards. Cowdrey's comment is:

> I was of little help to him since it was not until afterwards that I learned the rules to prevent a batsman having a runner.

This again seems a shade on the diffident side. May can be forgiven because he was poorly, and the laws of the game are complicated, but what are vice-captains for if they cannot help troubled captains in such moments of anxiety? However, Cowdrey carried on efficiently, even with the abundant help of Robins, till the rubber reached a successful close.

May was also captain seven times against New Zealand, and three times against India. Against New Zealand he won four matches in 1958, and would probably have won the fifth had it not been for the weather. This was not a good New Zealand side, compared with the formidable one they had produced in 1949. In two Tests at the end of the Australia 1958–9 tour, England won one by an innings and had the better of the second, which was drawn (May's scores in these matches were 71 and 124, not out). In 1959 he began the series against India with another hundred, and won the first three matches easily. Cowdrey took over when May was unfit, and won the last two equally easily. Neither of these two home rubbers, against New Zealand in 1958 and India in 1959, aroused much interest in England, nor were they much preparation for the tours to come in the following winters. It was about this time that people began to think of the possibility of the 'double tour', though it was not until 1965 that such a thing happened.

I am not quite sure that I have been fair to May, in this summary. He was a good captain, and a great batsman. I suppose the hesitations arise because he did not turn out quite as expected. Here he was, an amateur, a classical stylist, three initials and all, embodying a return to the old tradition – and, tactically, playing like a canny old pro. In his captaincy, he was Hutton's child. There was little observable difference in their approaches: but the caution which seemed natural and acceptable to Pudsey and Yorkshire did not sit so easily on Charterhouse and Cambridge.

Cowdrey, too, was one of the Hutton family – indeed, in a more personal sense, for in Australia, especially after Cowdrey's beloved father had died, early in the tour, Hutton had taken the young man – without fussing – under his wing. But Cowdrey would have been a cautious captain anyway, at least in Test matches. Of the 27 Tests in which he was captain, the first in 1959 and the last in 1969, only four were lost, but only eight were won. The wins were against India (twice), South Africa (three times), and Pakistan, West Indies and Australia once each. The losses were against West Indies and Australia, twice each. In only three rubbers was he captain throughout a series, against South Africa in 1960, against West Indies in 1967–8, against Pakistan in 1968–9. Against South Africa he won 3–0, against the West Indies he won 1–0, and in Pakistan there were three draws. But we ought to count his captaincy against Australia in 1968, when he would have led in all five matches but for injury: that rubber was drawn, 1–1, England levelling it at the Oval with only a few minutes of the match to go. These figures do suggest, what I am sure is true, that Cowdrey was a better captain when he had a full and regular responsibility, than when he was kept hopping in and out of the job.

He played in 118 Test matches, an astonishing figure, easily a record, beginning in 1954 and ending in 1975, and scored 7,865 runs, another record, at an average of 43·45. The last figure is some way from a record – a dozen and more men have surpassed it – but that was the price he had to pay for staying so devotedly in the game for so long. In all first-class cricket (I am assuming, in 1979, that he has finished it, though I would not risk a bet) he scored nearly 43,000 runs, with an average of 42·89. Thus his Test average was slightly higher than his average for all matches, which need not surprise us.

In writing about May, I have inevitably written a good deal already about Cowdrey. They were not only colleagues but close friends. Nor were they rivals, in the sharper sense. May's primacy was accepted between them, though it was also accepted that Cowdrey would in due course succeed him. It was his misfortunes thereafter that brought just a tinge of bitterness to Cowdrey's autobiography. He is a man from whom I have received many kindnesses, a man who will go the extra mile, and nearly everybody who knows him would say the same.

Cowdrey's misadventures, so far as captaincy went, started in the autumn of 1961, when he decided, entirely reasonably, that he would like a winter at home. Dexter went instead, losing in India and winning in Pakistan, and was reappointed at the beginning of the home series against Pakistan in 1962. Robins had now succeeded Allen as the chairman of selectors (the others were Insole, Bedser, and Watson), and this cannot have enhanced Cowdrey's hopes. A side was due to go to Australia in the autumn, and this was another summer with much controversy about the captaincy, as 1954 had been. Cowdrey and Dexter were obvious contestants, and again the name of Sheppard was brought forward. Sheppard had last played for England five years before, and was hard at work at the Mayflower Centre in the East End of London. But he could, if he so desired, legitimately take a sabbatical leave for the Australian tour, and there was obviously much to recommend him. The only drawback was that it could be no more than a one-tour appointment. There was much talk about the resentment of senior professionals at playing under a captain who was not a regular cricketer, and a parson at that, but it was arguable that Sheppard had the character to overcome that.

The idea was first widely bruited in an article by E. M. Wellings, the cricket correspondent of the London *Evening News*. Robins read the article and was taken by the idea. He took the view, which has nearly always been held, that winning a rubber against Australia was an end in itself, and if Sheppard was the best man to do it, and was able to go, then he should. Robins rang up Sheppard, who was out, and left a message asking him to ring back. There followed, as has been described once or twice in print, a comic interlude. Sheppard thought the message came from one of his parishioners, also called Robins, and it was several days before the misunderstanding was elucidated. However, in the end Sheppard did get in touch with Robins (Walter), and pacified him; and the upshot was that he did make himself available for Australia and, if it was wished, the captaincy. The story was soon out, and there was another press jamboree.

The first thing was for Sheppard to play some cricket and make some runs. In this he was for a while only moderately successful. Sheppard himself by mid-July felt it would be wiser to abandon the experiment. However, he had at least one more match to play, for he had been chosen for the Gentlemen against the Players, during which match the captain for Australia was to be named. He scored a hundred. By scoring a hundred in the same match in 1950, Brown had seized the captaincy, and there was a widespread feeling – which Robins, mischievously, encouraged – that Sheppard had done the same. But Dexter was appointed. Cowdrey was made vice-captain. Sheppard went too, and did well. It was all a little baffling. If the doubt about Sheppard was his form, why not choose him, when he had demonstrated he had found it? If it had been intended to appoint Dexter all along, why all the fuss?

In all the excitement, Cowdrey had been rather forgotten. Dexter had been captain in the first two Tests, and then Cowdrey given a chance in the third, Dexter playing under him. England won it easily enough, and though Cowdrey failed with the bat, that was of no significance. The real contest in the selector's minds, one feels looking back, was between Dexter and Cowdrey, and it went to the one who was thought to have the more commanding personality.

Dexter returned to the captaincy for the last Two Tests against Pakistan, a rubber easily won; duly went to Australia, where the series was drawn; picked up a 3–0 victory in New Zealand; and was captain again at home in 1963, losing 3–1 to one of the strongest of West Indies sides. There was a tour to India that winter. It was a short tour of a new pattern, with five Test matches crammed into eight weeks. Dexter decided against going as captain, and Cowdrey was invited. But Cowdrey had suffered a broken arm in the Lord's Test (that famous Test when, at the end, he went out to bat with his arm in plaster), had been out of cricket for the rest of the summer, and was still not completely fit when the team left (though he joined them, in an emergency, later). M. J. K. Smith was chosen. All five Tests were drawn, not a bad performance by an England side exceptionally smitten by injuries from the start. In 1964, Dexter resumed as captain, at home against the Australians, losing the only match finished. It was a narrow victory for Australia, which often had looked like going the other way. There was some criticism of Dexter's captaincy, but any losing captain has to face that. Not since Tennyson and Gilligan has a losing England captain received much praise.

That, as it proved, was the end of Dexter's Test captaincy, though not quite of his Test cricket. He had been adopted as Conservative candidate for a Cardiff division, facing one James Callaghan, and an election was imminent. So he could not accept the captaincy for South Africa in 1964–5, although in the end when it turned out he had not been elected to Parliament, he made the tour. Cowdrey, still bothered by injury, aged nearly 33 and doubtless feeling older, stayed at home. Smith was therefore the obvious choice, won the rubber 1–0, and it was a happy series, with nothing but compliments for the English captain. So Smith was captain again in 1965, the first of the double-tour seasons, winning all three against New Zealand, but losing the second against South Africa. Nevertheless, he had already been made captain against Australia (for some reason, which must have been a bad one, there were two English tours of Australia in three years, instead of the customary four), and did very well there, scoring runs, holding numerous catches at close short-leg, and establishing that cheerful relationship with his players which had been so noticed in India.

The rubber, like Dexter's, ended in a draw. After the first Test of the next home summer, against the West Indies in 1966, Smith was dropped from the captaincy. It proved to be his last match as captain, though – again like Dexter – not in Test cricket. Now, May had retired, Dexter had retired, Smith had been dropped: of the quadrumvirate, only Cowdrey remained. He was appointed captain for the second Test, at Lord's. This was only the second occasion, he felt, when he had been appointed England captain in his own right. The circumstances could have been more propitious. Smith had lost the first match by an innings, in three days, and failed with the bat in both innings, but he had a good record behind him. He was a warm friend of Cowdrey's, who had given him his Blue at Oxford, and been his vice-captain in Australia. It was thought that Smith, who wore glasses, and was never at his happiest against the fastest bowlers, of which the West Indies had several (though in fact it was Gibbs, the off-spinner, who got him out twice in the first Test), might not be the best man to lead in the circumstances. Cowdrey accepted the job, as was indeed his duty, since no other candidate was impressive, a little reluctantly he tells us – and I believe him – but now he had a real chance again. This was the moment, or one of the several moments, he might have seized. Perhaps this above any. But he had the difficulty, just as Smith had had in the first Test, that, taken all round, the other side was better, more considerably than captaincy could conquer, save by exceptional inspiration or exceptional luck. Cowdrey had no luck, losing three tosses running, managed a draw at Lord's but then lost the next two by an innings, and apart from a 96 in the third Test did not bat very well. For the fifth Test, the selectors dropped him, not only from the captaincy but from the side, and appointed Brian Close, the Yorkshire captain. The wheel had spun again, and England had a 'professional' captain for the first time since Hutton. There was much glee in Yorkshire when Close, in that last match (though the rubber was already lost), won England's only match of the series. A strange series it had been, in which England had had three captains, not by accident but by selectoral choice.

There was no tour that winter. Close continued to captain England in the following summer, winning three out of three against India and two out of three against Pakistan (neither of them, that year, very strong opposition). There could be no question that Close was the man to take England on the tour to the West Indies, the 'world champions' as it was commonly said, in 1967–8. Nor would there have been, but for an act of folly by Close in a county match at Edgbaston, when he flagrantly wasted time – and, less understandable but more damning, refused, when summoned by the Cricket Council to account for himself, to apologize.

This happened late in the season, just before the sixth Test, in which Close remained captain. The selectors (Insole was now the chairman) chose him for the West Indies, but the Cricket Council would not have it. There was really no one else, at such short notice, to captain the side, except Cowdrey. He had the experience. He had captained England in the West Indies before, when May was unable to complete the tour. He was approaching 34, but that was a year younger than Close. As captain of Kent, he had just won the Gillette Cup and taken them to second place in the championship. He had averaged 39 during the season. Cowdrey, for the second time in 18 months, in some embarrassment, accepted the England captaincy. His embarrassment would have been lessened if Insole, in an incautious press conference, had not revealed that the selectors, as opposed to the Cricket Council (who for various reasons had become the governing body for tours in succession to M.C.C.), would still have preferred Close. In the circumstances Cowdrey could not have been blamed if he had pulled a long nose at them, but he turned the other cheek, as a Christian should, and went out to the West Indies, and won the rubber.

Now, he felt, his position must be secure for a year or two. He outlined to the touring party his long-term plan for restoring England to the supremacy in world cricket. The West Indian part of it was secured, and in 1968, at home against Australia, although the rubber was drawn, England were obviously the unluckier side, and there were no serious complaints about Cowdrey. He took England to Pakistan in 1968–9, a shortened series because of Pakistan's internal troubles, in which he behaved with tact and bravery, and was naturally asked to captain England in the first Test of 1969, against the West Indies.

But here his luck, never his strongest point when it came to captaining England, at last expired. Near the end of May, he snapped an Achilles tendon in his left heel. That put him out for the season. The selectors appointed Illingworth to take his place. Illingworth had not played in much Test cricket till then, and what he had played had been only moderately successful. He had no regular experience of captaincy, and would not have been even a county captain had he not recently fallen out, over a contractual matter, with Yorkshire, and moved to Leicestershire, who shrewdly made him captain at once. Illingworth had had the best brain, apart possibly from Binks, in the Yorkshire side which Close had led with much courage and success. He was six months older than Cowdrey. Nobody imagined it to be any more than a sensible short-term appointment. In 1969, Illingworth led England to victory over the West Indies and New Zealand, 2–0 in each case, and his own contribution, especially with the bat, improved much with the new responsibility he bore. In 1970, when the South African tour was cancelled, England played a series against a side called 'The Rest of the World'. There was some marvellous cricket in these matches, which deserve to be ranked as Tests, in the same way as matches played by South Africa since they left the International Cricket Conference and were therefore unable to play Test matches, deserve to be. *Wisden* properly accords both sets of matches the status of Test cricket, and I have no time for those statistical or political bigots, on whichever side they may be, who argue otherwise. Not, one must remember, that it really matters in the least what the statisticians call a Test match and what they do not. But it is a nuisance to have to cope with more than one set of statistics. For myself, I follow *Wisden*.

Illingworth captained England again, against the Rest of the World. England were 1–1 after the first two matches, and the captain for Australia was to be announced during the third: a not unfamiliar situation, which might conceivably have been avoided. Cowdrey was playing again, bound to be picked again on his merits as a player if he wanted to go, and there was a general feeling, or perhaps I should say a general expectation, that on his fifth tour, three times vice-captain, he would take an England side to Australia. Cowdrey had been batting when the selectors reached their decision, just as Sheppard had been during the Gentlemen–Players match of 1962. When he came off (this is Cowdrey's own account) he was asked by A. C. Smith, one of the selectors, to have a word with Alec Bedser (now the chairman) in the secretary's office. Bedser was gracious. He said, 'We're sorry about this. We know what an ambition it was of yours, and how much it meant to you, but we've chosen the other fellow.'

Cowdrey, with goodness knows how much of a struggle, said 'Fair enough'.

He was asked to go as vice-captain, and, after slightly too long a delay, agreed. He and Illingworth did not strike up a happy partnership, but I am not suggesting it was just Illingworth's fault. Cowdrey never captained England again. But he continued as an England player, and, in the emergency of 1974–5, when the England batsmen were in physical and mental trouble against Lillee and Thomson, was summoned to Australia for the sixth time, as a replacement.

The history of the England captaincy, so far as Australia is concerned – for every England captain, at least in modern times, it is his crown to take a side to Australia – contains no comparable irony to that which harassed Cowdrey. Time after time, he seemed a certainty, and time after time something, or someone, got in the way. When this kind of thing happens so often, it may be that

> The fault, dear Brutus, is not in our stars
> But in ourselves

– perhaps diffidence did overcome him a little too often. But would he have been a better or happier man had he heeded Cassius's word? Brutus was not. Cowdrey was never an assassin, nor a schemer. If you put a dagger in his hand, placed him behind a cosy pillar in the Forum, and set somebody in an imperial toga loose before him, he would be merciful and stay his hand: yes, even if Caesar had something of an air of Walter Robins.

Just as writing about May involved writing about Cowdrey, so writing about Cowdrey has involved writing about nearly all the English captains up to the last few years. But they cannot be treated as so many appendices of Cowdrey.

Dexter, though no more like Cassius than Cowdrey was like Brutus, has certainly always had a lean and hungry look. Cowdrey has always had a reputation as a trencherman, but Dexter did not do so badly either. Indeed the first time I spoke to him was one day at Southampton, when, arriving rather late in the lunch tent, I was just in time to see Dexter, who had finished his own, gently drawing towards himself the plate of meat set before my place. He was a man of great energy, who enjoyed fielding all day – apart from the irritation that the other side was scoring runs – and needed plenty of grub.

Dexter played in 62 Tests, scoring 4,502 runs, at an average of 47·89, a very similar output to May's. He scored nine Test hundreds, a high proportion out of the 51 he scored in first-class cricket. The latter statistic reflects not only the relative brevity of his carrer, but a slight disdain for the magic three figures. He was, in some ways, a latter-day C. B. Fry. Disdain and scorn ran sparkling in their eyes. He was also a useful medium-paced bowler, even at Test level. I never thought him quite such a handsome batsman as Cowdrey, when Cowdrey was at his best – Cowdrey could bat much like Hammond – but Dexter played far fewer stodgy innings. Cowdrey, even in youth, was liable to long spells of introspection, of self-doubt. The arrogance of Dexter's batting agreed with one aspect of his character. He could bat as if he felt that no bowler had the right to exist on the same field, or the same planet. The effects on the bowlers were varied, but usually, from Dexter's point of view, successful. He hated being out as much as Boycott does, but very rarely gave any trouble to umpires. He did not welcome commiseration. Once at Taunton, in a Gillette Cup match, Sussex began badly, and Dexter himself was out for just a few. As he walked, head down, back to the pavilion, the members gave him the slight, sympathetic clap appropriate to a great batsman and a captain of England. He lifted his head and glowered at them. The look said, 'We'll beat you yet, you bastards' – which, as a matter of fact, they did. His autobiography is, in places, a sour book, especially when he comes to deal with the press (even Walter Robins comes off better). But that was written in 1966, and he has mellowed much since those days, partly no doubt because he has himself become a distinguished member of the press gallery.

Of his Tests as captain, he won nine and lost seven. The various tactical mistakes alleged against him, such as taking the new ball at Leeds in 1964, when Australia escaped from an unpromising position, were mostly *post hoc ergo propter hoc* criticisms. It was often said that he did not have sufficient confidence in his spin bowlers, but that was very much in the manner of his time, the Hutton style. His Test career began on a low note. He was chosen against New Zealand in 1958, and scored 52, but was not chosen for Australia. He was summoned there, however (he happened to be in Paris at the time), as a replacement. He did get into the England side for two Tests, scoring 1, 11, 0 and 6. He tells us that the only reason he was chosen was that he had been such a catastrophic twelfth man. Australians regarded him (Radley and Cambridge) as one of the old English public school jokes. Not until his great innings at Edgbaston in 1961, when he saved the match, did most Australians begin to respect him. By the end of his career they had begun to fear him, and were as relieved when he retired as

Englishmen were dismayed. A remarkable man, 'Lord Edward' (a term sometimes used sardonically and sometimes affectionately), and certainly one of the more interesting England captains.

M. J. K. Smith was also a remarkable man, though in a very different way. He was born at Leicester in 1933, and went to Stamford, which if not quite an Eton or Harrow was a respected public school. He went up to Oxford in 1953, and played in three university matches, scoring a century in each of them. He played for Leicestershire for a time, before moving to Warwickshire, of whom he soon became captain. He was very nearly as good a Rugby player as he was a cricketer, and one of my principal memories of him is when, at Twickenham, he played at fly-half outside Brace, and they got up to all sorts of tricks, anticipating many modern developments in the game, and Oxford had one of their best wins since the war. He was not so successful when he played for Leicestershire, and for England, without Brace, who of course is a Welshman, but the selectors (the Rugby selectors, I mean) might have persevered with him a little longer.

Michael Smith played in 50 Test matches, from 1958 to 1972, when he was recalled, not unsuccessfully, to help out a bothered English batting side. He scored 2,278 runs, average 31·63. In all first-class cricket, he scored almost 40,000 runs, average nearly 42. So he was one of those batsmen who did not do nearly so well in Test matches as in the others. His Test career was not helped by a tendency of selectors to drop him after a failure or two. It was his glasses, and his scholarly, distanced air – which the glasses enhanced – that made the heartier characters doubt him. Still, it must be admitted that he was not at his best against fast bowlers, especially when opening the innings, which he usually did in the early part of his career. He was probably more liked by his sides than any England captain since the Second World War. When he was captain, he won five Test matches and lost three, so he had a favourable balance, though there were certainly a lot of draws, out of those 25 matches.

John Woodcock, writing about Smith in the 1976 *Wisden*, asked the question 'Of how many cricketers may it be said, at the end of a long and distinguished career, that they made no enemies?'. Smith, he rightly suggests, was one of them. He adds 'It took some time to dawn that he was as good as he was, or such an excellent man.' Smith was, in some ways, an unconventional captain. He treated press conferences dutifully rather than enthusiastically. In moments of stress he would retire peacefully behind a crossword puzzle, before reaching a decision (though he would have solved the crossword puzzle as well). It is interesting, and curious, that so popular a captain – with the players, though less so with the press and the public – should not have been at all one of the 'Hi, everybody, give the boys some wine' types, though there have not been many of those about lately. He could take a party or leave it alone. He could, even more difficult, take a pressman or leave him alone. If I may return to John Woodcock's article –

No matter who he was with, or where it was, or when, he was always the same man – absolutely fair and as unselfish a captain as England ever had. His players knew exactly where they were with him, which meant every bit as much to them as their acceptance that he was a good enough cricketer to be in the side. Had he played as much for himself as the great majority of successful batsmen do, he would undoubtedly have scored more runs than he did.

John Woodcock is always, and properly, cautious in his compliments. He does not err on the lavish side. He writes about Smith, perhaps, with the added enthusiasm of a convert. It is, nevertheless, a fine and deserved tribute to an England captain whose merits have never been sufficiently recognized, except by those close to him. It would be wrong to say, though, that Smith was as good-looking a batsman, taking him all round, as May, or Cowdrey, or Dexter, or Sheppard. He was mostly an on-side player, a kind of superior Yardley or Insole. There was only rarely majesty in his batting. But majesty in batting, as we have noticed before and will yet notice again, does not constitute the sole qualification for an England captain.

Brian Close, who had become Yorkshire's official captain in 1963, and remained so until 1970, when he embarked upon another career with Somerset, whom he captained from 1972 until 1977, won six matches as captain of England and lost none. His choice as the England captain marked a return, less in tactics than in style, to the north-country professional touch. Raymond Illingworth, who succeeded him, after the last Cowdrey interlude, won 13 matches as captain, and lost nine, four of them against that exceptionally strong Rest of the World side.

In terms of a book such as this, we are now dealing with the day before yesterday, too near the events to have a proper perspective. In 1978 Close produced, with the assistance of Don Mosey, an autobiography. He called the book, with an heroic disregard for any sort of truth, *I Don't Bruise Easily*. I quote from a review which I wrote in *The Cricketer*, which I would not, at least as yet, change.

I am an admirer of Brian Close, as my writings over the years testify, though like most others I have had occasional reservations. I am a long-standing colleague and friend of Don Mosey. So it is reluctantly that I write that I found this rather a sad, sour book ... [which] leaves us with a less favourable impression of Close than we had already.

After retiring from cricket, Bradman wrote a book, *Farewell to Cricket*, in which he seemed to go through every slur cast on him during his cricketing career, and reject them all. This insistence on perennial innocence marred an otherwise splendid book, and much the same has happened this time. Besides, Bradman was Bradman, the greatest player of his time, and Close, though a notable player who did not have the best of luck, was no Bradman, nor even a Woolley, with whom he was compared in his early days. Close has no unquestionable position of strength from which to argue, and has been the centre, at least in England, of far more controversies than Bradman ever got into. It would have been gracious, now that his career on the field is over, if he acknowledged that his failure – only a failure in the sense that his rewards have never been the equal of his gifts – might have been due to defects of character, as well as luck.

Close's attempt to justify his conduct in the row at Edgbaston, which led to his loss of the England captaincy, is unconvincing even in his own terms. His defence is no more than 'two blacks make a white' (I suppose nowadays, in cricket, the more accurate phrase would be 'two whites make a black'). That other captains had deliberately wasted time, and were to do again, is not to the point. He had set, as a captain of England as well as Yorkshire, a particularly bad example. On top of that, he could not bring himself to say he was sorry, and cannot now: any family man should know that there are times when it is necessary to say you are sorry, even if you are still feeling cross. . . .

Close's description of his departure from Yorkshire rings much more truly, and harmonizes with Illingworth's experience. I wish A. B. Sellers would write a book, and put *his* side of the case. On the evidence we have so far, Sellers, the greatest, probably, of Yorkshire county captains, was not able to come to terms, or communicate easily, with the post-war generation of professionals.

There is something wrong here, or at least odd, since every Yorkshireman vows that dedication to his county means more than anything else in life. I think it lies in the curious dual nature of the Yorkshire temperament. It is the bugbear of Yorkshiremen that they always feel they have to behave like Yorkshiremen, or like their fixed belief in what a Yorkshireman should be: tough, ruthless, brave, mean. That most of them are not naturally like that at all is bound to cause tensions, especially when they have to strike public attitudes in such a passionate arena as the cricket field.

'I beseech you', wrote Cromwell to the Scots ministers before the battle of Dunbar, 'I beseech you, in the bowels of Christ, think it possible you may be mistaken'. . . . Although Close might think much the same himself, deep within that mighty skull, he would never let on.

It ought also to be remembered, however, and is brought out in the book, though not immodestly, that Close completely fulfils one Yorkshire ideal, that of physical courage. I remember writing, when the question of his recall to the Test team to face the fast bowlers of 1976 arose, that he 'would die in the breach rather than run away'. He damned near did. Brian Close will be remembered by cricketers, even Yorkshire cricketers, with lasting admiration and affection, less for his words than his actions.

I am not sure, reading it again, that I did proper justice to the Old Bald Blighter, who was absurdly left out of England teams when there were constant complaints that we had no batsmen who would stand up to fast bowling.

In the same year as Close's autobiography, there appeared a biography of Illingworth, written by Michael Stevenson, with the collaboration of his subject. This is part of what I wrote about it in a review for *The Times*.

Several times, an odd chain of circumstance has brought a cricketer to the captaincy of his country. Would Lord Hawke have led England, if his uncle had not died without an heir, thus putting the son of a Lincolnshire parson in direct line for the peerage? Would A. P. F. Chapman, if A. W. Carr had not dropped that catch in the first over, after putting the Australians in? Would Walter Read, had it not been for the argument and muddle which resulted in two English sides touring Australia at the same time? . . . Would C. Aubrey Smith, if he had not looked like a youthful Duke of Wellington? Would S. E. Gregory have captained Australia, if Frank Laver, the manager of the previous tour in 1909, had not refused to surrender the books to the Board of Control, thus precipitating a row which caused most of Australia's senior players to miss the 1912 tour of England? So we could go on.

The way in which Raymond Illingworth became England's captain was as odd as any of these. . . . The only thing I dislike about [Stevenson's] book is its title, *Illy*, illustrating as it does the curious infertility of the modern cricketer in nicknames. It might almost have been better called 'The Liver-Fluke', The liver-fluke (variety *alaria mustelae*) lives inside a mammal, such as a sheep. Its larva is excreted, and sets up house in a water-snail. After passing through the snail, it has to be eaten by a tadpole or frog, which in turn has to be eaten by a mouse, which in turn has to be eaten by a mink or weasel. It leaves the mink in due course and, all being well, is eaten by a sheep, where it breeds. Unless all these things happen to it, the fluke cannot complete its life-cycle. It is an appropriately named creature.

Not for a moment do I suggest that Illingworth's career has been parasitic. From what I know of the man, I like him very much, and I have always admired him as a cricketer, rather more than the England selectors did for a long time. But it was only by a succession of improbable chances that he became England's captain. May and Dexter had to leave the game early. Smith and Cowdrey, though neither could be called a failure, had to be judged not quite up to the job. Close had to have a spectacular and unnecessary row with the Edgbaston crowd, and with the London authorities. Then Cowdrey, restored to office, and seeming set in the job for several years, had to injure himself. Even then, Illingworth would hardly have been considered for the captaincy had he not had a disagreement with Yorkshire, when Close was still

211

in command there, which led to his joining Leicestershire and captaining them
. . . (perhaps Brian Sellers, after all, did Illingworth the best turn of his life);
and even then, though this can hardly be called luck, Illingworth had to show
not only shrewdness in captaincy, which few doubted he possessed, but talent
as a player which he had not consistently demonstrated, at Test level, before.
There were those who thought, in 1969, that Pocock, of Surrey, was as good
an off-spinner, and with more before him. One of the reasons it is difficult to
have a regular bowler as captain, is that it seals off a place, unless the attack is
to be unbalanced.

Illingworth's response to this problem was to score a great many runs, in
the middle of the order, often when the side was in trouble. . . . As a captain,
he was inclined not to bowl himself enough, but with his skill in other
departments, this hardly mattered (except no doubt to poor Pocock) and he
was always worth his place in the side. . . .

Illingworth first played for Yorkshire in 1951, when he was 19, and for
England in 1958, in one Test against New Zealand. He was chosen twice against
India in 1959, and did enough to go to the West Indies that winter. There he
played in all five Test matches, more valuably than his figures indicated. He had
four Tests at home against South Africa in 1960, two against Australia in 1961,
one against Pakistan in 1962. In 1962–3 he went on Dexter's tour, playing twice
against Australia, and three times against New Zealand. He was then out of the
England side until 1965 (one Test against New Zealand) and over the next few
years resumed his in-and-out pattern. In the period 1966 to 1968 he had nine
Tests at home, and none abroad. All this time, he was taking many wickets, and
scoring many runs, for Yorkshire. He was always at his most valuable in 'pulling
them over the hump' of the season, when the championship battles were at their
heaviest. But when he left Yorkshire for Leicestershire, his standing was that of a
very good county cricketer who had not quite made it in the highest grade. Of
course, he had, as an off-spinner, to face severe competition: Titmus, Allen,
Mortimore were around, apart from the rising Pocock. Michael Stevenson says,
'He rarely seemed able to play as well for nis country as he regularly did for
Yorkshire,' and attributes this not just to bad luck, but a 'natural tendency to
insecurity [which] was accentuated by the belief that he was only a stop-gap
selection.'

The honour of the captaincy produced the response, as it had done with
Hutton. He became only the fourth English captain since the First World War to
win the Ashes in Australia. The others, I remind you, were Chapman, Jardine,
and Hutton. All these men, even Chapman, the beatific Chapman, were subject
to controversy. So it was with Illingworth, who had an exceptionally heavy
burden to carry on his Australian tour. He did not get on too easily with his

manager, D. G. Clark, nor his vice-captain, Cowdrey; and this cannot have been entirely Illingworth's fault. His walk-off at Sydney, when Snow had got into a tangle with some spectators on the fence, was unwise, though no doubt it could have been theoretically justified. He may even have been right in saying that it got the match started again sooner than it would have done if the English team had stayed on. But there were many unhappy incidents on that tour. Though the bulk of the men were as loyal to him as could be wished, the senior professionals had not quite the character to give him the support he needed, and the strain told.

In the Lord's Test of 1971, against India, Snow knocked over Gavaskar, the non-striker, as both were chasing back towards the bowler's wicket. I was commenting on the radio at the time, and a right hash I made of it. I thought it must just have been a silly muddle, and made light of it. Trevor Bailey, graciously as ever, suggested that there might have been more in it than a muddle. At lunchtime, John Woodcock said, with an unusual air of gloom, 'This is the kind of thing that was always happening in Australia.' An exaggeration, obviously, but still an honest comment upon Illingworth's captaincy.

These two Yorkists, Close and Illingworth, have been the two best Yorkshire all-rounders since the war, both Test players, both England captains, nearly contemporaries. Close was born at Rawdon in 1931, Illingworth at Pudsey in 1932. Close retired from first-class cricket just a year before Illingworth did. They both spent their latter playing days in exile, though their homes have remained in Yorkshire (I don't know about the reaction of the Leicestershire committee, but the Somerset committee used to get quite cross about this, and demand undertakings that their captain should live in, or near, the county; undertakings readily given but unfulfilled).

It is worth remembering that Leicestershire had never won anything until Illingworth went there, and Yorkshire (I write in 1979) have never won anything since Close left.

Illingworth will take a high ranking among England captains, as anyone must who beat Australia in Australia, and drew with them at home. Close was not captain for long enough for us to make a proper judgment. The way in which he lost the job ('I am a strong-minded man; you are an obstinate fellow; he is a pig-headed ass', is Close's philosophy) suggests that even if that one had been smoothed, he would have got himself into some kind of trouble, sooner or later. You would not call Illingworth a pliable man, but he realised that there are times when you have to be generous, as well as times when you must be stubborn. When India had at last won a rubber in England at the Oval, and all the Indians in London were rejoicing, Illingworth, the defeated captain, addressed the spectators. He congratulated India very courteously, the better side had won on the day, et cetera, and drily added, 'Of course, they had the advantage of a home crowd'. He said it with a smile, and it went down well with the happy brown faces. Could Close have risen to such an occasion in such a friendly way? I doubt it.

How different the careers of these two men were! Close burst into glory: the double of 1,000 runs and 100 wickets in his first season; a century in his first first-class match in Australia. It was too much for a temperamental boy, and he never made his way back, despite that innings at Lord's in 1963, when he ran down the pitch to Wesley Hall, and despite the way he played the West Indian fast bowlers when he came back to the side upon the eve of his career. Illingworth, on the other hand, came along late, and did not miss his unexpected chance when it came. In their contrasting ways, both these men have given much service to English cricket, and much pleasure to its followers.

Illingworth's captaincy lasted from 1969 to 1973, with one interruption in 1972–3, when he took a winter's rest. A. R. Lewis led the England side to India and Pakistan, a stiff tour with eight Test matches. Lewis was widely, and reasonably, expected to be Illingworth's successor. He had never played for England before, but the quality of his batting was known and respected, and in fact he turned out to be one of the batting successes of the tour. He had been an admired captain of Glamorgan since 1967, taking them to the championship in 1969. He is a Welshman, educated at Neath Grammar School and Cambridge, where he was cricket captain in 1972 (he also won a Rugby Blue at full-back). He loves the Welsh and laughs at them, as the best Welshmen do. He likes to tell a story of how, when he was not playing too well and getting some criticism from the crowds, he went to Neath for a Glamorgan match, thinking 'Well, I shall be all right here'. He did not have a very successful match, and his captaincy was not approved, because Glamorgan lost. In the clubhouse afterwards, the *aficionados* decided that the match had been lost because of a dropped catch by a Glamorgan player in the deep, during the last innings. Tony felt it right to come to the support of the unfortunate fieldsman. 'Difficult one, that', he explained to his old friends, 'Swerving about in the wind a bit, you know. Wouldn't have liked to have had to catch it myself.'

'No, I dare say', said Old Friend No. 1. 'It would have knocked your bloody teeth out.'

In 1972, when he became captain of England, he was 34, and could hope for several years at the top. He lost the series in India – narrowly; England were very close to going two up. All the Tests in Pakistan were drawn. But it was a harmonious tour, and won Lewis many good opinions.

Alas! we were to see very little more of him, on the cricket field (though we continue to see, and hear, and read quite a lot of him off it). He played once under Illingworth in 1973 – chosen 'to learn', as the chairman of selectors, Alec Bedser, put it. He was chosen for the following match, despite a batting failure, but had to withdraw because of a leg injury. It seemed at the time a transient setback, but the injury proved troublesome, he was out for most of the season, never played for England again, and not much for anybody. This disappointment he accepted philosophically, but he was a major loss to English cricket, especially at that stage. A few years of Lewis, and the whole pattern of subsequent events must have been drastically changed.

Lewis had the widest culture, if he will forgive the word, of any captain of England since C. B. Fry. (Curiously enough, another man of letters, Brearley, was to turn up a few years later.) He must certainly be the best violinist among England captains, and he has the sensitivity which we expect from good violinists (perhaps unreasonably, but did not Colin Blythe, one of the most sensitive of left-arm bowlers, also play the violin?) Music would very likely have been Lewis's career, but for his cricketing abilities. Or writing: where his natural talent would surely have brought him success, apart from his reputation as a cricketer. His sense of humour is acute but always magnanimous, and this is one of the most precious gifts a captain can have.

I can say all this with the utmost sincerity, though I can already sense the word 'backslapping' hovering over the land. I can almost hear the beating of its wings, like the tread of Jim Swanton marching up the steps behind the commentary box at Leeds, to announce that a Test match was about to finish. Lewis was the first Glamorgan player to captain England. His opposing captain in Pakistan was another Glamorgan player, Majid Khan. Several Glamorgan members made the long journey to mark the occasion.

As a batsman Lewis did not, I suppose, have quite the range of strokes to be in the highest class. Perhaps, I ponder, it would be more accurate to say that he had all the strokes, but deployed some of them more securely than others. He had a noble off-drive, which occasionally reminded me of Hutton's. People laughed at me when I said this, and I am not enough of a technical buff to defend the point theoretically, but the clear impression remains. He had a lofted shot over short mid-wicket which was very much his own, and which brought him many runs. I have seen him use it to get off the mark, against captains unfamiliar with his methods. He was dignified but not stately, the Cambridge man at his best.

But as Lewis faded away from the field, he left the question: who would take England to the West Indies in 1973–4? There was still a case for Illingworth. He was now 42. In the Tests that season England had won against New Zealand, not without uneasy moments, and taken a thorough beating from these same West Indians whom they now had to face in the Caribbean. So there was also a case for a change from Illingworth. But to whom? It would not exactly be a giant stride forward if they chose Close, whose name was often mentioned. They decided in favour of change, and in favour of Denness of Kent. It was in one sense a logical solution, since Denness had been Lewis's vice-captain on the India/Pakistan tour; but Denness had not played in a Test match in 1973, and had therefore missed opportunities of assessing both the current England side and the prospective opposition. 'Bad tabulation there', as Lord Monomark put it.

Denness has been under-valued as an England captain, which does not mean to say that I consider him one of the great ones. He drew the rubber in the West Indies from a losing position, as Hutton had done, more than 20 years earlier. He was captain in 19 Tests, of which six were won and five lost. What is reckoned against him is the disaster in Australia in 1974–5, when Lillee and Thomson were too much for the England batsmen, himself included. Against anything less than the highest speed he was a very good batsman, and it was unlucky for him that his severest challenge came when Australia had their best pair of fast bowlers since Lindwall and Miller.

Denness was born at Bellshill, in Lanarkshire, in 1940, went to Ayr Academy, played for Scotland in 1959, and for Kent in 1962. He was not particularly swift to develop, and it was 1964 before Kent gave him his county cap. By 1970 he had made enough runs, most of them handsomely and on the off side, to be chosen for one of the matches against the Rest of the World. In all, he played in 29 Tests, scoring 1,704 runs at an average of 38·72. He was a fine fielder close to the wicket, indeed anywhere. A catch I saw him make in 1978 at Taunton, in the covers, when Vivian Richards was thundering along, is, I am sure, among the best half-dozen I have ever seen.

Denness was in many ways the kind of Scotsman that a long, though often false, English tradition depicts: a withdrawn man, a bit of a Buchan tight-lipped hero. As a leader, he could give his men devotion, and he had the Covenanting humility, as he showed when he consented to being dropped from the side in Australia. What he could not quite do was to manage a genuine, unforced geniality, with his team, and (what has now become, unfortunately, as important) with the press.

On the West Indies tour of 1973–4, Greig was the man for the press. The England recovery was widely attributed to Greig, sometimes in fulsome terms. He certainly played well in that series, and must have headed, by a wide margin, the averages for unofficial interviews. Still, Denness had actually been the captain, and was made captain again in the 1974 series at home, another double-tour season. He won against India 3–0. All matches against Pakistan – O familiar phrase – were drawn. Denness had done enough to deserve his trip to Australia. There were those who felt that the thrusting urgency of Greig might have been better suited to the occasion; there were those who felt that Illingworth, a great player of fast bowling, might have been recalled to the job, especially if he had been allowed to take Close with him. I was one of the latter camp, and was greeted with even heartier laughter than usual. But nobody knew how fast and fearsome the Australian bowling was going to be, and Denness had earned his chance. It did not make much difference. No England captain could have beaten Australia that season, without winning every toss on a fine day, and summoning up a storm towards the end of the second. The fast bowlers, as we have seen so often in this chronicle, from the days of Spofforth and Richardson, did it again. When you have two of them at a time, they are almost irresistible.

Although Denness had scored centuries both against Australia (with Thomson injured and Lillee able to bowl only six overs) and New Zealand, he gave way to Greig after one match of the 1975 series against Australia. This series followed the Prudential Cup and was limited to four matches. The first had been lost and the rest were drawn. Greig remained as captain in 1976 against the West Indies, and in the tour of India in 1976–7, losing the first series and winning the second. Then came the centenary match, then Greig's alliance with Kerry Packer and his departure from the English scene. He had captained England in 14 Tests, winning three and losing five. In all, he played in 61 Tests, scoring 3,695 runs, average 39·30, and taking 152 wickets, average 31·76. So his Test record was a good one – better, with the bat, than his record for Sussex.

Greig is a South African, born at Queenstown in 1946. As we have seen, it is not all that uncommon for an England captain to have been born abroad, but Greig's case was on a different footing from the others, in that he had learnt his cricket abroad. He played for Border in the Currie Cup before making his debut for Sussex in 1966. However, he was properly qualified for England, and was entitled to be considered for the captaincy on his merits. I remember John Woodcock writing that 'it could not be quite the same thing' for a South African to lead an England side. He came in for some criticism for making the remark, mild though his tone was. Events bore him out, but to many, Greig was the hope of English cricket in 1975 (he had been made captain of Sussex in 1973), and it must be said that, while he stayed, he served his adopted country well.

I shared in the general admiration, and had written this about him in *The Cricketer* in 1973:

In an era of tall men, it is still his height that strikes you, on the twentieth time of watching as much as the first. Find a dozen skeletons as long on a Pacific island, and you would declare you had found a race of giants. He is six feet seven and a half inches tall. Naturally, his height conditions his cricket. I doubt if a cricketer has any real advantage over others in being either tall or short (compare Woolley and Hendren) but it makes a difference to his style, and also to what spectators expect of him. Thus when Greig goes right down the pitch and gets hold of a drive, or when he leaps high in the air, or dives yards away to hold a catch, we say 'That's the advantage of being tall'; but when he is late on a yorker, or cannot hold a slip catch straight at his ankles (I am not suggesting he does either of these things often) 'Ah', we say, wiseacrely, 'that's the trouble with these tall men'. I heard this said once at Hove last season, so severely, that you would have thought the man ought to be doing something about it, going on a diet to lose a few inches of height.

(When we first saw him) his general physique had not quite grown to match his height; he looked like a cherub on stilts; but quickly the word went round that here was a fine player. He played for the county against Cambridge (he was still qualifying), scoring 51 for once out and taking 3 wickets. For the second eleven he scored 362 runs and took 42 wickets. In 1967, he was in the side for the first championship match against Lancashire at Hove, and scored 156 not out in less than four hours. Statham, Higgs and Lever were bowling. Later that season, also at Hove, he took 8 wickets for 25 in Gloucestershire's second innings, winning the match. He scored 1299 runs and took 67 wickets that season. His form was still in-and-out, and was to remain so for some time, but he had arrived.

In 1968 he did not do quite so well, but was still a redeeming part of a Sussex side for which everything went wrong (they were bottom of the championship). In 1969 he again scored 1000 runs, and took 69 wickets. Sussex did better but were still in the process of sorting themselves out, and so I suppose was Greig, who had to consider his cricketing future in difficult circumstances. He decided that he would play Test cricket, if chosen, for England. I have no idea what his motives were, but however you look at it, it must have been a courageous decision.

He was justified, so far as his cricket went, in the short term; and he has been abundantly vindicated in his belief in himself in the long term; but he must have had a few worried moments in between. In 1970 he was chosen for three of the matches against the Rest of the World. In the second Test at Nottingham, which England won (probably the best performance by an England side since the second world war) he had as much as anyone to do with the victory, taking 4 wickets in the first innings and 3 in the second. The batsmen whose wickets he took were Richards (twice), Sobers (twice), Kanhai, Engineer and Barlow. In the third Test he took no wickets, but scored 55 and 22. He took 4 for 86 in the first innings in the fourth Test at Leeds, but he did not bowl well in that innings. Indeed, he lost himself his place in the side, and we could see him doing it while he was bowling. When the Rest of the World batted on the morning of the second day, both the pitch and the atmosphere favoured fast-medium bowlers, but Greig, though he produced a good ball from time to time, could not find a steady length or line. I remember how Trevor Bailey was itching with irritation that he could not be bowling himself. Greig would no doubt have kept himself in the selectors' picture with some runs, but scored 5 and 0. So he was out of the last Test, and not chosen for Australia. He again scored 1000 runs in the season, and took 59 wickets, but his bowling average was higher than his batting. Yet he looked every long inch a cricketer, and his reputation as a close fielder (31 catches that year) was growing fast. If he was inconsistent, he was still young.

Perhaps he will look back on 1971 as the decisive season in his career. He still averaged fewer with the bat than the ball, but he scored a thousand runs and took 77 wickets; more importantly, bowling almost 800 overs to get them. Snow was flitting into and out of the Sussex side this season, and Greig had to carry the burden, both shock and stock as they used to say. The way in which he sustained his task put to rest any lingering doubts about his physical strength. Richard Hutton was preferred to him in the England side, but there was a general feeling that they were of much the same level, and that Greig would be the better when he got the best out of himself. Both went to Australia that winter with a Rest of the World side. No doubt both were chosen in the first place because of Australian determination not to pick a Rest of the World side that approximated to the real strength of the Rest of the World: but it did not turn out to be as pointless a series as was intended, and of the two English all-rounders it was Greig who made his mark. It was now we began to hear of those astonishing catches close to the wicket, his long shadow stretching across the pitch.

Thus to the series against Australia last summer, and against India and Pakistan this winter . . . I notice that the cricket correspondent of *The Times*, the Sage of Longparish, has spoken especially highly of him. (The Sage of Longparish is not himself a tall man, and has not always been enthusiastic about Greig in the past. What he really feels is that all the best cricketers are five feet three. A judgment from this quarter is therefore convincing.)

I have not, myself, seen enough of Greig's cricket to offer a judgment; except to say that whatever he is doing on the field, he is enjoyable to watch, and not just because that height catches the eye, nor that blond hair is so readily identifiable to a struggling commentator. He is a true athlete now; and still with a touch of the cherub.

I have thought that worth reproducing because it is so easy to forget in what high regard we held Greig less than a lustrum ago. And if his manner of leaving the job did not become him, and we inevitably tend to think of him as one who put his own career before the needs of his (adopted) country, that is only part of the picture. We must not forget the cherub as well as the imp.

The centenary Test was a moment of rejoicing and hope. Former Test cricketers were present in force: of the 244 living who had played for England or Australia, 218 were able to attend. The oldest Australian was Jack Ryder, aged 87, the oldest Englishman Percy Fender, aged 84. It was the idea of Hans Ebeling, who bowled for Australia over here in 1934, and was a vice-president of the Melbourne Cricket Club, to play a match to mark a century of Test cricket on the same ground which had seen David Gregory's team beat James Lillywhite's. It was an unusual but very fine match. Australia scored 138 and 419 for 9, declared. England scored 95 and 417. So Australia won by 45 runs: exactly the same result as 100 years before. No wonder Reg Hayter was moved to call the proud originator Hans 'Andersen' Ebeling.

9

POSTSCRIPT

Any postscript is nothing but a bloody anticlimax
Harassed *Times* copy-taker to harassed *Times*
reporter, *circa* 1970

It would have been pleasanter, as well as tidier, to have ended the story of the cricket captaincy of England in 1977. The events in world cricket since the Centenary Test require a book to themselves, and indeed have already received a good one, in *The Packer Affair*, by Henry Blofeld. I shall not rehearse them further, and as I write the problems are still unresolved. Greig, as he must have realized, ruled himself out of Test cricket by acting as Mr Packer's agent. The last few years have not been a happy period in cricket history, but something of the sort was bound to happen, one way or another, sooner or later. The structure of first-class cricket had become too far removed from the mood of an age in which sport has become society's golden calf.

One happy consequence was that Greig's departure gave Brearley an opportunity, which otherwise he could scarcely have expected, to become an England captain.

J. M. Brearley was born in Harrow in 1942, went to the City of London School and then to Cambridge, where he was captain in 1963 and 1964. He had an academic record of unusual distinction, and did not play cricket for much of his time after he had left Cambridge, becoming a lecturer in philosophy, until, after seeing his professional (i.e. non-cricketing) career safely launched, he became captain of Middlesex in 1971. He had been Greig's vice-captain on the tour which culminated in the Centenary Test, and was the obvious successor. He was captain against Australia in the summer of 1977, winning the rubber 3–0, with two matches drawn. That was, it seemed, a rather troubled Australian side, and would not in any case have been one of their best. But Brearley did all that was necessary as a captain, and averaged 27 with the bat, which was respectable.

The question that has been most often raised about Brearley is the old one: is he really good enough to be in the side? He was considered an outstanding batting prospect when he began his first-class cricket, but after his break seemed to have lost some of his fluency. Then he had a bad arm injury on the tour of Pakistan and New Zealand in 1977–8, and had to go home early, and could not score many runs for a long time afterwards. When, in Australia in 1978–9, he had a poor batting run in the Tests, the point about the quality of his batting was raised again, and after Australia had won the third Test, suggestions were made that he ought to drop himself from the side.

Brearley's own view is that 'a captain is an all-rounder'. His phrase may not be semantically precise, but his point is clear: that a batsman's ability as a captain must be taken into account as one of his assets, just as a man's bowling, or fielding, or wicket-keeping should be taken into account, even if there might just be a better specialist batsman about. This view will find much confirmation in the foregoing pages.

Still, it was a nuisance that Brearley did not score more runs, and it was felt by some, especially in the north, that Boycott had a good claim to the captaincy, when it came to taking England to Australia in the autumn of 1978. Boycott had been the hero of the 1977 series, scoring his hundredth hundred, before his own people, in the Leeds Test. But he had been out of the England side, at his own public request, when the going was hard (Greig put it more brutally), and when he did captain England, in New Zealand after Brearley's injury, New Zealand had their first win. He was not popular with his fellow-players – though his technique was almost univerally admired – in the Yorkshire or the England team.

Early in the 1978 season, I wrote this piece in *The Spectator*. They headed it 'North v. South', and it reflects many things that I have described in these pages.

The arguments about the England captaincy next season are well under way; or, at least, both sides are suggesting that there is nothing to argue about. Why, we are asked, should there be any hesitation in choosing Brearley, assuming he is fit and in tolerable form? He beat the Australians, and did as well as anyone could be expected to do in Pakistan. In the present English batting side, he is obviously worth his place. If it had not been for his unlucky injury, no question would ever have arisen. End of discussion.

Hard luck on Brearley, no doubt, agree the Boycott supporters. But it so happens that the injury has brought the natural captain of England to his rightful place at last, and there is no point at all in messing Boycott about any more. End of discussion.

All sorts of other things will be brought into the argument as it develops, some of them ungraciously, but those are the essential positions. When you come to more detailed examination, the trouble is that so much of the evidence can be interpreted in more than one way. Boycott, they say (chiefly) in the south, let England down by leaving the Test team at the time he was most needed, because he was scared of the fast bowlers. The first part of this accusation may be true. As for the second part, I do not profess to understand Boycott's motives for withdrawing, and I doubt very much whether he does himself, but they were certainly more complex than fear.

Brearley, they say (chiefly) in the north, would never have been in the England side at all, had it not been that Lord's wanted an 'establishment' captain in the old amateur tradition. He was only a second-bester to start with. All right, he hasn't done so badly, but they would never have thought of him if he hadn't been a fancy-cap. As against this, Brearley, though he certainly had the misfortune to be educated at Cambridge, is not at all the kind of man whom Yorkshiremen identify with the establishment. His views might be described in many ways as leftish. He markedly did not join in the Packer hunt last summer, keeping a cool, impartial attitude, one fitting to an England captain – and much needed, after the contortions of Greig.

Then there is the question of experience. Boycott has been captain of Yorkshire since 1971, the same year as Brearley became captain of Middlesex, but Boycott has a much wider and longer knowledge of Test cricket, and its special stresses. On the other hand, Brearley has led Middlesex to several successes, and Boycott – some of whose teams, on the face of it, contained a lot of talent – has not done the same for Yorkshire. So you can also take that both ways.

. . . I would not be altogether surprised if at any time Brearley decided he had had enough Test cricket. He is not the man to relish a public debate of this kind, any more than David Sheppard was. But it would make a fine conclusion to his career, to hold the Ashes in Australia, before he turns his mind to more important things than cricket. I wonder what his old Cambridge opening partner, Craig, thinks. Craig, another exceptional batsman and scholar, felt that a few years of first-class cricket, while interesting, were enough.

I have one suggestion to make. The old match, North v. South, should be revived this season. It could still be fitted in, with an effort. Brearley would captain the south, Boycott the north. They might even choose their own sides. I do not suggest that the winner should automatically be captain, but if the selectors are in any doubt, it might help them to make up their minds. Test trials do not usually attract much attention nowadays, but I bet that one would.

I suppose it would be cowardly not to declare my preference, though it is early days and much may happen. I am a Yorkshireman, but I am on Brearley's side. Maybe if winning, or at least avoiding defeat, is all that matters, he would not be the best choice. But it is not. After all, we sometimes beat Australia, and they sometimes beat us, and the operation would be pointless were it not so. A happy tour next winter, a popular touring side, is, in the present state of international cricket, more important than who holds the Ashes. Brearley is of course not nearly so good a batsman as Boycott, nor quite so utterly dedicated to the game. Boycott might be the harder man to beat, but I have never known it suggested that anyone on his own side has deliberately run Brearley out.

The selectors took the same view, and the arguments about whether Boycott should captain England were soon swallowed in the arguments about whether he should captain Yorkshire.

Thus Brearley became only the fourth captain in this century to win two rubbers against Australia, and the only one but Hutton to win them consecutively. He must be tempted to go on and try for a third. Any hesitation about placing him in the front rank arises because of doubts about the quality of the opposition he has had to face. But a captain can do no more than win the matches he has to play. The difference between his reactions to the possibility of being dropped and those of Denness, who had a similar problem on the previous tour, is an illustration of what helps to make a captain.

I wrote, in the flush of the Australian victory, that he had 'illumined the art of captaincy', and I think it was true. But his career is not, as I write, concluded, and I do not attempt an assessment of it. When the balances come to be weighed, they can hardly fall against him.

And so we say farewell to the captains of England, a not unattractive company. Farewell to John Davis, the first man to realize that sport could be exported; to William Clarke, who so cunningly bowled out, and fascinated, the countrymen; to Grace, who embodied the countrymen's revenge; to Stoddart, the Victorian masher; to the Edwardians, the Georgians, and the neo-Elizabethans: MacLaren in his grandeur, Jackson coolly winning matches, Warner doing his honest best, Fry surveying the scene from an Olympic height, brave Douglas putting himself on to bowl before Barnes, the improbable Tennyson, playing Gregory and MacDonald with one arm; the genial Gilligan; Chapman winning match after match and holding catch after catch. Farewell (though not yet, for he still thrives, down in Cornwall) to the theoretician Wyatt, to the ruthless – though loved by those who knew him best, even if they were Australians – Jardine; to the amiable and sporting Allen, the mighty and moody Hammond, the unlucky but cheerful Yardley, the resilient Brown, the steady hero Hutton: to the post-war Cambridge captains, a good lot from May to

Brearley, to Oxford's more diffident post-war contribution, with Cowdrey and Smith. I am surprised, looking back on this book, how much it confirms the old university joke: 'The Oxford man may feel he owns the earth, but the Cambridge man feels that he doesn't care a damn who owns it'. Compare, for instance, Jardine and Dexter.

And then the professionals: Shaw must have been an adventurous and courageous man to have managed those early tours, though you would not have applied either term to that remorseless bowling, dead on a length on or just outside the off-stump. There was his colleague Shrewsbury ('Give me Arthur!') with an inner anxiety which belied his outward calm. They were the men who did as much as anybody to get international cricket moving. Long afterwards, there came Hutton, and later again, Close and Illingworth, Yorkshiremen all, with the professional touch.

Some of the England captains have been, or it has been said of them, too tough; some have been too nice; some have been better at captaincy than cricket, and some better at cricket than captaincy; some have been rogues, not in the worst sense of the word – 'that sly rogue Cupid', who pierced hearts; rogue elephants, stricken deer who left the herd – some have been flannelled fools, as Kipling called them, and some have been fools in the way the saints were called fools; some have been wise men. All, we may be sure, even those of the briefest tenure, have come in for severe criticism from those who played under them, those who watched them, and those who wrote about them. Anyone of whom it can be truthfully said that 'nobody ever said an unkind word about him' was not a Test match captain, or come to that any kind of a cricket captain. The man who keeps his sensitivity, but keeps it under a thick skin, is the kind likely to be best at the job; though he will suffer.

I doubt very much if Test cricket will survive for another hundred years, in anything like its present form. Nor do I share the view that the playing of Test cricket is a major blessing to humanity. But I would conjecture that so far, Test matches, and this mixed company of men who have had the responsibility of leading England in them, have produced more pleasure than pain, and even (not quite the same thing) done more good than harm.

INDEX